DOMESDAY BOOK

THROUGH NINE CENTURIES

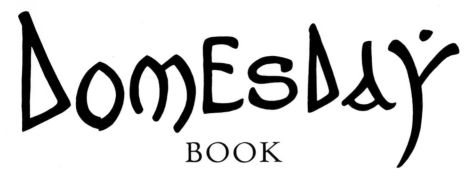

DOMESDAY
BOOK

THROUGH NINE CENTURIES

ELIZABETH M. HALLAM

PUBLIC RECORD OFFICE

THAMES AND HUDSON

© Crown copyright 1986. Published by permission of the Controller of
Her Majesty's Stationery Office.

First published in the United States in 1986 by
Thames and Hudson Inc., 500 Fifth Avenue,
New York, New York 10110

Library of Congress Catalog Card Number 85-51625

Printed and bound in Spain by
Artes Graficas Toledo S.A.
D.L. TO-1699-85

Table of Contents

Preface

During the 1886 Domesday celebrations at the Public Record Office, Hubert Hall, an assistant keeper, stood in the gallery of the Round Room and addressed a distinguished gathering on the official custody of Domesday Book. Most of his speech was concerned with precisely where Domesday had been kept in the twelfth century, but he also made some mention of its reputation and uses throughout the subsequent centuries. That was, he suggested, a topic greatly neglected by historians. Since then, considerable interest has been shown in Domesday Book's practical value during its first century, but its later history remains largely uncharted. Even the Public Record Office handbook *Domesday Rebound* and V.H. Galbraith's *Domesday Book, its Place in Administrative History* treat it in only the broadest outline, and both works raise as many questions as they answer.

This book, written in celebration of the nine hundredth anniversary of the Domesday survey, takes up Hubert Hall's challenge of a century ago. It begins with William the Conqueror and with the making of Domesday, a conundrum which Domesday scholars have since Hall's day made impressive progress in solving. The physical nature of Domesday's two volumes is discussed, and the text is compared with analogous records produced by other European states in the middle ages. The contentious matter of Domesday's practical usefulness in the twelfth century is next examined, and some new evidence from the thirteenth century is adduced to suggest that the survey's importance between 1087 and 1272 has hitherto been underestima-ted. From Edward I's reign, the sources for Domesday Book as a working record become copious. The procedures for citing it for administrative and legal purposes are examined, and examples are given from the thirteenth to the seventeenth centuries to show the variety of issues in which it was of value. It was most important for verifying ancient demesne, a tenure which brought special legal privileges with it and which was of practical value into the nineteenth century. The ravelled history of that tenure is traced in outline to show that Domesday remained necessary to its proof. The survey continued to be cited in court into the present century and remains acceptable legal evidence, but in the reign of Elizabeth I its potential as a historical source was first clearly recognized. Ever since, it has been discussed in numerous antiquarian and historical writings and in a variety of polemical tracts. Its text became better known after the publication of an edition in 1783 and of a photozincographic facsimile in the early 1860s.

From the thirteenth century, Domesday Book had its permanent home at

Westminster, but it travelled with the royal household on a number of occasions in the middle ages. Later it was taken to Hatfield, Nonsuch, Bodmin and Shepton Mallet to escape plague, fire and war, and to Southampton to be photographed in the open air. But through all its vicissitudes it has been treated with the utmost care by its custodians, who have always regarded it as the greatest of all the national records. It is, indeed, one of the few documents to achieve a reputation which transcends its contents, remarkable as they are. It has always excited awe and admiration. To the conquered Anglo-Saxons it was a symbol of Norman oppression, for late-fourteenth-century villeins it held out the hope of escape from the burdensome labour services demanded by their landlords. By the seventeenth century, it was generally considered to be an encyclopaedic account of life in the Conqueror's reign; in the mid-Victorian era it became a cult object, encased in an impractical and sumptuous binding. By 1900, Domesday studies were a major, established field of historical endeavour; the current analysis of Domesday's text by computer is further enhancing its reputation. But whether it is viewed as the focus of a myth or as a practical administrative record, Domesday Book and its history through nine centuries provide a richly rewarding study.

1. *Great Domesday and Little Domesday on the chest in which they were kept during the seventeenth and eighteenth centuries.*

Domesday Book:
Some Facts and Figures

Origin Survey ordered by King William the Conqueror, Christmas 1085.

Aims of the survey To discover the resources and taxable values of manors and boroughs; to ascertain what lands each tenant-in-chief held and what he owed to the king; to settle who were the rightful holders of land; to satisfy the king's curiosity.

Survey finished (? and Little Domesday completed) ? August 1086.

Great Domesday left uncompleted ? September 1087.

Where written	Great Domesday: ? Winchester.
	Little Domesday: ? in the three counties covered.
Number of volumes	Two; Great Domesday and Little Domesday.
Number of leaves	Great Domesday: 413.
	Little Domesday: 475.
Materials	Parchment (the skins of sheep); black and red ink.
Dimensions	Great Domesday: *c.* 15″ × 11″.
	Little Domesday: *c.* 11″ × 8″.
Number of scribes	Great Domesday: one, with annotations in another hand.
	Little Domesday: about six.
Script	Caroline minuscule.
Language	Latin.
Number of words	*c.* two million.
Countries covered	England south of the river Tees; a small part of Wales.
Counties covered	Little Domesday: Essex, Norfolk, Suffolk.
	Great Domesday: all the rest of the English counties, excluding Durham and Northumberland, are covered or represented. 28 Cumbrian and 142 Welsh places appear, as do some of north and all of south Lancashire (between the Mersey and Ribble rivers). Total: 37 pre-1974 counties.
Total places named	13,418.
Major places omitted	London and Winchester.
Information given	Names of landholders in each county (king, bishops, abbots, lay magnates); the manors which each held and their values, and the names of their subtenants (the pre-Conquest landholders and values are often given, and sometimes those for just after the Conquest); the names of many boroughs and details of their customs.
	The numbers of freemen, sokemen, unfree peasants and slaves on each manor (but information on population figures is incomplete); the resources of each manor, including land use, plough teams, livestock and appurtenances such as mills; manorial values and geld (i.e., tax) assessments.

Bindings	Twelfth century (perhaps before 1100); 1320; sixteenth or seventeenth century; 1819; 1869; 1953; 1985.
Names	*c.* 1100 first called a book (*liber*); *c.* 1179 first called Domesday, signifying the Book of Judgment.
Where kept	Late eleventh to early thirteenth century: Royal Treasury at Winchester, then London, then Westminster, but frequently on the move. Thirteenth century: Treasury of Receipt at Westminster (probably in the Chapel of the Pyx), but still peripatetic on occasions. Sixteenth century: Tally Court, Westminster. *c.* 1740s: Chapter House, Westminster. 1859: Public Record Office, Chancery Lane, London.
First printed	Ed. Abraham Farley, 1783 (also used in recent Phillimore volumes).
Principal translations	*Victoria County History* (revised for new Alecto Historical Editions version) and Phillimore volumes.
Facsimiles	Photozincograph (1862); Alecto Historical Editions (1986).

Acknowledgments

I would particularly like to thank Dr D. Bates, Dr P.A. Brand, Professor C.N.L. Brooke, Dr D. Carpenter, Miss C.M. Hallam, Dr P.J.A. Levene, Mr C. Lewis, Professor H.R. Loyn, Mrs C. Thorn, Dr F. Thorn, and my colleagues Mr J.D. Cantwell, Dr T.M. Chalmers, Miss M.M. Condon, Dr D. Crook, Dr G.H. Martin and Mrs A. Nicol for their valuable advice and encouragement. Further debts are recorded in the footnotes below. Of the many others at the Public Record Office who have helped with this book at its various stages, I would particularly like to mention Mrs J.M. Cox and Mr R.V. Weygang for arranging its publication, Dr P.M. Barnes and Dr R.F. Hunnisett for their unstinting textual criticisms, Mr J. Millen for his excellent photographic work, and Mrs L. Rees and Mrs B. Saddington for typing the text. The maps have been drawn by Mrs J. Fahy. Thanks are also due to the staffs of the Bodleian Library, British Library, the Cambridgeshire Record Office at Huntingdon, the Law Society Library, the Royal Historical Society and the Society of Antiquaries of London for their co-operation and assistance.

Crown copyright material is quoted with the permission of the Controller of H.M. Stationery Office. The agreement of the Oxford University Press and of Macmillan Publishers Ltd to the reproduction of the quotations on pages 32 and 100–102 respectively is gratefully acknowledged, as is that of all those who have supplied photographs and who are thanked individually below on page 217.

Much of this book has been written at home in the evenings, and I am very grateful to my husband, Mr T.S. Smith; to our children, Timothy and Emily; and to our nanny, Miss A.C. Price, for their forbearance and support.

NOTE

All documents cited are in the Public Record Office and all books mentioned were published in London unless otherwise stated. The county boundaries are those preceding the 1974 reorganization. Spelling and punctuation in quotations from sources in English have where necessary been modernized.

CHAPTER I

The Making of
Domesday Book

Domesday Book is very much an expression of the will of one of England's harshest and most able monarchs, William I. The colophon, or tail-piece, of Little Domesday Book tells us that

In the year one thousand and eighty-six from the Incarnation of Our Lord, and in the twentieth year of the reign of William there was made this survey, not only through these three counties, but also through others.[1]

The making of an inquiry of such scope and size was perhaps the most dramatic and durable public gesture of a man who dominated the politics of western Europe in the later eleventh century. Born in 1027 or 1028, the illegitimate son of Robert I, duke of Normandy, and Herlève, probably a tanner's daughter from Falaise, he succeeded to his father's title in 1035. The accession of a minor whose claim was dubious provoked war and disorder. With the support of a powerful group of Norman magnates, of the Norman Church and of the French king, William's feudal overlord, the young duke survived. After the decisive defeat of his most dangerous enemies in 1047, William was threatened by invasion from the count of Anjou and by hostility from the French king, but he managed to unite his own nobility in defensive campaigns. He also made an advantageous marriage to Matilda of Flanders in the early 1050s, although many contemporaries regarded the union as unlawful on grounds of consanguinity. In the 1060s, the tables were turned: unopposed by Philip I, the new young king of France, the duke took the county of Maine from the counts of Anjou, campaigned successfully on the Breton marches, and established a claim to the throne of England by the oath of fealty given to him by Earl Harold Godwineson. King Edward the Confessor's death in 1066 and the rapid coup by Harold meant that William had to fight to substantiate that claim. Luck as well as ability was clearly on his side in the battle near Hastings which marked the culmination of his series of conquests and which he followed up with ruthless brutality. The bastard duke had now acquired a crown – a source of great prestige – and perhaps the wealthiest and most coveted state in western Europe.[2]

For the rest of his life, William the Conqueror, as he is familiarly known, strove to maintain and consolidate his immense gains. To the periodic threats posed by the

2. Detail from the twelfth-century Chronicle of Battle Abbey, depicting William the Conqueror enthroned.

French and Scandinavian kings were added, later in his life, problems arising from the dubious loyalty of his eldest son, Robert Curthose, and his followers. It was in conducting a violent and forceful campaign against Philip I of France, now his great enemy, and Robert, that William was to receive his fatal injury at Mantes in 1087. He died shortly afterwards, still far from being a spent force. The power of his personality emerges clearly in the description given by the Anglo-Saxon chronicler:

This King William of whom we speak was a very wise man, and very powerful and more worshipful and stronger than any predecessor of his had been. He was gentle to the good men who loved God, and stern beyond all measure to those people who resisted his will. . . . Also, he was a very stern and violent man, so that no one dared to do anything contrary to his will. He had earls in his fetters, who acted against his will. He expelled bishops from their sees and abbots from their abbacies, and put thegns in prison. . . . Amongst other things the good security he made in this country is not to be forgotten, so that any honest man could travel over his kingdom with his bosom full of gold: and no one dared strike another, no matter how much wrong he had done him.[3]

This was the man who was widely admired and feared, who was celebrated by two contemporary Norman biographers, William of Jumièges and William of

Map 1. *England and Normandy at the time of William the Conqueror.*

3. *Scene from the Bayeux tapestry, showing William the Conqueror giving arms to Earl Harold.*

4. *Another scene from the Bayeux tapestry, in which Duke William exhorts his men before the battle of Hastings.*

Poitiers, and whose stylized and triumphant image was immortalized in the embroidered narrative of the Bayeux tapestry.

Kings Henry I and Philip I of France, William's neighbours and rivals, by contrast went virtually unnoticed, and although that was to some extent the result of the weakness of French royal power, which was little greater than that of the leading vassals, it is more indicative of the Conqueror's outstanding reputation. As duke of Normandy, he was in theory subject to the French kings, but strove constantly to emphasize his princely, later royal, powers and attributes, and went well beyond the pretensions to quasi-royal status held by other great French nobles, such as the counts of Anjou and the dukes of Burgundy. He was a man to whom the trappings and outward signs of strong rule were of the greatest importance.[4]

One such symbol was William's new Norman 'capital' at Caen, which later became the seat of ducal government. There he built an imposing castle and he and his wife founded two major abbeys, one as his burial place, the other as hers. All these buildings may be seen as symbols of William's authority in the duchy.[5] By the end of his reign, the English countryside also bore many visual reminders of the Norman presence, among them Windsor Castle, securing the Thames valley, and the great stone keep of the White Tower in London.

5. *The White Tower, Tower of London, in the eighteenth century.*

The king, however, made an audacious gesture in founding an abbey on the
battlefield at Hastings between 1067 and 1070. In the twelfth century, its monks,
anxious to claim judicial rights and to gain favours from the Conqueror's successors,
put together a highly inventive chronicle and forged foundation charters to
perpetuate the idea that it had been created by the king in atonement for the
bloodshed at Hastings. Scanty earlier sources present a quite different picture. The
Anglo-Saxon chronicler, for example, stresses that the house was built 'in the same
place where God permitted [William] to conquer England'.[6] Even the Battle
chronicle emphasizes the difficulties presented by the high, waterless site to the
builders and the monks alike. The cause of the problems was the king's insistence
that the high altar should be sited on the very spot where Harold had fallen. Taken
with the most striking feature of all, the naming of the house as Battle Abbey, this
marks out the monastery, supposedly a symbol of holy peace and prayer, as a
memorial of martial victory and conquest.[7]

The Domesday survey was an equally dramatic gesture of a quite different sort.
The Anglo-Saxons were well accustomed to literate administration using their
native tongue, and to the holding of royal surveys of tax liability, the results of which
had been preserved in the royal treasury at Winchester.[8] For some administrative
purposes, however, Anglo-Saxon England operated more as a confederation of
counties, and within them of hundreds, than as a centralized kingdom. The
Normans appear to have retained many of the old English forms and methods of
government, but to have instituted a new and, for its time, vigorously centralized
administration.[9] Domesday Book, intended as the final uniform summary of an
inquiry planned and controlled from the centre, was a symbol of the new order.

The detail and thoroughness of the Conqueror's work seem to have frightened
and alienated the native population. The Anglo-Saxon chronicler, whose account
of William's reign is pervaded with gloom and hostility, wrote of the survey:

He sent his men all over England into every shire and had them find out how many hundred
hides there were in the shire, or what land and cattle the king himself had in the country, or
what dues he ought to have in twelve months from the shire. Also he had a record made of
how much land his archbishops had, and his bishops and his abbots and his earls, and . . .
what or how much everybody had who was occupying land in England, in land or cattle,
and how much money it was worth. So very narrowly did he have it investigated, that there
was no single hide nor a yard of land, nor indeed (it is a shame to relate but it seemed no
shame to him to do) one ox nor one cow nor one pig which was there left out, and not put
down in his record: and all these records were brought to him afterwards.[10]

Such feelings of fear and awe soon led the English to call the final version of the
survey 'Domesday Book', because it reminded them of the familiar and frightening

6. Detail from the twelfth-century tympanum of Barfreston church, Kent, depicting the Last Judgment.

image of the Last Judgment, described in Revelation and painted or carved in many parish churches.[11]

William's contemporaries, then, were much impressed by his wide-ranging and unprecedented survey. His reasons for making it, however, were concerned far more with power than with image. They were also complex, as is shown by the many facets of the finished text; indeed, attempts by historians to categorize Domesday Book as either a financial or a feudal document have been defeated by the very diversity of the information which it contains. The survey must instead be seen in the general context of William's conquest and administration of England.

In consolidating his position, the king had crushed the opposition with characteristic ruthlessness. He needed to keep his wealthy kingdom firmly under control, the better to pursue the interests of his Norman patrimony; and because there was a purposeful and growing hostility from his neighbours in France, much of his time was spent in his duchy. In England, the rebellion of the earls, suppressed in 1075, was followed by further unrest in the north in 1080; and in 1085 there was a major threat of invasion from Scandinavia when Cnut of Denmark, in alliance with Olav of Norway and Robert, count of Flanders, assembled a seemingly invincible fleet. In the event, Cnut was prevented from sailing by the uprising in Denmark which was to lead to his untimely death, but William was alarmed by the danger and, assembling a massive and costly mercenary army in northern France, brought it across to England and billeted it on his barons. The difficulties and uncertainties involved may have underlined the lack of reliable information about English landholding, and may have given an impetus to the launching of the Domesday survey.[12]

William's military campaigns were extremely costly, and it has been argued that a reassessment of the landholders' liability for Danegeld, that lucrative Anglo-Saxon tax on land, took place roughly concurrently with the Domesday survey and may well have been connected with it.[13] The content and arrangement of Domesday Book, however, suggest that it was far more than a geld book. William was famed and feared for his avarice and, in the wider fiscal aspects of the inquiry, aimed to obtain a valuation of estates and to allocate a new fiscal rating. That involved the counting not only of lands but of livestock and aroused the terror, and perhaps even the violence, of the Anglo-Saxons. It is this material which makes Domesday Book an invaluable statement about the wealth of England and its rulers.

The Anglo-Saxon chronicler had a straightforward explanation of the need for the survey. William, he said, wanted to know 'about this country – how it was occupied or with what sort of people.'[14] Edward the Confessor had installed Normans rather than Anglo-Saxons in a few important ecclesiastical and lay offices; but William's reign witnessed the complete eclipse of the Anglo-Saxon aristocracy by death in battle or rebellion, by exile or by banishment, and its replacement by a group of northern French barons, the Normans, Bretons, Flemings and others who had come over in his army. This dispossession was not immediate, but took place gradually in the wake of uprisings and rebellions, particularly those of 1067–71. The result was a highly complex and confused pattern of landholding, leading to many uncertainties as to legal title – further complicated by the hostility of the native population – and to numerous lawsuits.[15] At least since Cnut's reign, questions about possession of land had often been settled by referring to tax lists,[16] and after 1086 Domesday Book, as an indisputable record of who had held each manor at the time of King Edward and who in 1086, would have readily resolved such issues. William's own position as the rightful heir of Edward the Confessor, and that of his barons as the successors of the Anglo-Saxon earls and thegns, were also strongly emphasized, the power won by the sword thereby being portrayed as legitimate. Harold's reign was ignored, and Harold himself was almost always referred to only as 'earl' and not 'king'.

An allied question was one of feudal rights. In many parts of France, feudal ties were used by the lesser nobility to cement alliances of mutual benefit or protection, spreading gradually upwards through society. In Normandy, by contrast, and to an even greater extent in England, they were employed as an instrument of royal authority, imposed from above. An under-tenant had to pay homage, fealty and services to his lord, a tenant-in-chief, but he also owed a higher allegiance to his king; thus, in 1086, the more important lesser tenants affirmed that obligation at William's Lammas court in Salisbury.[17] The arrangement of each county section of Domesday Book is very revealing about the higher reaches of the social hierarchy and organization. Except in the case of two counties, Shropshire and Cheshire, the lands of the king come first; they are followed by those of the ecclesiastical landholders, the bishops and abbots, ranking next to, and controlled by, the king; and finally the estates of the lay lords are listed.[18] The king and his family possessed about one fifth of the land in the counties surveyed, a striking increase compared with the previous reign; the Church about one quarter; and another quarter was in the hands of the dozen leading tenants-in-chief.[19] Domesday Book is thus a clear and practical list of holdings and a statement about power in the England of 1086.

One of the most remarkable features of the Domesday survey is the speed with which it was compiled. It was at his 1085 Christmas court in Gloucester that William 'had much thought and very deep discussion about this country – how it was occupied or with what sort of people. Then he sent his men all over England into every shire.'[20] The colophon at the end of Little Domesday tells us that the survey was made in 1086, and its analysis and codification into Great Domesday Book were almost certainly nearing completion in September 1087, when the Conqueror died. Only the returns for Essex, Suffolk and Norfolk had not been put into their final condensed form, but were left in last draft. They were later bound into a separate volume, Little Domesday.[21]

Such rapidity of action can only have been made possible by pre-existing lists of hundreds, vills and tenants, as well as by a highly efficient method of collecting new and correcting old information, particularly in the face of what often must have been bitter hostility from the native population. The eleventh-century Anglo-Saxon fiscal administration was able to control the coinage and levy the Danegeld on a regular basis; and the Normans seem to have preserved that system and to have utilized it to the full. A reassessment of the Northamptonshire geld payments was made in the years before 1086, and another, wider-ranging, adjustment took place concurrently with Domesday.[22] Such activity needed and produced records, some of which were probably kept at Winchester and some in the counties, and these were a vital source of background information to the makers of the Domesday survey. Dating from earlier in William's reign, and some perhaps from the Anglo-Saxon past, they fell into two broad categories. One consisted of tax lists (kept locally by the sheriff) and other taxation records, of which examples are a Kentish list preserved in a later copy and a Yorkshire assessment incorporated in Great Domesday itself.[23] They recorded liability for geld; and some were arranged, as Domesday Book was to be, by counties, tenants-in-chief and manors, while others were listed by hundreds, then tenants and manors. They were of various dates and gave only a partial record of fiscal obligations. A second, more miscellaneous, group of documents described the royal estates in each county and the values of their farms (i.e., rents), and listed dues and charges from the boroughs.[24] But even with such background material, the task facing the royal administration in 1086 was daunting.

The near-contemporary account of Robert, bishop of Hereford, described the way in which the king's servants worked. The king, he said, had the inquiry carried out in two stages. His men

made a survey of all England; of the lands in each of the counties; of the possessions of each of the magnates, their lands, their habitations, their men both bond and free, living in huts or with their own houses and lands; of ploughs, horses, and other animals; of the services and payments due from each and every estate. After these investigators came others who were sent to unfamiliar counties to check the first description and to denounce any wrongdoers to the king. And the land was troubled with many calamities arising from the gathering of the royal taxes.[25]

Initially, then, the royal officials perhaps sought returns of estates, rights and dues from each landholder and from each shire and hundredal administration, all of which could later be tested in court.[26] The whole of England south of the river Tees, the limits of the shire system, was divided into circuits, for each of which was appointed a panel of three or four royal commissioners drawn from the ecclesiastical and lay aristocracy. Map 2 represents the most likely arrangement of seven circuits, although there may have been as many as eight or nine.[27] The commissioners visited each shire in turn and dealt with a formidable amount of business at special enlarged sittings of the county court. Juries from the hundreds or wapentakes (in former Danish areas) and representatives from each manor came before them and deliberated upon, and added to, already existing material. That took only a matter of months and the participants must have adhered to a carefully prepared programme. There must also have been set criteria for establishing the values and the fiscal assessments of estates, because, at least in the Essex returns, these figures show a close correlation with manorial resources. Procedures seem to have varied from shire to shire, but the sequence of manorial entries in the resulting documents may have followed the order of earlier fiscal records. In some areas, the as yet unsorted returns may have been arranged by tenants within individual hundreds and wapentakes; in others, they were ordered according to tenants within the county at large but were resorted according to hundreds and wapentakes. The importance of the hundreds as fiscal and legal units of local administration is underlined in both arrangements.[28]

The survival of the texts of two surveys which are connected with the earlier stages of the Domesday inquest does much to elucidate the way in which it was made. The *Inquisitio Comitatus Cantabrigiensis* is probably a later copy of a part of the original returns for Cambridgeshire. It does not describe the king's nine manors which were,

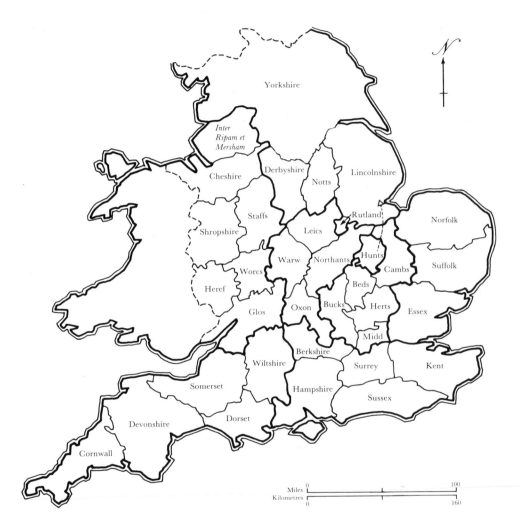

Map 2. *Domesday counties and possible circuits.*
    (The thick lines denote the possible boundaries of the circuits.)

as it shows, covered in a separate return, but otherwise it gives lists of manors arranged by hundreds and with considerable detail about livestock.[29] The other is the *Inquisitio Eliensis*, a collection of returns for the abbey of Ely, probably first copied in 1086–87, but preserved in three later manuscripts. It draws its material from six counties and three circuits.[30] Its prologue provides an invaluable account of the way in which business was conducted in court and even gives the names of the jurors in the hundreds.

Here follows the inquiry concerning lands which the king's barons made according to the oath of the sheriff of the shire and of all the barons and their Frenchmen, and of the whole hundred court – the priests, reeves and six villeins from each village. They inquired what the manor was called; who held it in the time of King Edward; who holds it now; how many hides there are; how many ploughs in demesne and how many belonging to the men; how many villeins; how many cottars; how many slaves; how many free men; how many sokemen; how much woodland; how much meadow; how much pasture; how many mills; how many fisheries; how much has been added to, or taken away from, the estate; what it used to be worth then; what it is worth now, and how much each freeman and sokeman had or has. All this to be recorded thrice: to wit, as it was in the time of King Edward, as it was when King William gave the estate, and as it is now. And it was also noted whether more could be taken from the estate than is now taken.[31]

The main text of the *Inquisitio Eliensis* appears to derive from the next stage of the inquest: the refining and recasting of the material into draft returns for the circuits. It suggests that the checking and sifting of the information were carried out differently in the three circuits it covered, and also points to the continuing involvement of great landholders.[32] That involvement allowed several other religious houses as well as Ely, and some lay tenants, to collect their own private Domesdays for their records. Examples are some near-contemporary parts of the Feudal Book of Abbot Baldwin of Bury St Edmunds, which seem to derive either from the first returns for the monastery's land or from the next stage of drafting;[33] and a section of the thirteenth-century cartulary of the Braybrooke family, listing the Cambridgeshire estates of Guy de Reimbercourt, the first source of which was probably the original returns.[34] Such landholders were also involved in the commissioners' adjudications of numerous disputes both about estates and about rights as diverse as the levying of tolls and the provision of a horse for military service. Many such wrangles were still to remain unsettled when Great Domesday was compiled, and thus appear in its text.[35]

A letter from Lanfranc, archbishop of Canterbury, written at some stage of the inquest proceedings, brings the involvement of the tenants-in-chief to life. He is replying to an inquiry from one of the royal commissioners of the Essex, Norfolk and Suffolk circuit who was evidently very persistent in cross-checking his materials. Lanfranc writes:

I confirm that in those counties in which you have been assigned the duty of making an inquest I have no demesne land; all the lands of our Church in those parts are entirely given over to providing food for the monks. The brother who is bringing you this letter has told me a great deal in your favour, too much to be set out here within the brief limits of a letter. May almighty God, whose memory nothing escapes, recompense you according to his knowledge many times over, and be your vigilant helper at all times to defend you from every evil machination.[36]

It is not known how many drafts lay between the first set of returns made to the shire court and the final format of Great Domesday, and it is probable that here again there were variations between the circuits. The original of a massive and valuable return for much of the south-western circuit, the *Liber Exoniensis* or Exon Domesday, has survived and provides vitally important information. The major part of the volume is a survey of boroughs and manors, arranged by landholders, fiefs and

7. *Page from Exon Domesday, giving part of the description of the count of Mortain's Somerset lands.*

within those by county and then by hundred. It answers the same questions as Great Domesday but at greater length, giving, for example, details of livestock and the names of tenants. All of the returns for Somerset and Cornwall and the majority for Devon are there, but those for Dorset and Wiltshire have mostly been lost and only a few appear. Other material, including a geld inquisition of about 1084–86, is also included in Exon. The work of several scribes, parts of the volume are untidy and contain corrections and additions, but much is written neatly. P.H. Sawyer and more recently C. and F. Thorn suggest that, rather than being only the penultimate draft behind the final Domesday version, as many scholars have believed, Exon Domesday, including its sections now missing, was used directly by the Exchequer scribe in making his compilation.[37] Eventually, once Exon's immediate usefulness was over, it probably passed to Exeter Cathedral, where it is known to have been preserved at least since 1669. It was not, however, bound up until the fourteenth or fifteenth century.[38]

Little Domesday, which is the final return for the eastern circuit, covering the counties of Essex, Suffolk and Norfolk, has remained with Great Domesday in official custody throughout the nine centuries since it was made. It contains far more detail than its companion, but its arrangement by counties, landholders and manors is the same. It was hastily copied by several clerks and contains many errors which remained uncorrected. Its headings were carefully rubricated, that is, marked in red ink, to expedite reference to it and to give it a more formal appearance, probably when it was adopted as part of the final record of the survey after work on Great Domesday was abandoned. The colophon, which states that the survey of England was made by King William in 1086, implies that all the final drafts were completed in that year, perhaps even by 1 August when the king received his oaths of homage from many important under-tenants.[39]

Great Domesday Book is the final summarized version of all the circuit returns save the one for the eastern circuit. Written in county sections quire by quire, rather than as one volume, it was compiled by one man and checked and annotated by another. These important and trusted, but anonymous, officials performed their task either at Winchester or, just possibly, in the shires, but it remained uncompleted, probably as the result of King William's departure for Normandy at the end of 1086 or of his death in the following September. Its highly abbreviated text follows the very questions which, according to the *Inquisitio Eliensis*, the royal commissioners asked. Most of the superfluous detail of the kind found in Exon Domesday or the *Inquisitio Eliensis* is ruthlessly, and in general systematically, pruned away to leave clear and easily usable entries. The material has a clear hierarchical arrangement and follows a set order in all but six shire sections. First in each county quire or quires comes a description of the main town or towns, then an outline list of

8. *Part of the list of royal lands in Norfolk, as shown in Little Domesday.*

landholders, and then the manorial descriptions, beginning with the king's estates and normally working through the holdings of his ecclesiastical and lay tenants. The boroughs are not, however, given uniform treatment, perhaps because they were not initially intended to form part of the survey, but were added when it was already under way. Indeed, the cities of London and Winchester are missing altogether. One reason may be that there was already enough information about them elsewhere,[40] another that, as with the eastern circuit, the work was never finished.

As well as such omissions, there are other problems with the text of Great Domesday, such as certain discrepancies in the type of information that is included and apparent inconsistencies in some manorial descriptions. There are gaps in several entries and undigested extraneous information in others. That may be the result partly of the rapidity of Great Domesday's compilation, and partly of the probable unavailability of fair and final drafts for at least some of the circuits.[41] Such complications make the interpretation of Domesday Book particularly difficult, but they do not diminish its value. It is a vitally important description of England's lands and of those who held them at a critical moment in its history; and it was produced by a royal administration which had an authority and capacity to rule which were unrivalled in north-western Europe.

Although Great Domesday Book was intended primarily as a work of practical reference and lacks the splendid illumination and fine penmanship of contemporary bibles and psalters, considerable care went into its making. It is written not on the vellum used for ceremonial volumes, but on parchment, which was suitable for

9. *Page from Great Domesday, describing royal lands in Yorkshire.*

administrative records because any erasures showed plainly upon it.[42] That used for Great Domesday's 413 leaves is of good quality and was made from the skins of between five hundred and a thousand small sheep, probably from Dorset, Hampshire or Wiltshire. The yellowish discolouration of the pages, particularly, as would be expected, on the grain side, is a clear sign of the considerable extent to which the book has been used through the centuries; but the oil from many human hands has also given the parchment a smooth and glossy feel. Some of the folios at the beginning and the end of the volume are of poorer quality and were probably added later, but several show signs of heavy use, particularly f. Hv, on which is written a table of contents. The 475 parchment leaves of Little Domesday are coarser and heavier and were not pared down as much as those in the larger volume. Nor do its pages, which have remained relatively clean, show signs of the frequent and regular use to which Great Domesday has been put.[43]

There are also considerable differences in the way in which the quires of the two volumes are made up. Great Domesday, with its many insertions and marginalia, shows all the features of being an abbreviation rather than a copy. Although in six cases a county section begins in the middle of a quire and seems closely connected with the one before, as, for example, with the overlap of Devon and Cornwall, all the others are self-contained within one or more quires of various sizes. In many cases, extra sheets were inserted for additions, a sign of the revisions which took place while the work was being compiled. Most of Little Domesday's quires are of eight leaves, and only a few extra pages were inserted. Although it is the work of several scribes, there are few additions or marginalia or variations in the number of lines to the page, all of which implies that it is a fair copy of an existing text.[44]

The logical geographical order in which the booklets of Great Domesday were later bound up[45] does not reflect the order in which they were originally made. Close examination of the rulings and the number of lines of writing on the page[46] suggests that the scribe probably began his task of abbreviating the final circuit drafts with circuit III, covering Middlesex, Hertfordshire, Buckinghamshire, Cambridgeshire and Bedfordshire. These quires were written in a large, careful hand with forty-four lines of writing on most pages. That was also the case for most of the next circuit, VI, for the counties of Huntingdon, Nottingham, Derby and Lincoln, but in one of its counties, Yorkshire, the scribe began to compress his work, ruling and filling almost fifty lines to the page. The quires for circuit I, containing Kent, Sussex, Surrey, Hampshire and Berkshire, where there are again about fifty lines to the page, were probably the next to be written; and those for circuit IV (Oxford, Northampton, Leicester and Warwick) show even greater economy, with between fifty-one and fifty-nine lines to a page for the first three counties and no rulings at all, but a closely written text, for the last. The final pattern of closely written pages persists for most of circuit II, containing Wiltshire, Dorset, Somerset, Devon and Cornwall, in which only the Wiltshire pages are ruled, and for all of circuit V, for Gloucestershire, Worcestershire, Herefordshire, Staffordshire, Shropshire, Cheshire, and the lands between the Ribble and Mersey rivers. The last sections were evidently compiled in great haste: there is considerable variation in the size of the writing, many additions, and much compression of material into the existing space.[47]

The style of writing in both Great and Little Domesday is that of the ubiquitous Caroline minuscule, but with rustic capitals for many of the rubricated headings. The main hand of the larger volume, which is in two columns, is idiosyncratic and slightly more advanced in form, perhaps being in the style in use at the royal

.XXI. TERRA ECCLE DE LANHELE. IN CELFLEDETORNE HD

Eccla S Mariae de Lanhele ten Estune. Goda comitissa tenuit T.R.E. Ibi .IIII. hide. In dnio sunt .III. car. 7 .VI. uilli 7 un miles cu .II. car 7 dim. Ibi .VI. serui. 7 .III. ancille. Valuit .C. sol. m̄ .IIII. lib.

.XXII. TERRA SCI EBRULFI. IN BOLELORD HD

Eccla S Ebrulfi ten de rege Rauuelle. Wluuard tenuit T.R.E. Ibi .X. hide. In dnio sunt .IIII. car. 7 .XVI. uilli 7 .II. bord cu .VI. car. Ibi .IIII. serui. Val 7 ualuit .X. lib. hoc M̄ nunc geldauit.

.XXIII. TERRA ECCLE MONIALIU DE CADOMO IN CIRECESTRE HD

Ecclā monialiū de Cadomo ten de rege Penne. Eberie. Ibi .III. hide. In dnio sunt .III. car. 7 .II. uilli 7 un faber cu .III. car. Ibi .XX. serui. 7 molin de .XL. den. Val 7 ualuit .III. lib. IN LANGETREV HD

Ipsa eccla ten Hantone. Goda comitissa tenuit T.R.E. Ibi .VIII. hide. in dnio sunt .V. car. 7 .XXXII. uilli 7 .X. bord cu .XII. car. Ibi pbr 7 .X. serui. 7 .III. molini de .XL.V. sol. .XX. ac pti. Silua .II. leuu lg 7 dimid leuu lat. Valet .XXVIII. lib.

.XXIIII. TERRA ECCLE DE TROARZ. IN LANGETREV HD

Ecclā S Martini de Roarz ten Horslei. dono regis. 7 Goda tenuit soror R.E. Ibi .X. hide. In dnio sunt .IIII. car. 7 .VI. uilli 7 .II. bord cu .VI. car. 7 un radchenist. de .VI. den. una domu in Glouuecestre de .VI. den. Ibi .I. molin de .L. denar. Valuit .XII. lib. modo .XIII. lib.

.XXV... TERRA ROGERII COMITIS. IN GERSDONES HD

Comes Rogerius ten Hantone. 7 Turold de eo nepos Wigoti.

.XXVI. TERRA HUGONIS COMITIS. IN BISELEIE HD

Comes Hugo ten Biselege. 7 Rob de eo. Ibi .VIII. hide. In dnio sunt .IIII. car. 7 .XX. uilli 7 .XXVIII. bord cu .XX. car. Ibi .VI. serui. 7 .IIII. ancille. Ibi .II. pbri 7 .VII. radchenist bntes .X. car. 7 alii .XXIII. hoes reddtes .XL.IIII. solid. 7 .II. sextar mell. Ibi .V. molin de .XVI. solid. 7 Silua de .XX. sold. 7 In Glouuec .XI. burgses reddtes .IX. den. Valuit .XXVIII. lib. Modo .XX. lib.

IN LANGETREV HD
do com̄ ten Westone. Elnod tenuit T.R.E. Ibi .II. hide geld. In eps 7 ht̄ HD

Ibd ten ipse comes .I. hid ad Rochā leuenod tenuit de rege E. 7 poterat ire quo uolet. H tra geld. Ibi sunt .IIII. bord cu .I. car. 7 .III. ac pti. Val .XX. sol.

Ibd ten ipse com̄ dimid hid. quā Roc de Laci cā iuniat ad Egesuurde. teste comitatu. Val .X. sol. 7 geld.

Ipse comes ten Capedene. Harold tenuit. Ibi .XV. hide geldant. In dnio .VI. car. 7 .I. uilli 7 .VIII. bord. cu .XXI. car. Ibi .XII. serui. 7 .II. molini de .VI. sold. 7 .II. denar. Ibi .II. ancille. Valuit modo .XX. lib. IN LANGETREV HD

Ipse com̄ ten .II. M̄ de .IIII. hid geldant. 7 .II. hoes de eo. Elnod 7 Leuuin tenuer T.R.E. Non fuer 7 respondep de his duo. sed p hoes comitat appciant .VIII. lib.

.XXVII. TERRA COMITIS MORITON. IN WITELAI HD

Comes Moriton ten Langeberge. Toui tenuit T.R.E. Ibi .II. hide. In dnio sunt .II. car. 7 .II. uilli 7 un bord cu .I. car. 7 .III. serui. Valuit .IIII. lib. 7 .XL. sol. 7 geld.

.XXV. TERRA ECCLE DE CIRECESTRE IN CIRECESTRE HD

Ecclā de Cirecestre ten de rege .II. hid in elemo sina. 7 de rege E. tenuit geras ab om̄ csuetudine. Ibi sunt .VI. ac pti. Val 7 ualuit hoc .XL. sol.

TERRA RENBALDI PBRI. IN GERSDONES HD

Leuenot tenuit. Ibi .V. hide. In dnio .I. car. 7 .II. uilli 7 .I. bord 7 pbr 7 duo alii hoes. Int om̄s hnt .II. car 7 dimid. Ibi .VI. serui. Valuit .VIII. lib. modo .III. lib.

.XXVII. Renbald ten Oaŭille de rege. Godric tenuit T.R.E. Ibi .IIII. hide 7 una V. In dnio .II. car. 7 .VIII. uilli 7 .I. bord cu .VI. car 7 pbro. Ibi .VIII. serui. 7 .II. molini de .X. solid. 7 .XX. ac pti. Val 7 ualuit .C. solid.

Ist Renbald ten Daireille. Elaf tenuit de comite Tosti. Ibi .VII. hide. In dnio .IIII. car. 7 .VI. uilli 7 .II. bord 7 pbr cu .V. car. Ibi .XV. serui. 7 molin de .V. solid. 7 .X. ac pti. Val 7 ualuit .VIII. lib. IN CIRECESTRE HD

Ist Rainbald ten in Nortcote .I. hid. Godric tenuit T.R.E. In dnio e una car. 7 .II. uilli 7 .II. bord cu .I. car. Ibi .VI. serui. Val 7 ualuit .XL. solid. hic raiñ poterat ire quo uolebat.

Ist Rainb ten Prestetune. Elaf tenuit T.R.E. Ibi .VIII. hide geld fuer dnio. In dnio sunt .III. car. 7 .VII. uilli 7 .II. bord cu .VI. car. Ibi .XX. serui. 7 .XII. ac pti. Val 7 ualuit .VIII. lib. Ipse Elaf poterat ire quo uolet.

.XXX. TERRA GISLEBERTI EPI LISIACSIS. IN LANGETREV HD

Hugo maminot ten Rednescote de Gisleb epo lisiacsi 7 ipse de rege. Ibi .II. hide. In dnio sunt .II. car. 7 .I. uilli 7 .II. bord 7 pbr cu .I. car. Ibi .II. serui. Valuit .III. lib. modo .III. lib. Leuuin tenuit de rege .E.

Ist hugo ten de ipso epo Lesseberge. Leuuin tenuit. Ibi .V. hide. In dnio e una car. 7 .V. uilli 7 pbr cu .II. car. 7 .VII. serui. Valuit .X. lib. modo .V. solid. IN GRIBOLDESTOV HD

Ist hugo ten Sopeberie de eod epo. Aluuard tenuit T.R.E. Ibi .V. hide geld. In dnio sunt .II. car. 7 .III. uilli 7 .II. bord cu .II. car. Ibi .IIII. serui. 7 .XX. ac pti. Silua aliquatu. Valuit .VIII. lib. modo .IIII. lib.

.XXXII. TERRA WILLELMI DE OW. IN BLICHELEV HD

Wills de Ow ten Stanhes. Toui tenuit T.R.E. Ibi erant .VII. hid. In dnio su. .III. car. 7 .VII. uilli 7 .V. bord cu .IIII. car. Ibi .II. serui. 7 .II. molini de .XVI. solid. 7 .VI. denar. Ibi .XX. arpenz uinee. Val 7 ualuit .VIII. lib. hoc M̄ geldat. IN TEBELGE HOND

Ist Wills ten Aluredestone. Bondi tenuit T.R.E. Ibi .III. hide geldant. Nil ibi e in dnio. sed .V. uilli 7 .II. bord hnt .III. car. Ibi piscaria de .XII. den. 7 .X. ac pti. Silua dimid leuu lg 7 dimid lat. Valuit .XX. sold. modo .XX. sol. Henric de Fereriis calumiat eam bondi tenuit. Wills antecessor tenuit h̄ d de Lunesi.

Ips W. ten ibid .II. hid geld. 7 ibi sunt .III. uilli cu .II. car. Val 7 ualuit .X. sold.

Ips W. tenuit Wicberie. 7 Radselmeti ante eu. Alestan tenuit T.R.E. Sic est iussu regis in foresta sua. Ibi erant .VI. hid 7 geld. 7 ualet .LX. solid. Modo ñ est nisi piscaria de .X. solid.

Ist W. ten Rossluesston. Bricric f algari tenuit. Ibi .II. hide. Nil ibi e in dnio. nisi .V. uilli cu .V. car. 7 una piscaria in Sauerna de .V. solid. 7 molin de .XL. denar. Val 7 ualuit .XX. solid. h tra geld. IN KIFTESGATE HD

Ist W. ten in Sibelia una V. 7 dimid geldant. Saigar tenuit. Ibi .I. uilli cu .I. car 7 .II. piscarie. Val 7 ualuit .X. sol.

Ist W. ten Dentesborne. Alestan tenuit T.R.E. Ibi Cirecestre HD. Ibi .V. hide 7 dim geld. In dnio sunt .II. car. 7 .VI. uilli 7 .III. bord cu .V. car 7 dimid. 7 .II. serui. 7 molin de .V. solid. hoc M̄ ten Radulf de Willo .V. geld. sed ipse geld regi de .III. hid. VI francig ten 7 dimid hid de isa tra. 7 ibi hnt .I. car cu suis hoib3. Tot T.R.E. ualeb .X. lib. modo .VIII. lib.

Ist W. ten in Toruentone .I. hid. 7 hertb de eo. Leuric tenuit T.R.E. 7 poquit ire quo uolet. In dnio e una car. 7 .XL. solid. modo .XX. sol. IN LANGETREV HD

10. *(Opposite) Page, apparently written in haste, from the Gloucestershire section of Great Domesday*

11. *The 'Tudor' covers of Domesday Book. The boards of the smaller volume are the medieval ones, which were re-used.*

court. The hands of Little Domesday, which is written in single column, are rather closer to their Carolingian exemplars; and it is striking that, in later centuries, officials with the task of producing copies in Domesday script normally followed the letter forms of the smaller volume.

It has often been assumed that Domesday Book remained unbound until well into the thirteenth century. Yet a different conclusion has recently emerged from examination of the oak boards of Little Domesday's earliest surviving cover, for they, and hence the first binding, date certainly from before 1220 and probably from the twelfth century. Domesday was described as a book (*liber*) in the reign of Henry I, and perhaps it had already been bound by then.[48] It is known that in 1320 William 'le Bokbyndere' was paid 3s. 4d. for rebinding and repairing Little Domesday, probably for the first time;[49] and a new cover was placed on it during the Tudor or, just possibly, the Stuart period, over the Romanesque boards, apparently leaving 'le Bokbyndere's' work undisturbed.[50] No similar evidence has been found for Great Domesday, although it would probably have first been bound at roughly the same time as Little Domesday, on seven bands corresponding to the earliest lines of sewing holes. The 'Tudor' binder replaced them with five bands, and used new beech boards as the basis for the finely decorated cover.[51] Since then both volumes have been rebound four times: in 1819, 1869, 1953 and 1985.[52]

Domesday scholars have through the centuries rightly stressed the unusual and unique features of William the Conqueror's survey. An assessment of its historical importance would, however, be incomplete without a look at where it stands in relation to other medieval European surveys. The rulers of republican and imperial

Rome had made regular use of fiscal censuses, a practice also employed by their Byzantine and Arab successors in the Eastern Empire.[53] In the West, by contrast, the necessary administrative capacity was lost. However, in the late-Roman period, many great landowners had kept their own estate inventories as a by-product of the census, a practice which survived after the census disappeared. The revival of the Western Empire by the Carolingians in the ninth century brought with it a resurgence of official surveys. Imperial administrators, perhaps influenced by the value of private land-lists, used surveys to achieve a great variety of purposes: to describe manors, to assess the value of property, to inquire into market rights. Many of their inquiries involved commissioners, the sworn inquest and written returns.[54]

With the collapse of the Carolingian Empire there also disappeared the practice of making royal surveys, but from the ninth century to the twelfth the Church in north-eastern France, Italy and the Rhineland preserved the tradition in its estate surveys (known as polyptychs or *descriptiones*). As an example, the polyptych of the abbey of Prüm in Lorraine, the text of which dates from about 893, was compiled from returns from commissioners who were sent around all the abbey's vast and scattered estates to collect information about manors, mills and other sources of income. The final version was written not, as normally, in a roll but in a book, and was thought to be as much a public as a private record.[55] No evidence has survived for similar contemporary surveys of the lands of English abbeys, and there are few signs of direct Carolingian influence on the administrative practices of the Anglo-Saxon kingdom. Nevertheless, the similarities between the régime of the Carolingians of the ninth century and the English of the eleventh are arresting.[56]

The administration of Edward the Confessor and William the Conqueror does, however, seem to have been unique in the north-western Europe of the later eleventh century in its ability to assess and levy taxation on the basis of written records. For example, in France, a kingdom far less centralized than England, no royal survey of any scope was made until 1204, after the conquest of Normandy from King John. That inquest, made for King Philip Augustus, took until 1211 to complete, and was followed immediately by the first in a long series of revisions. Yet it was no more than an outline list of lands and their holders, distinguishing between the cities, castellanies and estates in the royal demesne and those held by the great ecclesiastical and lay barons.[57] It was the product of an expanding royal administration with a capacity to innovate comparable to that of Henry I of England,[58] but which did not produce a survey with either the scale or detail of Domesday until as late as 1327–28. This was *l'état des paroisses et des feux*, commissioned by King Philip VI, a full description of royal rights in the levying of hearth tax, and covering the whole kingdom apart from six great fiefs, some lesser lordships and the royal appanages. The material was collected from the localities by royal officials, then returned to the royal accounting department (*chambre des comptes*) in Paris and finally copied into official registers for future reference.[59] A fundamental and continuing contrast between the French and English kingdoms is revealed by the inability of the French king to levy taxes or to collect information inside the lands of his greatest barons.

The most direct near-contemporary comparisons with Domesday Book come not from north-western Europe but from other Norman and Frankish kingdoms in the Mediterranean. In Sicily, the Norman administration was, like its ecclesiastical architecture, an exotic and eclectic mixture of Byzantine, Arabic and Norman elements. Fiscal records had possibly been kept by the ducal administration in Normandy in the eleventh century,[60] but undoubtedly had been in Sicily, where early Norman descriptions were derived from Muslim and perhaps from Byzantine material. In the twelfth century, the Norman kings kept records in their treasuries which listed boundaries, the names of serfs, the values of estates and the details of land use, and which were used to settle land disputes and to register sales.[61] There was a similar pattern in southern Italy, and also in the Latin kingdom of Jerusalem, where the twelfth-century Frankish rulers allowed the existing Muslim financial administration to continue to keep records of land, boundaries and services and to account for revenues collected by royal agents, while at the same time carrying out their own surveys of the crusader population and lands.[62]

Domesday Book is thus neither unprecedented nor wholly isolated, but it has special qualities which set it apart from those other surveys. In 1844, a celebrated French scholar who had worked extensively on polyptychs commented that, of all of them, 'the most wide-ranging and the most remarkable, if not the most ancient, is without any doubt the description which William the Conqueror, king of England, had made of the lands in his kingdom'.[63] The detail contained in Domesday Book, the coverage not merely of the royal estates but of all the land, the several different sets of questions — fiscal, feudal, tenurial and legal — which it answers, the systematic analysis of information there, the sense of administrative purpose and royal direction which it conveys, have all combined to make it a unique record. So also has its reputation, fostered by the royal administration, as the source of final judgment from which there could be no appeal. It is such qualities, too, which have, over the centuries, turned what was a pragmatic exercise in the gathering of information into a 'most venerable monument of antiquity',[64] a distinction which fiscal records can only very exceptionally achieve. Although it has remained a working document through its nine hundred years, the 'Domesday myth' has also endowed it with symbolic attributes of many different kinds and has given it the reputation for containing an apparently limitless fund of information. The following account of Domesday's history will contain many examples of the intrusion of this myth into administrative reality.

CHAPTER II

The Reputation and Uses of
Domesday Book, 1087–1272

Domesday Book and its importance to the royal administration were eloquently described by Richard Fitz Neal, King Henry II's treasurer.

There are several things in the vaults of the Treasury, which are taken about the country, and are locked up and kept safe by the treasurer and chamberlains . . ., such as the king's seal . . ., Domesday Book, the roll of demands, which is called the 'writ of farms'; the great yearly rolls of account, a multitude of charters, counter tallies and rolls of receipts, royal writs for the issue of treasure, and sundry other things which are needed for daily use while the Exchequer is sitting.

Domesday Book . . . is the inseparable companion in the Treasury of the royal seal. The reason for its compilation was told me by Henry, bishop of Winchester, as follows. When the famous William 'the Conqueror' . . . had brought under his sway the farthest limits of the island . . ., he decided to bring the conquered people under the rule of written law.

To give the finishing touch to all this forethought, after taking counsel he sent his most skilful councillors in circuit throughout the realm. By these a careful survey of the whole country was made, of its woods, its pastures and meadows, as well of arable land, and was set down in common language and drawn up into a book; in order, that is, that every man may be content with his own rights, and not encroach unpunished on those of others. The survey is made by counties, hundreds and hides. The king's name heads the list, followed by those of the nobles who hold of the king in chief, according to their order of dignity. The list is then numbered, and the matter in the actual text of the book relating to each tenant is easily found by the corresponding number.

This book is metaphorically called by the native English, Domesday, i.e., the Day of Judgment. For as the sentence of that strict and terrible last account cannot be evaded by any subterfuge, so when this book is appealed to on those matters which it contains, its sentence cannot be quashed or set aside with impunity. That is why we have called the book 'the Book of Judgment', . . . not because it contains decisions on various difficult points, but because its decisions, like those of the Last Judgment, are unalterable.[1]

The passage comes from Fitz Neal's *Dialogus de Scaccario* (Dialogue of the Exchequer), which was completed in its original form in about 1179[2] and was copied and used by generations of Exchequer officials. The value and interest of the passage about Domesday Book, including the discussion of counties, hundreds and hides which follows it, were recognized by many later keepers of Domesday. In

Elizabeth I's reign, Arthur Agarde, a deputy chamberlain of the Exchequer and a noted scholar, was the first to use this evidence to explain the purpose of the Domesday survey, and in 1617 John Bradshaw, one of his successors, copied the passage into the preliminary pages of Great Domesday itself.[3] Bradshaw reproduced the thirteenth-century version from the Black Book of the Exchequer, a remembrance book which had been in regular use at the Exchequer for many centuries.[4] He wrote in a quasi-Domesday script and introduced some minor variations, and his version of the text was recopied by other, later, Domesday custodians.[5]

12. *Extract from the Black Book of the Exchequer, describing Domesday Book. The text dates from the twelfth century, but this copy is from the thirteenth.*

13. *The same passage as in Plate 12, as copied out by John Bradshaw into the preliminary pages of Domesday Book. It was written in 1617, but imitates the calligraphical style of Domesday itself.*

The explanation in the *Dialogus* of how Domesday Book acquired its name is of particular interest. Richard Fitz Neal knew of and understood the awe in which the native English still held it almost a century after its making, which led the Exchequer officials to adopt the metaphor of the Last Judgment, calling it the Book of Judgment. From the thirteenth century, it almost invariably appears in official documents as 'the book which is called Domesday' (*liber qui vocatur Domesday*). Some later chroniclers and antiquaries were to offer a different and erroneous explanation of how the book was named. John Stow, an assiduous Elizabethan peruser of earlier chronicles and histories, wrote that he had discovered in

the book of Bermondsey, [that] this book [i.e., Domesday] was laid up in the king's Treasury (which was in the Church of Winchester, or Westminster), in a place called *Domus Dei*, or God's house, and so the name of the book [was] therefore called *Domus Dei*, and since, shortly, Domesday.

The Bermondsey book may well have been a fourteenth-century cartulary of the abbey, which is now lost, but the extent to which Stow embellished what he found there is not clear. His was a story which had many later echoes:[6] Sir Richard Baker, for example, writing in the seventeenth century, said that Domesday 'was known by the English as Domesday Book instead of *Domus Dei* book, for that it was laid in the church of Winchester, in a place called *Domus Dei*'.[7]

Although without etymological foundation, these stories were accurate about the city in which Domesday Book was first kept. For about the first hundred years of its existence it had its permanent home in the royal treasury at Winchester, along with earlier fiscal lists and perhaps some of the records on which the Conqueror's survey had been based. As the *Dialogus* suggests, the Exchequer often moved with the king on his travels, and Domesday Book and other records needed for financial business were frequently in the royal baggage train. Probably by the end of Henry II's reign, the principal royal treasury was no longer at Winchester but in London at the Temple and the Tower, from where it moved again, this time to Westminster, in the early thirteenth century.[8] The Exchequer likewise gained a more permanent home in Westminster under John and Henry III, but royal government was to remain peripatetic for centuries, and Domesday Book was on many occasions to be moved, together with all the other records and paraphernalia needed for Exchequer business.[9] In 1194, King Philip Augustus of France lost many important royal records when fleeing from the battle of Fréteval, and it is fortunate for posterity that Domesday was not with King John's treasure and regalia which were engulfed by the quicksands of the Wellstream in 1216.[10]

Although the English may have adopted the title 'Domesday' within a generation, until the end of John's reign royal officials and monastic chroniclers knew the records connected with the inquiry by a variety of other names. To Domesday's makers it was a 'survey' (*descriptio*),[11] and to William Rufus's administrators, the king's 'writings' (*brevia*), an expression which matches the terminology of its own text.[12] From about 1100, there are references to the 'book' (*liber*)[13] or 'document' (*carta*)[14] of Winchester or belonging to the king or treasury. From about the mid-twelfth to the early thirteenth centuries, the most usual description of Domesday is either the Winchester or the king's 'roll' (*rotulus*).[15] One annalist described it as 'the book called the king's roll'.[16] The name Domesday used by Fitz Neal does not appear in an official document until 1221.[17]

It is, however, often very difficult to discern precisely which records lie behind the names.[18] Hemming, a monk of Worcester who compiled a cartulary in the years around 1100, drew on Domesday material and distinguished clearly between Domesday Book and earlier fiscal lists preserved in the royal treasury.[19] An Abingdon monk, writing perhaps forty years later, gives extracts both from 'the writings of the king's treasury' and from Domesday Book, which he describes as 'another book of the royal treasury from the time of King William ..., [which] contains an abbreviation of hides'.[20] It has been suggested that many apparent references to Domesday Book in royal writs could apply to the earlier surveys as well or better.[21] So too could the later description of Winchester roll or rolls.[22] Indeed, the chronicle forged at Crowland Abbey in the later middle ages to substantiate the tenurial claims of its inmates suggests that, in the twelfth century, the term 'Winchester rolls' was applied both to the fiscal lists, organized by counties and hundreds, which went back to the reign of Alfred (a major piece of exaggeration, but a story which was to die hard),[23] and to Domesday Book, which shared their name because it was modelled on them.[24] The matter is complicated yet further by the advent of official abbreviated versions of Domesday Book, listing only landholders, manors and hides. The earliest was probably made during Henry II's reign and, with its successors, was used for at least a century as a finding aid, a summary of the more cumbersome original.[25]

Descriptions of the making of the Domesday survey occur in a number of chronicles and narratives of the period. They derive from two sources already quoted above: the contemporary account by Robert de Losinga, bishop of Hereford, and the version in the Anglo-Saxon Chronicle, written about thirty years later for Peterborough Abbey.[26] Robert de Losinga had added his passage on the survey to a shortened version of the celebrated Universal Chronicle of Marianus Scotus. A full copy of the same chronicle found its way to the cathedral library at Worcester, where Robert's friend Wulfstan was bishop until 1095, and to it was subsequently added an abridgment of Robert's passage:

William, king of the English, had all property in all of England surveyed: lands, men, all animals, all habitations from the greatest to the least, and all rents which all the estates could render. Consequently the land was vexed with many calamities.[27]

It was from these additions to the works of Marianus that a later chronicler at the same monastery (probably John of Worcester and not Florence of Worcester, as for long thought), writing in about the 1120s, derived his version of Domesday's making:[28]

King William had all England surveyed: how much land each of his barons possessed, how many enfeoffed knights, how many ploughs, villeins, animals and livestock each possessed in his kingdom from the greatest to the least, and how much each estate could render in rents. Consequently the land was vexed with many calamities.[29]

Another historical compilation, made probably at Worcester between 1125 and 1140, contains a different explanation in a passage translated into Latin from the old English of the Anglo-Saxon Chronicle.[30] Some extra explanatory material was added, including the information that the king 'ordered that all should be written in one volume, and that the volume should be placed in his treasury at Winchester and kept there'.[31]

The passage on the genesis of Domesday in Henry of Huntingdon's history of England, first completed in the later 1120s, draws on both the Hereford-Worcester and the Anglo-Saxon Chronicle versions. It describes how

that most powerful king sent his justices through every shire or county of England, and had inquiries made by sworn inquest about how many hides (that is to say ploughlands each sufficient for one plough in the year) there were in each village, and what livestock. He also made inquiries about how much each city, castle, township, village, marsh and wood was accustomed to render each year. All this information was written down in records which were brought to the king, and placed in the Treasury where they are used to this day.[32]

This version of events proved highly acceptable to Henry of Huntingdon's literary successors; and it was to appear with only minor variations in numerous subsequent works, from that of Robert of Torigni, abbot of Mont St Michel, writing in the mid-twelfth century,[33] to those of the St Albans historian, Matthew Paris, writing in the mid-thirteenth. Matthew reproduced the story in three separate chronicles. The first, dating from the 1240s, was his Great Chronicle.[34] To the second, his History of the English, written in the 1250s, he added a marginal memorandum: 'Note that then was made the great book which is kept in the Treasury at Westminster and is called Domesday, and is so named because, like the Day of Judgment, it spares no-one.'[35]

A further addition is: 'Here the manifest oppression of England began', a comment found again in his third account in the Epitome of Chronicles[36] and perhaps influenced by the Anglo-Saxon chronicler's version. Certainly it springs also from Matthew Paris's implacable hostility towards a strong royal power and detestation of all royal taxation, which he saw as extortion – feelings which coloured and enlivened his works.[37] Thus, many centuries before the Levellers were to rail against the oppressions of the 'Norman yoke', a highly influential English Benedictine chronicler was representing the Domesday survey as a cruel and tyrannical act by a conquering king.[38]

From the late thirteenth century, Domesday was frequently to be called on to provide proof of landholding, tenures and boundaries.[39] It is far more difficult to assess its value to the royal administration earlier on, during its first two centuries, and to ascertain whether it was a working record or merely an outmoded relic with an inflated reputation. To V.H. Galbraith, 'the making of Domesday Book was not the conclusion but the beginning of its history'.[40] For S.P.J. Harvey, Domesday Book stands as 'an epitome of the administration and policy of Anglo-Norman governance of England',[41] and she has demonstrated its importance in the earlier twelfth century. W.L. Warren considers that 'for a century after its completion Domesday Book was sacrosanct: it was the administrators' bible'.[42] However, an entirely different approach was adopted by H.G. Richardson and G.O. Sayles. They saw Domesday Book as

an inestimable boon to a learned posterity, but a vast administrative mistake. Devised, as the Domesday survey obviously was, to augment the king's already swollen revenue, we cannot guess to what practical purposes its findings could have been put had he survived. ... The fruit of a personal whim of the king, ... within a generation Domesday Book itself had become a historical monument, respected but unused.[43]

That point of view has more recently been echoed by M.T. Clanchy. He argues that Domesday Book 'was founded on a misconception of how to use writing in royal administration [and was] too precocious'; not until two centuries after its making, when the royal administration consulted documents as a matter of routine, did it become of any practical use.[44] If such views as these were fully accepted, it could well be argued that Domesday Book was of greater value as a working record during the twentieth century than during the twelfth.[45]

So striking a diversity of opinion has been possible mainly because of the complexity of the evidence. As well as the testimony of Richard Fitz Neal, it consists of extracts from Domesday and its associated records which were copied into cartularies and other documents; of legal records in which Domesday evidence was cited; of the Herefordshire Domesday, a twelfth-century Exchequer record; and of the abbreviated versions of Domesday Book. The cartulary and other copies, many now known as 'satellite surveys', are difficult to interpret, and the relative scarcity of surviving twelfth-century writs citing Domesday has made it difficult to establish a continuous pattern of use. Furthermore, the Domesday abbreviations have never been properly evaluated, yet they contain vital evidence about the uses of Domesday Book in the thirteenth century which enables us to make a fuller assessment of its value during the whole of its first two hundred years.

It is a mistake to regard Domesday Book as an isolated record, as an experiment which was ahead of its time, because other analogous documents were produced by the royal administration both before and after it. Just as it had official precursors in the earlier fiscal assessments and lists of manors, so, after its completion, the royal administration continued to produce similar records on a lesser scale. Among those are the lists of lands and vills in Leicestershire, Lindsey and Northamptonshire made in the early twelfth century;[46] a list of the lands of Robert de Bruis added to the pages of Great Domesday in the 1120s;[47] and the Winchester Domesday, compiled in about 1110 to remedy the omission of that city from Domesday Book and based probably on a pre-Conquest list of tenements.[48] There is also a legal context in the lawsuits involving religious houses such as Ely, Worcester and Christ Church, Canterbury, in the years before the inquest.[49] It was these and other religious communities which took extracts and made summaries of Domesday material in its various forms for preservation in their muniments and, in some instances, for use in later legal battles. Despite Domesday's exceptional qualities, it therefore fell within a general pattern of records produced by the royal administration.

Copies of Domesday material which survive in cartularies and legal records are an indication of the importance attached to Domesday by the Crown's tenants-in-chief. They had had a considerable involvement in its making, many acting as commissioners and having access to the written returns. A number of extracts from records connected with the Domesday survey were made, presumably on their behalf, and preserved by being copied into cartularies for future reference. The passage in the thirteenth-century Braybrooke cartulary is a rare instance of the survival of a Domesday document in a lay register;[50] for far more have come down to us in the cartularies made in the scriptoria of religious houses. Ecclesiastical documents have been better preserved than those of lay families, but the discrepancy may also stem from a greater contemporary interest among churchmen in the survey's records. To monastic administrators, accustomed to the idea of using written records as evidence of their rights, it must have seemed prudent to keep copies of Domesday documents alongside their earlier geld assessments or royal charters. In such a way were some of the major 'satellite' surveys preserved, together with many other fiscal, manorial and feudal lists, some earlier than the Domesday survey, others later, and some roughly contemporary.[51] Thus, parts of the Feudal Book of Abbot Baldwin of Bury St Edmunds, a complex and puzzling document, appear to have been based closely on Domesday material. However, other parts, made at about the same time as the Conqueror's survey, seem not to derive directly from it.[52] Somewhere between these two extremes comes material in the archives of Christ Church, Canterbury (the monastic cathedral),[53] St Augustine's Abbey at Canterbury,[54] Abingdon Abbey,[55] Bath Cathedral Priory[56] and Evesham Abbey.[57] The *Inquisitio Eliensis* is similar, but was perhaps expanded by the monks for the use of royal administrators sent in by Ranulf Flambard during the episcopal vacancy of 1093.[58]

One of the most important of these compilations came from Worcester Cathedral Priory, where in about 1100 the monk Hemming copied a dossier of recent documents into the cartulary which he had made in defence of the rights of the monks. Since 1087, the community had suffered financially from its heavy hidation under the survey, and worse had befallen in 1095, when the then vacant bishopric fell into the hands of the rapacious William Rufus. Not content with enjoying the profits of the vacant see, the king, with the help and counsel of Ranulf Flambard, levied a relief from the abbey's sub-tenants, provoking strong hostility from the community.[59] The arrival of Bishop Samson (1096–1112), who had court connections and access to official records, enabled Hemming to include parts of the Domesday survey in his cartulary, together with lists of lands seized from the monastery by the Danes and Normans and material on a long-running dispute with Evesham Abbey.[60] Hemming's Domesday documents included a slightly augmented version of the Great Domesday entry for Oswaldslaw hundred and a highly abbreviated version of the entry for the lands of the bishopric of Worcester.[61] Although the latter differs significantly in its wording from the later official Domesday abbreviations, Galbraith suggested that it could nevertheless have been based on a Domesday abstract used at court.[62] But it is far more likely to be a résumé made by Hemming himself,[63] because the first official Domesday abbreviation was probably not compiled until the reign of Henry II, more than fifty years later.[64]

Documents collected by tenants-in-chief were intended to be used, and among the surviving writs and charters from the reigns of William Rufus and Henry I, which must represent only a proportion of those originally drawn up, there are a number of references to the citation of Domesday evidence by monastic communities in support of their rights. In 1091–96, St Swithun's Cathedral Priory, Winchester, used Domesday records, which were readily available to its monks, to prove that the Conqueror had granted it the churches of Lydeard St Lawrence and Angersleigh in

Somerset. Shortly after that, in 1099–1100, the monks similarly made certain their claim to Hayling Island, originally given to them by Queen Emma.[65] The abbey of St Benet of Hulme, Norfolk, used the survey between 1093 and 1100 to repossess land in Winterton and Burgh St Margaret, evidently seized from it, perhaps by Earl Hugh of Chester.[66] There may be an analogy here with the Anglo-Saxon administrators' practice of allowing the use of fiscal records as evidence in the settlement of land disputes.[67] In 1127, Ely Cathedral Priory obtained a writ stating that all barons and knights who were holders of lands listed in Domesday Book as lying within the fee of Ely were still to hold them from the same church and bishop.[68] Domesday was used also to determine matters of taxation. In 1127, the Augustinian canons of the newly founded priory at Plympton obtained an exemption from paying geld at Wembury and Colebrooke, Devon, because their lands there were not listed in the hidage of the 'king's document'.[69] The bishops and the monks of Worcester Cathedral Priory also found Domesday's evidence of considerable value. In 1111, Bishop Samson used it to prove that certain lands had to pay geld with his own estates, and between 1114 and 1133, a successor established by it that he should pay geld on no more than $387\frac{1}{2}$ hides.[70] Between 1109 and 1114, the monks of Worcester likewise secured their right to church scot.[71] Feudal and judicial obligations could similarly be proved by recourse to Domesday Book. The abbot of Abingdon cited Domesday evidence in 1111 to prove that the manor of Lewknor in Oxfordshire owed suit of court and various dues not to the hundred court of Pirton, but to that of Lewknor in which the abbey had seventeen hides.[72]

Although there is a gap in the evidence for the later years of the twelfth century, similar use of Domesday Book was made at its very end. In 1199, Samson, abbot of Bury St Edmunds, vouched the survey to prove that the manor of Heacham in Norfolk was within the liberty of the abbey and that therefore a knight of the bishop of Ely who had exercised judicial rights on land of the manor had acted unjustly.[73] In the next year, Robert the Chamberlain cited it to show that his land in Marston, Lincolnshire, had from the time of the Conquest been held directly from the king.[74] Between 1198 and 1214 Master William of Potterne, a career ecclesiastic, informed Robert, prior of Bath, that

I have found in Domesday Book that the town of Bath with Easton used to geld with the shire of Somerset for twenty hides. There are also in the said town forty messuages which pay four pounds a year. There are also seven empty houses and a house which a certain interpreter holds for two shillings. The barons of the province also have in the same town fifty shillings. Farewell.[75]

There is also a tantalizing entry in a 1221 plea roll: 'Remember to look up Domesday Book for the bishop.' This is the first time that Domesday is so called in an official document, and it is probably the first official search of Domesday Book ever to be recorded.[76]

Interesting evidence about how Domesday was regarded at the court of Henry II and ample corroboration of Fitz Neal's description of the book's contemporary uses in the Exchequer are found in the Herefordshire Domesday. It is a formal and embellished copy of Domesday's Herefordshire folios, which was apparently made in the Exchequer in the 1160s at the behest of one of the officials there. The shire chosen and the list of royal oblations which are included in the volume link it with Master Thomas Brown, the king's almoner and the holder of considerable property in Herefordshire. Thomas had served and gained valuable experience at the court of King Roger II of Sicily, from which he had subsequently been exiled, and became one of Henry II's most trusted Exchequer officials. His volume is an elegant one, indicative both of his personal standing and of the veneration with which Domesday Book was regarded, but there is also much of practical interest in its marginal annotations. They are of two kinds, the geldable values of the estates and the names of their recent holders, and they look very much like an attempt to bring Domesday's information up to date and into line with current Exchequer preoccupations.[77]

14. *Page from the Herefordshire Domesday,*
summarizing the Great Domesday information
on royal lands.

The experiment appears, however, to have been abandoned in its early stages. There are obvious reasons. The format of Domesday Book was not one which readily lent itself to updating, and the mass of detail in its text concealed the information about landholding, manors and titles which was felt still to be important. Those elements were therefore extracted into summarized versions of the survey.[78] Such abbreviations were probably not intended as a substitute for Domesday Book, which furnished the only acceptable legal proof, but were made and copied as repertories, or finding aids, to Great and Little Domesday. Far more portable and easily reproduced, they contained key information for immediate administrative use. The earliest to survive dates from the latter half of the twelfth century, and gives a summarized version of the Kent folios. Although now mounted in a volume, it was originally made as a roll, probably in the Exchequer, for the use of a sheriff or another county official.[79] Its text is fuller and closer to that of Great Domesday than are those of the later abbreviations.[80]

Two thirteenth-century abbreviations of the whole of Domesday Book have survived, as well as a third which is now incomplete. All are similar in layout and appearance, but comparison of their texts suggest that they were not copied one from another, but that they derived, whether directly or indirectly, from a common exemplar, now lost. The most striking is the Exchequer *Abbreviatio*, written in a formal hand and sumptuously illuminated: a document fit for a king. The handwriting suggests that it was made in the first half of the thirteenth century, possibly in the scriptorium at Westminster Abbey. The main part has initial letters picked out and illuminated in gold, red and blue, and illustrations of the king, archbishops, bishops and lay barons at appropriate places in the text. Even more splendid are the two folios later added to the front of the volume, which contain scenes from the life and miracles of St Edward the Confessor.[81] The whole was obviously intended to be a fine and elegant manuscript, both in homage to the reputation of Domesday and to please the patron for whom it was compiled.

The Exchequer *Abbreviatio* was, however, intended primarily to be a working volume. In the main body of the text, each reference to the king is marked in the margin either with an 'r' for 'rex' or with a symbol, occasionally in red for greater emphasis. Against other entries 'nᵃ', signifying 'nota', is elegantly written, again sometimes in red. Some such marginal notes mark lands in dispute in 1086, others the estates of the counts of Mortain, which had been in contention following the French conquest of Normandy in 1204. There is a 'c' by one Westminster manor, perhaps denoting that a certificate from Domesday had been obtained for the entry.[82] Finally, and most helpful for dating, 'A's are written against every entry relating to Count Alan of Brittany, whose lands were a major Domesday estate known in later centuries as the honor of Richmond. At the beginning of 1241, the honor of

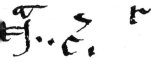

Richmond was in the king's hands; in May of that year it was granted to Peter of Savoy, the king's close kinsman, favourite and adviser.[83] He was briefly sheriff of Kent in 1241–42, and he is known, some years later, to have cited Domesday in the King's Council against his tenants.[84] In the 1240s, too, Henry III was deeply involved in enhancing the cult of Edward the Confessor: a new shrine for the saint's remains was commissioned in 1241 and, from 1245 onwards, vast sums were made available for rebuilding the whole of Westminster Abbey in his honour.[85] Taken together, the evidence suggests that the Exchequer *Abbreviatio* was commissioned shortly after the honor of Richmond was granted to Peter of Savoy and completed fairly soon afterwards, to be used by Peter or perhaps presented to the king. In it, the cult of the Confessor meets with and enhances the cult of Domesday Book.

The two other thirteenth-century abbreviations, one preserved at Margam Abbey,[86] the other perhaps at Neath Abbey[87] were probably copied somewhat later than the Exchequer *Abbreviatio*. The handwriting in both is fairly formal and their initial letters are picked out in blue and red, giving them a very similar appearance. They also have much in common with the Exchequer *Abbreviatio*, but it is uncertain whether either or both were made officially. Both have liberal marginal annotations, some contemporary, not matching one another or those of the Exchequer version. Many of those in the Margam manuscript have been partially erased.

Although it is missing substantial portions at its beginning and at its end, the provenance of the Margam manuscript is not in doubt. The way in which it came into the possession of a remote Welsh abbey has, however, always been something of a puzzle,[88] but it contains some hints which may link it with the associates of the future King Edward I in the Welsh marches whose families had connections with the monastery. The Clares, earls of Gloucester and Hertford, were patrons, albeit rather distant, of Margam Abbey.[89] Richard de Clare (1230–62)[90] was powerful at a national as well as at a local level. During the wars between the king and the barons in the later years of Henry's reign, Richard's loyalties shifted away from the king and towards the opposition. After his death in 1262, allegedly by poison at the table of Peter of Savoy, he was succeeded by his son Gilbert.[91] The Margam abbreviation could well have been made for the use, both official and unofficial, of the Clare family, especially as those marginalia which were not erased show a strong Gloucestershire interest. Later, once its usefulness was over, it might have been given to Margam Abbey by one of the Clares. It would, however, have been of far more use to Tewkesbury Abbey, their most favoured religious house, and so perhaps it was simply left behind for safe keeping.

The other abbreviation, known as the Domesday Breviate, has survived complete with later additions to the pages before and after the summarized Domesday text. Like the Margam manuscript, it has many additions and annotations, including

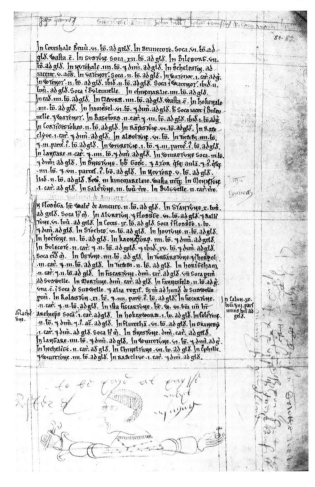

19. *Page from the Margam abbreviation, describing lands in Nottinghamshire and showing marginal additions.*

dots against entries that were probably to be checked and hands pointing to others that were of particular importance. The original scribe had also marked each occurrence of the Braose lands with 'Br' in the margin. The manuscript was therefore a useful guide to the former Braose holdings, and the additions in its last folios are also connected with the affairs of that family. A series of transcripts of legal records, charters and historical notes, they were probably collected by an Anglo-Norman clerk for an inquisition into marcher rights in the Gower which began in 1300, the principal disputants being the Braoses and the earls of Warwick. Like the notes in the front of the volume, they were probably compiled in 1298–1300, but the preliminaries consist of annals, prognostications and prophecies which emanated from the abbeys of Strata Florida, Margam and Neath. The Neath monks held lands

20–22. Pages from the Domesday Breviate, showing marginal jottings and annotations. The 'Br' signs signify the Braose holdings.

in the Gower and were tenants in turn of the Braoses and of the earls of Warwick, and the manuscript may have been preserved at that abbey.[92]

As in the case of the Herefordshire Domesday, the existence and use of abbreviated texts of Domesday Book are an important testimony to the value of the original record to the king's court and government. The marginal annotations in the three thirteenth-century abbreviations suggest strongly that Domesday was in widespread use to check on whether lands rightfully belonged to the king or to one of his tenants-in-chief.

Analysis of the evidence thus suggests a clear pattern to the use made by the royal administration of Domesday Book during its first two centuries. Much of the survey's detailed information about land values and tenurial arrangements was of immediate importance, but rapidly went out of date, to be replaced with material produced by other royal inquiries. However, as a guide to royal resources and baronial holdings, Domesday maintained its usefulness to government, as it was to do in subsequent centuries.

Domesday Book was of immediate practical use as a list of what estates were worth. The Anglo-Saxon chronicler tells us that in 1087 William the Conqueror began to sell his lands on as hard terms as he could.[93] The Domesday information must have helped him to do so, for it provided him with a full inventory of the values and resources of royal manors. That was an approach which was continued and abused by William Rufus, with the aid of his ruthless and able right-hand man, Ranulf Flambard, who was known as the king's 'exactor' and was famed and feared for his avarice on the king's behalf. Domesday enabled him to check the value of estates granted or farmed out and of incoming feudal incidents, such as relief paid by heirs as they inherited, which was often based on the annual value of estates.[94] One recently discovered example of a land transaction concerns the manor of Haddenham in Buckinghamshire. William the Conqueror had granted it to Rochester Cathedral Priory for his own lifetime, and Rufus, at the suggestion of Lanfranc, archbishop of Canterbury, agreed to make the gift permanent. Characteristically, a payment was demanded, and the sum was fixed at £40, the value of the manor in Great Domesday. A demand to build a castle was also made.[95]

The sums levied from vacant bishoprics and abbeys may similarly have been based on Domesday figures. This was an area of financial activity which Flambard exploited to its furthest limits and about which contemporaries made harsh criticisms. Bishoprics and abbeys were deliberately kept vacant and their revenues were retained by the crown or farmed to the highest bidder. By the end of his reign, Rufus was said to hold a total of fourteen of these major benefices.[96] As a result, the already existing tendency to divide monastic estates between the bishop or abbot and the monks was accelerated; and many of the surviving Domesday copies and extracts were made by monks in defence of their claims. Others, such as the *Inquisitio Eliensis* and perhaps the *Domesday Monachorum* of Christ Church, Canterbury, may be connected with official attempts to value the estates.[97] Information about land values in Domesday Book was, however, rapidly superseded. The pipe roll of 1129–30, the English royal administration's first set of 'accounts', reveals that many estates had been alienated by the crown since 1086. The establishment of the system of accounting as exemplified in that pipe roll happened probably in the early years of the twelfth century. It was part of a major reorganization which brought with it many changes in the face value and the renders of estates remaining in royal hands.[98]

Further, it was only for a few more decades that Domesday's evidence about the identity of landholders was to remain of use. The marginal entries giving the names of their successors in the Herefordshire Domesday may mark an experiment by the royal administration in the 1160s to see if Domesday's tenurial information could be brought up to date. The Crown would have needed recent information about which lords held which lands and the piecemeal surveys carried out in some counties since the Domesday survey were not adequate. But the format of Domesday must have proved unsuitable for such a purpose, and in 1166 writs were sent out to all the tenants-in-chief, great and small, asking them to list the lands held from them, the names of their tenants and the amount of service owed. The returns, known as the *Cartae Baronum*, gave Henry II all the information he needed in order to levy aids and services.[99] The *Cartae* were to remain in use well into the thirteenth century, and the royal administration continued to make additional feudal and fiscal surveys, to be brought together in 1302 in the Book of Fees.[100]

Domesday Book thus lost its usefulness as a practical feudal guide during Henry II's reign, but, as already shown, it remained of value as a record of the lands and rights which pertained to feudal honors. From 1087 onwards, the tenants-in-chief referred to the survey for such a purpose and maintained its importance; but the Crown was equally zealous in preserving the feudal status quo. When an honor escheated or was forfeited to the king, the sheriffs in each county would have needed instructions as to which manors made up the estate. Arranged as it was by counties and honors, Domesday book provided a list to hand.[101] The marginalia in the thirteenth-century abbreviated versions show Domesday to have been used to check the lands and rights of the honor of Richmond and of the estates of the Braose family, and there are many other less immediately comprehensible markings in all the manuscripts which imply that it was used to verify other similar matters. Indeed, so lasting was the influence of Domesday Book as a blueprint for the feudal geography of England, that many of the great baronial holdings were to remain virtually unchanged throughout the middle ages.[102]

Domesday Book also retained some importance into the late twelfth century as a list of hides or carucates. These fiscal units, which were listed in the abbreviated text and were added for emphasis in the margin of the Herefordshire Domesday, were the basis for the assessment of Danegeld in the twelfth century. Danegeld was a tax imposed regularly by the English government at least since the late tenth century, and it remained a vital component in the royal revenues until the reign of Henry II. Some reassessments had taken place after 1086, but only in a piecemeal fashion, and much of the tax was raised on the Domesday valuations of hides and carucates.[103] Although it was not levied after 1162, there are signs that its yields had remained high, and Henry II made unsuccessful moves towards collecting it again between 1173 and 1175. Moreover, in 1193, the same assessments were used in the imposition of the carucage tax for King Richard I's ransom.[104] When particular magnates were excused from paying geld on their demesne lands, the sheriffs had to be notified, and Domesday must have been a useful starting-point for the barons of the Exchequer in determining the manors involved and their values.[105]

In the reign of Henry I, the Crown began also to exercise the right to tax its demesne tenants and likewise the boroughs, which under Henry II were gradually absorbed into the royal demesne. Such taxation, like the feudal aid, was to be used as a replacement for Danegeld. Known first as an aid or gift, and from later in the twelfth century as tallage, the tax on the demesne was normally imposed when-ever the Crown levied feudal aid or scutage. The boroughs gave little resistance, but rather more was met from the rural demesne. During Henry III's reign, attempts were made to realize the full potential of the tax on the rural manors of the king's present and former demesnes (the ancient demesne),[106] except in cases where the tallage had been specifically granted out. It was also raised from lands temporarily in the king's hands, as during an episcopal vacancy.[107] Domesday Book, which gradually became the proof of ancient demesne, was, in conjunction with later Exchequer records, an obvious and comprehensive source of information about lands formerly held by the Crown.

The Crown's development of the profits of taxation from the later twelfth century was part of a new approach to its own resources. At intervals from Henry II's reign onwards, Exchequer officials made inquiries into usurpations of royal rights, resources and estates, among which the *quo warranto* proceedings had emerged by 1200. *Quo warranto* provoked considerable hostility in the 1230s, but even more inquiries were held in the 1240s and 1250s.[108] The significance of the proceedings is not easy to assess because, unlike those of Edward I's reign, they are imperfectly documented. It is, however, clear that the royal officials, whether barons of the Exchequer or itinerant justices, were, as later, charged with discovering by what warrant the lands or franchises were held. A royal charter was adequate evidence;

otherwise the plea of holding by ancient tenure (*per antiquam tenuram*) was allowable if verified.[109] In some cases, landholders claimed liberties going back to the Conquest, and the Domesday survey was the obvious place to check such claims.[110] The royal officials also must have needed lists of earlier royal lands and rights in order to inquire why those were royal no longer,[111] and, although there was no shortage of more recent material, Domesday Book, as a record of a time when far more manors had been held by the king, would have produced potentially more favourable results. Marginal annotations in the Exchequer *Abbreviatio*, such as 'R' in the margin whenever the king is mentioned, and '*nota*' alongside the sections dealing with royal lands and beside a number of ecclesiastical estates, appear to connect it with the *quo warranto* campaign. In 1257, the bishops and abbots protested angrily to the king about the attack upon their liberties by the *quo warranto* proceedings, which, they said, were an infringement of Magna Carta.[112]

From the 1250s, Domesday Book began to be cited directly in administrative records, and the uses made of it were similar to those implied by the abbreviations. Thus, in 1256, the inhabitants of Chester were ordered to pay for the repair of a bridge in the town, because the king had learned from consulting Domesday Book that it was their obligation.[113] Royal servants in the Exchequer were required to search it in 1267 to ascertain what customs and services the men of Boycott, Buckinghamshire, had rendered to the king's predecessors.[114]

In 1259 the king granted Simon de Montfort, earl of Leicester, and his wife ten manors from which they were to draw five hundred marks annually, provided that those manors were not royal demesne. The Exchequer officials checked them all in Domesday Book to discover whether or not they were listed there as *terra regis*. That process, and examination of other, later evidence, proved that the majority of the manors were rightfully royal demesne and that the earl was entitled only to three: Dilwyn in Herefordshire, Bere Regis in Dorset, and Gunthorpe in Nottingham, shire. The incident, recorded on the memoranda roll, clearly demonstrates Domesday's value as the starting point for any official inquiry into earlier royal and baronial holdings, and confirms its role as suggested by the Exchequer *Abbreviatio*.[115] The baronage similarly recognized its importance. In about 1266, the notoriously rebellious Robert de Ferrers, earl of Derby, vainly attempted to grant his principal castle at Tutbury to Gilbert de Clare, earl of Gloucester and Hertford. The lands, franchises and appurtenances which went with it were to be 'as in the document [*lettre*] of King William the Bastard', very probably a reference to Domesday Book.[116]

There were also signs during the last two decades of Henry III's reign of a new use for the Conqueror's survey as proof of ancient demesne, the privileges attached to which evolved gradually during the thirteenth century.[117] The normal method of proof before the 1270s was by the sworn testimony of a jury. Under Edward I, it was to be Domesday Book which usually provided the evidence, as it did occasionally in Henry III's reign. The earliest known case concerns a group of villeins of the manor of Carlton in Yorkshire, who were trying to establish that they were privileged tenants of ancient demesne. In the course of litigation which had begun in 1249, they cited Domesday Book twice. The first attempt, in which they argued that Carlton was an appendage of the manor of Drax, which was ancient demesne, failed because no reference to Carlton could be found in Domesday Book. Such was their conviction, however, that they

gave ten marks to the lord king to have another certificate from the said great book which is called Domesday ... which said that, having consulted the rolls, and the book called Domesday, [the barons of the Exchequer] had found that Carlton had not been the ancient demesne of the king's predecessors. ...[118]

Their villeinage tenure was therefore confirmed.

These villeins showed what many others were later to share with them: an almost unshakable belief that Domesday Book would prove their case and release them from burdensome dues and services.[119] But, again as later, Domesday Book could also be used by great lords to prevent such claims from being realized, as when, in 1259, Peter of Savoy, by then surely a Domesday expert, cited it in the King's Council to prove that his manor of Witley in Surrey was not ancient demesne as his tenants asserted:

on the contrary, it belonged to the barony of the Eagle, which was at one time the king's escheat of the lands of the Normans [i.e., forfeited after the loss of Normandy], and was given to Peter by the present king. As to the truth of this, he puts himself on the book called Domesday.

The Domesday evidence having been examined in full, the case went against the villeins.[120]

Far from being an outmoded relic, Domesday Book was thus of continuing practical importance during the twelfth and thirteenth centuries, particularly as a record of royal and baronial holdings and of ancient tenures and rights. It was also a document with legendary attributes, treated with special reverence and increasingly cited in court, more in hope of its powers than in knowledge of its contents. To some degree, Domesday's significance as a working record may have been sustained and increased by the special veneration in which it was held. However, the writs of Henry I, the Herefordshire Domesday, the various abbreviations and the plea rolls and memoranda rolls of Henry III not only corroborate the testimony of Richard Fitz Neal about Domesday's use in government, but also show that its importance was practical as well as symbolic.

CHAPTER III

Domesday Book as a Working Record, 1272–1700

In the later middle ages, Domesday Book was widely regarded as being of the greatest practical value. For certain groups of peasants burdened with intolerable labour services, the purchase of a certified copy of its text held out the hope of a better life and of just retribution against their landlords. Nor was their faith in Domesday diminished by their frequent, although not invariable, failure to obtain the judgments they wanted; it tended, rather, to convince them of the corruption of the judiciary.[1] The burgesses of expanding market towns believed, rather more accurately, that by buying a Domesday extract they could claim freedom from paying taxes on trade throughout England, a privilege which, although expensive for the claimants, was widely sought from the fourteenth century to the sixteenth.[2] To great and long-established landlords, Domesday seemed to provide an inventory of their rightful holdings as in 1086 and to give a record of the customs and services owed to them by their tenants. Such an attitude, which contrasts with that of the peasants, is vividly summed up by a fourteenth-century register of Waltham Abbey.

Many advantages may arise from the possession of the copy, because it shows how the manors of this Church were held before the Conquest and at the Conquest. It also shows how many hides there are in each manor, and, if the king should wish to tallage his realm by hides, by how many hides our manors are taxed, even though this church is free by charter of the tallage of hidage. It also shows what status the tenants of our manors have by right. I do not say 'what status they have at present', because, by the longstanding passivity and negligence of their lords or bailiffs, they are now much freer than they should be, to the disinheritance of the Church and the peril of the souls of those who ought to have provided a rapid remedy. If, God forbid, any malicious plea should ever in future be raised by anyone to take away the possessions of this Church, the extract shows which words in the books or rolls should be used as evidence, and likewise any advantages or gains which may be brought to this Church. Many other uses may be found for such a copy; and let it be known that these things which are here noted from the Book of Domesday are written word for word. Nor do I advise that these memoranda should be allowed to fall into the hands of the unfaithful, in case perhaps they might plot something sinister to the prejudice of this Church, from which many inconveniences, costs and trouble might arise.[3]

Domesday extracts therefore were intended to be used for legal purposes, to claim or to maintain rights and privileges, and in the later middle ages were widely cited in court by the Crown and by people at all levels of society save the wholly unfree. Such extracts are found in abundance in monastic and borough archives. Domesday copies appear in the pocket-sized and easily portable register of Peterborough Abbey, made in the thirteenth century,[4] the cartularies of Blythburgh Priory[5] and Ely Cathedral Priory[6] dating from the fourteenth, and the fifteenth-century breviary of Muchelney Abbey.[7] The inhabitants of Reading[8] and Ipswich[9] were among the many towns which obtained extracts and preserved them in their archives. The city of London tried to have a similar copy made in 1428, but nothing about the capital was found, or indeed existed, in the volumes.[10] Analogous evidence for Domesday's use by lay families is much rarer, but the estate book of Henry de Bray, compiled in the early fourteenth century, and the fifteenth-century cartulary of the Tropenell family both contain Domesday extracts.[11]

As before 1272, Domesday Book continued to be of interest to chroniclers. Many, such as Walter of Hemingbrough, who wrote in the late thirteenth century, reproduced Henry of Huntingdon's account with minor variations.[12] Monastic writers also began to find or to invent ways in which Domesday was relevant to their own histories and holdings. Thus the annals of Bermondsey, compiled shortly after 1432, accurately reported that in Domesday 'the king held the manor of Bermondsey, where a new and beautiful church had recently been constructed in honour of St Saviour'.[13] The Dunstable annalist copied the proceedings of a court case of 1289 in which Domesday was cited,[14] while the authors of the Crowland chronicle, forged in the fifteenth century but purporting to date from the twelfth, implausibly claimed to have consulted the original in London. They fabricated the evidence of the abbey's liberties which they said was drawn from it.[15]

The fifteenth century saw the beginnings of a more systematic collection and interpretation of information about historical and topographical matters, an approach known as antiquarianism. The works of John Rous contain an early example of its application to Domesday Book. Rous, who lived by the patronage of the Beauchamp and Neville earls of Warwick, wrote a history of England to celebrate kings, great churchmen and the founders of towns. He took evidence from Domesday Book to describe the destruction of twenty-six tenements in Warwick for the enlargement of the castle in the Conqueror's reign; and yet his account of Domesday's making was still derived almost verbatim from Henry of Huntingdon.[16]

So magisterial had Domesday's reputation become that, from the thirteenth century onwards, many other documents were given its name to endow them with a special and binding importance. Among them were the Domesday rolls of Chester, used for recording charters and other particularly important records of the palatinate;[17] the thirteenth-century Domesday survey of the lands of St Paul's

Cathedral;[18] and the sixteenth-century Great Domesday Book of the borough of Ipswich.[19] Such wide use of the name to cover many different kinds of document further enhanced the standing of the original Domesday Book, but also strengthened the common misapprehension that it contained a virtually inexhaustible and encyclopaedic store of useful evidence.

As a source for proving ancient demesne, a matter involving relatively little interpretation, Domesday Book deserved its outstanding reputation; but analysis of other cases in which it was cited suggests that its reputation was inflated well beyond its practical value. It was called upon in court on many occasions in the later middle ages in suits involving boundaries, land and tenures, but in a substantial proportion of actions its evidence proved of little value, either because it was irrelevant, having been superseded by later developments, or because it could not be readily understood or interpreted. As the Conqueror's reign receded ever further into the past, the text of his survey became progressively more obscure. In 1337, for example, it was consulted to determine whether or not the lands of the late Roger de Huntyngfeld in Boxworth, Cambridgeshire, had been held directly from the king. Domesday listed the manor under the holdings of Robert Gernon, but the treasurer and barons of the Exchequer, after consulting diligently with the king's justices, were unable to put any interpretation on the words 'except as they sounded'. They therefore advised that the king's rights should be maintained until any contrary evidence could be found.[20] A few years later, in 1341, a lawyer pleading before the justices disputed the Crown's intention to cite Domesday in a case without having first provided a certified copy of the relevant passage. The book was, he stated, 'before time of memory, and so it is the secret of the king which does not lie in our cognizance, and to which we ought not by law to be put to answer'.[21] Such examples suggest that the very obscurity of the Domesday text may have heightened the veneration in which the book was held, and it is striking that both litigants and royal officials, particularly from the Exchequer, continued to have faith in the efficacy of its evidence.

The problems and ambiguities in Domesday Book, which have fuelled a modern historical industry, thus presented major problems to the generations of justices and administrators who had to use it as a legal record; and Domesday case law is often confused and contradictory. The complexity could, however, be turned to the king's advantage. For example, the question of which lands formed the ancient demesne of the crown was given a wide interpretation at times when assessments for taxation were being made, because such estates paid at a higher rate. Conversely, when the privileges of great landholders were threatened by the claims of villeins to the privileged status of ancient demesne, the justices took a far more restricted view of it.[22] Yet neither such legal inconsistencies, nor the diminishing frequency with which it was cited from the sixteenth century onwards, alloyed the universal respect in which

Domesday Book was held in the middle ages and beyond. Indeed, from the late sixteenth century, its reputation was enhanced in another way by the work of scholars and antiquaries, who began to reveal its unique value as a historical source rather than as a legal record, and whose work will be considered in due course. The continuing pattern of use of a record with so great a reputation necessitated strict arrangements for its care, custody, copying and citing. The resulting rules and procedures remained unchanged for centuries.

From the reign of John to that of Victoria, Domesday Book had its permanent home at Westminster in the Treasury of the Receipt of the Exchequer. It was probably stored in the Chapel of the Pyx at Westminster Abbey, home of the royal regalia and treasure, until at least the late fifteenth century; by 1610 it had been moved into the Treasury of Receipt premises,[23] and in 1631 it was said to be in the first treasury of the Court of Receipts,[24] known as the Tally Court. On many occasions, although

23. *The abbey and palace of Westminster in the seventeenth century.*

24. *The Chapel of the Pyx, Westminster, in the seventeenth century.*

25. A seventeenth-century engraving of the Great Fire of London.

probably not invariably, it travelled with the Exchequer and was used for administrative business. When, in the later years of his reign, Edward II took many of his key administrative officials north during the Scots wars, Domesday went too, with the other records needed by the Exchequer. In 1300, it was at York on two occasions[25] and once at Lincoln,[26] and in 1303 it was back at York again.[27] Edward II moved the Exchequer for similar reasons, and the author of the Annals of St Paul's notes that in 1319 'the clerks of the Exchequer left London for York with twenty-one carts carrying rolls and Domesday Book'.[28] Such migrations became less frequent in subsequent centuries, but were still made in response to a particular emergency. In Elizabeth I's reign, the Exchequer officials went to Hertford on several occasions, presumably to escape the plague. A draft list of the records taken with them, dating probably from 1582 or 1592, notes *inter alia* the two volumes of Domesday Book.[29] They must also have been included when, in September 1666, the removal took place of

the said Receipt of the Exchequer, the officers with His Majesty's treasure, records and all other things belonging to the said office, from Westminster to Nonsuch for the servicing of the same in the time of the late dreadful fire of London.[30]

From the later thirteenth century, Domesday Book was one of the records in the custody of the two clerks or deputies of the chamberlain in the Receipt of the Exchequer, who had responsibility for making searches and for providing copies. In

1279, they were given the right to levy fees.[31] The Parliament of 1372 ruled that all legal records could be searched and exemplified (i.e., copied and certified as accurate) for all who paid the charges, whether the evidence went for the king or against him.[32] The duties of the deputy chamberlains, which were to remain almost unchanged until 1826, were threefold: striking tallies, making copies of the records, and keeping custody of them.[33] William de Boveye, an Exchequer clerk who in 1332 was given a special payment for extracting a list of towns from Domesday Book for tallage assessments, was almost certainly a deputy chamberlain, and the names of his successors are known in continuous sequence from the end of the fourteenth century.[34]

In the later middle ages, the deputy chamberlains made two different kinds of copy of the records in their charge. One was produced for, and sold by, the Exchequer, and gave the required extract from, or full copy of, a text. In the middle ages, that was for reference purposes only; thus, in 1394–95, the citizens of Norwich paid 6s. 8d. for such an extract from Domesday Book.[35] A few have survived in the original,[36] and others have been preserved in copy, as in monastic cartularies.[37] By the reign of Elizabeth I, such Domesday extracts had evolved into fully certified copies with legal validity, written in quasi-eleventh-century script and signed by the deputy chamberlains, as is shown by an example from 1572.[38] In the seventeenth century, the drawing up of these Exchequer exemplifications was a skill jealously

26. *Exchequer exemplification, made in 1572, of entries from the Domesday section for Cheshire.*

guarded by the deputy chamberlains. They were compiled according to a set format, as is demonstrated by the inclusion of detailed instructions for their making in a register of searches begun in 1685.[39] The less ornate certified copies available from the Public Record Office today are the direct descendants of such Exchequer exemplifications, but since 1838 they have been verified by assistant keepers and since 1958 they have been made by photographic process rather than by hand.

The second kind of copy which the deputy chamberlains made was a return on a writ. Such a certificate, which had the same format as those sold directly to private individuals, was not sold but was sent into Chancery, where it was used either for administrative or for legal purposes[40] or as the basis of formal letters patent of exemplification. In the middle ages, the purchase of Chancery letters patent was the only way of obtaining a certified copy, and Chancery exemplifications of Domesday were issued from the thirteenth century onwards in quite substantial numbers. They became less popular after 1500 and were gradually superseded by Exchequer exemplifications, but were still required for some purposes at least until 1656.

The writ which was used by Chancery to summon a Domesday extract was a particular kind of *certiorari*, which ordered information and which had, from about 1280, had a multitude of applications.[41] The version most frequently used in connection with Domesday was a demand to establish whether or not a given place was ancient demesne of the Crown, the proof being in the survey's pages. Variant writs were used to find out whether a manor had belonged to a particular honor or by what tenure it was held. Lists of particular tenants-in-chief's holdings or of certain types of land, such as forest, were among other kinds of Domesday information demanded by writs of *certiorari*. The forms of the writs ordering the consultation of Domesday had become fixed by 1300 and remained unchanged for centuries.[42] The late example reproduced here dates from the Commonwealth period, when English replaced Latin for official records, and shows the way in which the information was requested. Issued in 1656 in Oliver Cromwell's name, it tells the treasurer and chamberlains that a reply is required as to whether or not a group of Norfolk manors are ancient demesne of the Crown. They are therefore commanded to search Domesday Book and to certify Chancery of what they find, returning any copy with the writ.[43] The writ had always to be sent back to Chancery. If nothing was found in Domesday Book, an endorsement to that effect was made upon it; if a relevant Domesday passage was identified, it was carefully copied on to a certificate which was attached to the writ. The forms which the endorsements and the headings written above the Domesday extract should take had reached their final style by the late thirteenth century and were regarded as being of such moment that, in the fifteenth, they were noted as exemplars in the Black Book of the Exchequer, the book of memoranda and precedents kept by the deputy chamberlains.[44]

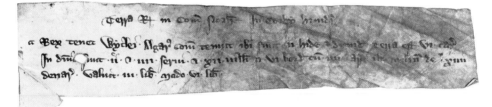

27. *Writ of* certiorari *(1656), ordering a Domesday extract to be made. It was issued in the name of Oliver Cromwell and was written in English.*

28. *Return on writ of* certiorari, *giving an extract from Domesday for Wiltshire. It was made in 1377.*

29. *Return on writ of* certiorari, *describing Weekley in Northamptonshire and made in 1307. The writing is deliberately archaic.*

The handwriting of the Domesday returns provides an interesting reflection of how Domesday was regarded by its custodians. For most of the middle ages, the returns were made in a fashion similar to copies of other documents. In this respect, Domesday Book was just another working record, albeit atypical. The example shown in Plate 28, from 1377, a year in which a relatively large number of Domesday certificates was produced by the deputy chamberlains, is in its handwriting and layout very similar to all the other extracts they made.[45] At the top is a heading stating that the Wiltshire section of Domesday Book contains the following information under the rubric of the king's lands. Then comes the extract for Melksham copied from Great Domesday.[46] Around 1300, some Domesday certificates were produced with handwriting of a somewhat antique appearance, as though the clerk had tried to imitate the Domesday script. There is a contrast between the working Chancery hand of the writs and the careful lettering of the Exchequer Domesday returns, such as the example of 1307 (Plate 29) giving the Domesday entry for Weekley in

Northamptonshire.[47] Not all Domesday extracts made at that time were of such a kind, but there are copies in other records which also contain the special lettering.[48] That suggests an antiquarian tendency in one or more of the royal clerks of the day, which must have stemmed from a particular interest in, and reverence for, Domesday.

From the 1470s, the deputy chamberlains again began to use an antique script in their Domesday returns, imitating the actual letter forms of the original as closely as they could. The certificate of 1488, illustrated in Plate 30, is an early example. The uneven lettering suggests that the scribe was still somewhat unsure of himself.[49] A later return made in 1629 and signed by John Bradshaw, a deputy chamberlain, according to the procedure introduced in Elizabeth's reign,[50] shows an altogether more elegant and practised script (Plate 31).[51] Bradshaw's predecessor, Arthur Agarde, a scholar and record keeper of great ability,[52] had laid down strict instructions for the making of Domesday extracts, as well as for the handling of the book itself, as is demonstrated by the passage reproduced in Plate 32, taken from one of his works.[53]

Such direct imitation of the Domesday script has a certain calligraphical interest, but also holds a much wider significance. The deputy chamberlains saw Domesday Book and the Black Book of the Exchequer as 'the two most ancient and most used records of England',[54] but gave only Domesday the honour of a full and painstaking reproduction. Nor was the use of the Domesday script confined to the making of certified copies: a memoranda roll of 1577, for example, has a similar extract in Domesday writing, perhaps written by, or copied from an extract made by, Arthur

30. *Return on writ of* certiorari, *describing Lewisham in Kent; made in 1488 in a quasi-Domesday script.*

Agarde.[55] Such letter forms were also employed in copies made for private individuals for legal or antiquarian use and indexes to Domesday made by the deputy chamberlains at least until 1700.[56] The Conqueror's survey was thereby honoured by its custodians above all the other records in their charge.

31. *Return on writ of certiorari of 1629, showing a practised quasi-Domesday script. The manor described is Kirton in Lindsey, Lincolnshire, and its outliers.*

In searching the Booke of *Domesdei*, is to bee avoyded, laying bare hands or moysture, vpon the writing thereof, and blotting.

In copying of Notes, out of the same Booke of *Domesdei*, you must write it as neare as you can, to the Letter thereof, obseruing both the great Letters, and the poynts therein, which are prickes with a Pen: thus,

32. *Instructions for writing Domesday script, from a treatise by Arthur Agarde published in 1631.*

From the thirteenth century, fixed fees were payable to the deputy chamberlains for searching and making extracts from the documents in their care. Their table of fees produced in 1692 quotes charges which were said to have been the same as at the beginning of Elizabeth I's reign: 4s. 8d. for searching Domesday, fourpence for copying each line, two shillings for examining and signing a copy and 16s. 8d. for a certified copy.[57] The charges were lower for short extracts than those for other records, despite the extra labour involved in making them, probably because Domesday was more straightforward to search. Less was charged during the Commonwealth, but the Restoration saw the return of older, higher levels of payment. The discrepancy between the prices for copies and searches of Domesday and for those of other records persisted into the nineteenth century.[58]

Many of the Domesday certificates returned into Chancery were used for making letters patent of exemplification for individuals or for groups who needed a copy with legal validity.[59] The document reproduced in Plate 33 is an original Chancery exemplification of a Domesday extract, drawn up in 1424 for the inhabitants of Godmanchester in Huntingdonshire. Issued in the king's name, it greets all those whom it shall reach and states that a certificate sent into Chancery by the treasurer and chamberlain has been inspected. The text of the Great Domesday extract for Godmanchester follows and is said to be exemplified at the request of the men of the manor. The great seal of England is attached at the bottom.[60] Although it is rare for such original exemplifications to have survived, we know from references in the Chancery rolls that they were issued in considerable numbers. Sometimes the full text was enrolled on the Chancery patent rolls or on the Exchequer memoranda rolls, and on a few occasions it was endorsed on the Domesday certificate,[61] sources which collectively show that the format of the letters remained unchanged throughout the middle ages and beyond.

The obtaining of Chancery exemplifications from Domesday was a slow and costly business. A fee had to be paid at the Exchequer for a search in the book, a process which in 1429–30 cost the University of Oxford 20s. 0½d.[62] Chancery's cumbersome machinery had also to be set in motion by a fixed payment, further fees being charged for the letters patent. Only the most favoured could gain exemption from the standard levies for Chancery exemplifications, which had to be paid whatever the record to be copied,[63] and which in the later middle ages amounted to 16s. 4d. to the Crown plus two shillings to the chancellor.[64] The accounts of the hanaper, the office which collected the fees for the sealing and issuing of writs,[65] give lists of the names of all those who bought exemplifications and other letters patent, but unfortunately do not usually show either why such letters were purchased or which documents were exemplified in them.[66] It is thus not possible to quantify the demand for Domesday by determining what proportion of all the exemplifications

33. *Chancery letters patent made in 1424
and giving a Domesday exemplification.
Such originals have survived very rarely.*

contained extracts from the Conqueror's survey rather than from other records. However, numerous *certiorari* writs and returns still survive out of the large number which must have been issued, and give copies of a wide range of documents.[67] Examination of these suggests that, in some years, particularly in the fourteenth century, that proportion, and thus Domesday's perceived value, must have been quite considerable. Moreover, the reasons for the purchase of the exemplifications may on occasions be deduced from other evidence, as will be shown in many of the cases discussed below.

Some possessors of Chancery examplifications safeguarded their position yet further by making an additional payment for the enrolment of their exemplifications on the patent roll. Administrative instructions and documents benefiting the Crown were copied there as a matter of course, whereas those which favoured private individuals were normally entered subject only to fee.[68] The example in Plate 34 is an enrolment on the patent roll of a Domesday exemplification for the manor of Torksey in Lincolnshire, made in 1342 at the request of John Darcey le Cosyn of Torksey.[69] By the end of the fifteenth century, the practice of enrolling exemplifications had ceased, although other letters patent which cited Domesday extracts as the basis of a grant of privileges, such as freedom from toll, continued to be registered.

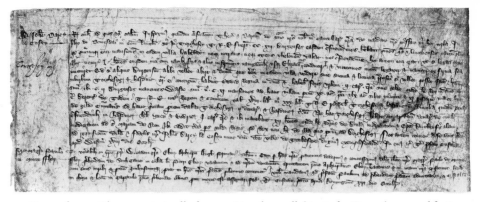

34. *Extract from a Chancery patent roll of 1342, giving the enrolled text of a Domesday exemplification.*

Not all the Domesday extracts returned into Chancery were used to make exemplifications. Many were required for current administrative business and others for sending on to various royal courts. Until the end of the sixteenth century, Domesday Book was in normal circumstances directly available only for Exchequer business, and elaborate procedures were needed to forward its evidence elsewhere. The least complex were those involving Chancery, which, as the department receiving the returns on *certiorari* writs, could readily use those extracts in its business without further bureaucratic impediment. Chancery sometimes needed Domesday evidence for use in inquiries into tenurial or other matters ordered by royal writ and carried out by an escheator or other royal official. The Domesday certificate was sent into the county together with other background evidence, and, once the inquisition was completed, was returned into Chancery with the resulting records. In 1356, for example, a complex series of inquiries was held as a result of a dispute between the heirs of the greedy and powerful knight John de Molyns, who had recently died. One of the matters at issue was whether or not the manor of Hatfield Peverel in Essex was held directly from the Crown and a writ was issued to the Exchequer officials asking them to search relevant records, including the Book of Fees, for evidence. The return begins with brief extracts from the Book of Fees and the Red Book of the Exchequer, and then turns to Domesday Book, which is described in some detail using the wording of the *Dialogus*. The relevant extract for the manor of Hatfield Peverel follows, and then, as a coda, the passage from the *Dialogus* which equates the verdict of Domesday with the Last Judgment. The Chancery officials are thereby implicitly castigated for not specifying Domesday Book in their writ.[70]

A Domesday extract might equally be needed as evidence for formal legal proceedings in Chancery. From 1354 to 1356, for example, a case was heard involving what the Crown considered to be the illegal seizure of the manor of Wilton in Pickering, Yorkshire, by Thomas and Walter de Heslarton. The escheator had taken custody of the manor on the grounds that it ought to have been held directly from the king, and a Domesday certificate was produced which listed Pickering as the king's land in 1086. The case was then transferred into the court of King's Bench and had to wait for its resolution until 1359, when it was found that, despite the Domesday evidence, Wilton should have been held not from the king but from the earl of Lancaster.[71]

A Domesday certificate might also be required for proceedings initiated in the courts of King's Bench or Common Pleas. The officials of the courts had to approach Chancery, which, having produced a return on a writ of *certiorari*, then issued another writ transferring the *certiorari* and return to the court.[72] The procedures were, however, cumbersome and delays could easily result. In 1339, for example, a lawsuit turning upon whether or not Dymock in Gloucestershire was ancient demesne was held up by the repeated failure of the treasurer and chamberlains of the Exchequer to return their *certiorari* and relevant Domesday extract.[73] Sometimes the full text of the writ and return was recorded with the account of the case on the plea roll, but on other occasions a much briefer reference was made to the search of Domesday Book and the results. Thus, in a description of a celebrated case of 1312 involving a dispute over the services owed by the villeins of Ogbourne St George and Ogbourne St Andrew in Wiltshire to their landlord, the abbot of the Norman monastery of Bec, the tenants are said to have 'called upon the record of the book of Domesday' in evidence. What was found there was not given in full but was merely summarized.[74]

No conclusive evidence has been found for the production of Domesday Book itself in any court other than the Exchequer until the seventeenth century, when the concept of trial by Domesday Book apparently emerged. A treatise of the 1620s, listing the duties of the deputy chamberlains of the Exchequer, described one of their duties as follows: 'They wait on the court of Common Pleas with the book of Domesday on all issues [turning on the evidence of] Domesday, and as the vice chamberlain informs, the court gives judgment.'[75] One such case, to resolve whether or not a manor was ancient demesne, was heard in the court of Common Pleas in 1611, and Domesday Book was carried into the court by a porter.[76] Similar facilities were probably not normally given to the other courts, and exemplifications from Domesday Book have been made for use as legal evidence until the present day.

It is a relatively straightforward task to work out the procedures for citing Domesday in Exchequer, Chancery or other courts, but, given the number and variety of lawsuits in which its evidence appeared, it is far less simple to ascertain its practical, as opposed to perceived, value in settling disputes. However, the cases in which it was called upon fall into broad groupings: those involving landholding, rights and services, and boundaries; those connected with forests and with ecclesiastical matters; and those relating to ancient demesne. The last is discussed at some length in the next chapter, but analysis of examples in the other categories will demonstrate both the value and the limitations of the Domesday evidence to those who sought to use it.

The royal forest in the middle ages was primarily a legal concept. It was not necessarily an area covered with trees, but a tract of land, some of which might be wooded, reserved for royal hunting and subject to the forest laws originally introduced from Normandy by William the Conqueror. Although Domesday tells us a great deal about woodland (*silva*), it is not always very explicit about forest areas (*foresta*), apart from the New Forest, which is clearly delineated.[77] Later searches for relevant information about the forests in Domesday Book were thus often unlikely to succeed; but the survey was nevertheless used as evidence in the crisis over the forests in 1299–1300.

In the 1290s, the relationship between Edward I and his barons had become increasingly strained as a result of the king's unpopular and expensive hostilities with Philip IV of France, who was trying to reclaim Gascony from the English Crown. In 1297, Edward, in the hope of appeasing the English nobility, agreed to confirm Henry III's charter regulating forest boundaries and rights. If any practical results were to be achieved by that confirmation, the precise boundaries of the forest jurisdiction had to be determined; by 1299, the matter had become a test of the king's good will. In that and the following year, perambulations (i.e., reviews and inspections) of the forest boundaries were made, and in March 1300, a full confirmation of Henry III's charter was sealed.[78] The five groups of justices making the perambulations from March 1300 were each equipped with lists of woodland in the royal demesne taken from Domesday Book, which, together with extracts from charters and earlier perambulation records, were collected from the Exchequer at York in May.[79] A number of roughly contemporary summaries of woods and forests extracted from Domesday Book have survived, and one at least may be the material used by the justices in the inquiry.[80] The four clerks involved in the labour of extracting the Domesday information were paid 42s. 8d. for their pains.[81]

In 1316, Domesday Book was put to similar use during another major perambulation of the forests. In January of that year, Edward II, anxious for revenge after his recent defeat by the Scots at Bannockburn, summoned Parliament to try to obtain a grant of taxation to supply his army. One part of his response to baronial demands for reform was to promise that Edward I's forest ordinances would be observed, and that a new inquiry into royal forest rights would be held in order to restore to the forest law any lands alienated before the issue of Henry III's charter. A great number of earlier rolls and records were called as evidence, and the Exchequer officials were asked to have Domesday Book and other records searched and to notify the Council of what they found.[82] For several counties, the resulting Domesday evidence was checked against records of earlier perambulations, but verification was not possible for Warwickshire because no evidence about the forest there could be discovered in Domesday.[83]

Forest status could be a crucially important factor in determining lawsuits. In a protracted case beginning in 1336, the inhabitants of three Oxfordshire villages, namely Stonesfield, Charlbury and Combe near Woodstock, were trying to confirm for themselves the special privileges and status of tenancy in ancient demesne which had been allowed in the 1270s on rather uncertain grounds.[84] The evidence of Domesday Book and of other records, including an inquisition held at Woodstock in 1337, established that Woodstock was in the demesne forest of the king but that the other three villages were not; indeed, Charlbury was not in Domesday at all. The people of Combe, however, found a way of overturning Domesday evidence. They agreed that, in Domesday Book, Combe was unequivocally a holding of the bishop of Bayeux, but argued that more recently, in the time of Henry III, it had been absorbed into the forest of Wychwood and that the tenants who asserted it (i.e., cleared it) had been granted privileges of ancient demesne by the Crown. Despite Domesday Book's importance as evidence of ancient demesne, their argument was accepted.[85]

Royal rights in forest areas subsequently diminished in importance, but were given an unexpected revival in the reign of James I, when the king was searching for extra revenues to avoid relying on Parliament. His officials began to recover Crown lands on his behalf which had been occupied illegally by their current holders; the forests, where land had been reclaimed for cultivation over many centuries, were an obvious starting-point. In about 1617, the king's lawyers accused the people of Havering, a substantial royal manor formerly in the forest of Essex, of occupying 11,533 acres illegally. They were, it was claimed, entitled only to 1,200 acres, as was proved by Domesday Book, in which the manor was assessed for ten hides; other records allegedly backed up that case. The assumption was that, as was usual, each hide had represented 120 acres. The free tenants of Havering responded that they had always held a far greater number of acres,[86] but they failed to show that the Crown had made a mistake in its calculations. A detailed survey of the manor made for its holder, Queen Philippa, in about 1355, and ironically known as 'le Domesday', would have been of great value to their case. Not only did it prove that the Havering hides were far larger than the norm, each containing about 480 acres, but it also showed that, when it was made, the tenants and under-tenants had held 11,850 acres in the manor with undisputed title.[87]

As the Domesday survey shows, the eleventh-century English Church controlled a high proportion of the land, and despite papal threats and pronouncements to the contrary, William the Conqueror maintained a powerful control over his archbishops, bishops and abbots. In subsequent centuries, the impact of Church reforms and the growth of papal government lessened the tight royal grip to a degree, but set against that were the continuing ability of the king to dictate or influence many high-level ecclesiastical appointments and his place as the leading patron of the religious orders.

The nature and extent of royal rights over the Church were often a matter of disagreement, and Domesday Book could be called on, with varying success, to resolve them. In 1266, a dispute had arisen between the king and the priory of Lenton in Nottinghamshire over the right to present (i.e., nominate) the parish priest of St Mary's in Nottingham. A writ to the Exchequer asked for Domesday Book to be searched to confirm that the presentation belonged to the Crown, but, although the return showed that in 1086 there had been a church in the town which was under the royal aegis, its dedication, and hence its identity, was not specified. The king still maintained that the right was his, but in 1267 he granted the priory, to which he had already given funds for building works, the right to present during his lifetime.[88]

35. Henry III as the founder of Westminster Abbey, from Matthew Paris's History of the English.

In 1314, Edward II claimed the right to present to the parish church of Washingley in Huntingdonshire, because the lord of the manor, a minor, was in royal wardship. The claim was opposed by the child's mother, Elizabeth de Washingley, on the grounds that the advowson was not one of the manorial rights but was held in socage tenure from the abbot of Crowland for the nominal yearly rent of a rose; that the tenure had been arranged before the reign of Richard I, the limit of legal memory; and that the abbot had granted the advowson to Richard de Washingley and his heirs in exchange for some land in the village. Domesday Book was consulted and it was found that a church in Washingley was among the appurtenances of the manor; but Elizabeth asserted that, although at that time the church had been connected to the manor, the link had subsequently been severed. Because she could not provide a record of the creation of the socage tenure, however, judgment went against her. The Common Pleas entry of this case gives the full Domesday extract, which may be translated as follows:

Land of the king's thegns. In Washingley Ketelbert had two and a half geldable hides. Land for four ploughs. He now holds of the king and has there one plough and ten villeins with four ploughs. There is a church there and a priest; and twelve acres of meadow; and woodland pasture, seven furlongs in length, ten and a half in width. In the time of King Edward and now it is worth ten shillings.[89]

The version given in the Year Book, which records the discussions of the lawyers on points of law, is strikingly different.

Grimbald of Washingley holds of the king in chief one virgate and ten perches of land and a chantry for a priest and the advowson of Washingley by the service of going with us in our army, and it is worth ten shillings a year.[90]

The Year Book version bears virtually no resemblance to the Domesday entry, but the writer was interested only in the finer points of the law and not in factual details.

Ecclesiastical lords on occasions used Domesday Book to try to escape secular exactions. In 1333, Henry of Casewick, abbot of Crowland, who is known to have pursued his monastery's claims with great vigour, petitioned Parliament, complaining that he had been unjustly asked to pay a feudal aid, for the marriage of the king's eldest daughter, from the Lincolnshire manors of Witham and Langtoft, whereas they had been held in free alms since the abbey's foundation and no service was due from them. The treasurer and chamberlains of the Exchequer, he submitted, had searched their records, and Domesday Book and other early documents clearly upheld the abbey's case. The matter was remitted by Parliament to the Exchequer, where, after lengthy searches in the records and a reconsideration of the Domesday evidence, no precedent was found for freeing the abbot from the aid. He was, however, permitted to take the matter further in the royal courts, and, although in 1346 he was still paying aids on Langtoft, by 1407 his successors had carried the day and were holding it in free alms.[91]

Like lay lords, monastic houses had to be vigilant to avoid encroachment by royal officials on their lands and rights. In 1332, the prior of Otterton in Devon had considerable success in defending his rights in East Budleigh and a fishery at the mouth of the river Otter against the claims of the escheator. They had been seized by the Crown under the Statute of Westminster II, which allowed lands granted in return for spiritual services to be recovered if those services had not been performed for two years or more. An inquisition carried out by an earlier escheator had established that the priory, a dependency of the abbey of Mont St Michel in France, had been founded by King John, who had granted the monks Otterton, Sidmouth and East Budleigh in return for their future distribution of alms to the poor; because that service had been discontinued, the lands had been seized. The prior now claimed that the manors of Otterton and East Budleigh had been conferred on Mont St Michel by William I, with no service of almsgiving attached. The Exchequer officials found from various records that Henry I, rather than John, had granted East Budleigh as part of an exchange of lands, but also discovered from Domesday itself that Mont St Michel had indeed held Otterton in 1086.[92]

It was not only in the middle ages that Domesday was used in an attempt to settle ecclesiastical matters. In 1592, after the Church had undergone radical change from the Reformation and the dissolution of the monasteries, Domesday was proffered in the Exchequer by the warden and fellows of New College, Oxford. The matter at issue was whether or not their parish of Brill, Buckinghamshire, included the manors of Oakley and Boarstall with glebes and tithes. To prove that it did, New College had collected a substantial number of copies of relevant documents, including a Domesday extract made by Arthur Agarde. That was unhelpful, because it showed that, in 1086, Brill had been held by the king and Oakley, a separate manor, by Robert d'Oilly; Boarstall was not in Domesday. The warden and fellows, nevertheless, by using later evidence, managed to obtain a decree in their favour.[93]

A similar case involving Domesday evidence was heard in 1656. A Master Boden had been appointed rector of the parish of Saints Peter and Paul in Bath, with the chapel of Whitcombe. The inhabitants of Whitcombe refused to pay him their tithes, alleging that theirs was a separate parish. A copy of the relevant Domesday extract was obtained, which showed, not very usefully, that the church of Bath held Lyncombe; other evidence convinced the court that the chapel was part of the parish, and the defendants were ordered to pay their tithes.[94] Domesday had proved wholly irrelevant to the proceedings.

An important area of Domesday's use concerned rights over land tenure and services and such related issues as the position of ancient administrative boundaries. In the reign of Elizabeth I, many manors changed hands by sale or lease; and some at least of the relatively numerous Domesday exemplifications of that period[95] probably represent the attempts of their new owners to obtain a formal record of their rights. The request in November 1585 for a Chancery exemplification for Feckenham in Worcestershire[96] is a likely example. This Crown manor had been granted by Queen Mary in 1558 to Sir John Throckmorton, his wife and heirs, but in 1584 his son Sir Francis was executed for his notorious plot against Elizabeth I. His wife Marjorie was allowed to retain possession of Feckenham for her own lifetime; but in August 1585 Elizabeth granted its reversion on Lady Throckmorton's death to Sir Thomas Leighton and his wife, the queen's kinswoman. Lady Throckmorton clearly intended to exploit her rights to the full, and in the next few years, to the fury of the Leightons, cut down trees in the park and sold the timber. The request for a Domesday exemplification as proof of the ancient-demesne status of the manor may have been made by either side, anxious to prove its rights and privileges, or perhaps by the tenants, anxious to prove theirs.[97] Domesday's potential value as legal evidence was clearly widely recognized by such landowners. In notes on the descent of lands in Shropshire to Sir Henry Vernon, drawn up after 1588 for a suit between Richard Nethway and William and Anne Dey, the evidence of Domesday Book about the hidation of the manor of Pontesbury is erroneously quoted.[98] Thus, although the sixteenth and seventeenth centuries saw a growing interest in Domesday Book for antiquarian purposes, it was still regarded as of value for determining questions of land and rights.

Its heyday in that respect had come in the later middle ages, and in particular during the fourteenth century. One area of contention concerned the boundaries of counties and franchises. For example, in 1335 the lords of the Welsh marches presented a petition in Parliament complaining that their franchises were being abused by neighbouring sheriffs, who were bringing their tenants to justice even when crimes had been committed in marcher land where English law did not apply. They asked that if those tenants could prove that their misdeeds had occurred in the marches rather than in the counties, their cases should of right be heard in the appropriate marcher court; the boundaries between the shires and marches were to be determined by Domesday Book or, failing that, by other records.[99] One such case, which gives a good illustration of the problems involved, began in 1335, when a royal writ was sent to the sheriff of Shropshire, ordering him to take over an appeal made by Joan de Middleton against some fellow inhabitants of Montgomery, concerning the death of her brother. The sheriff at first felt unable to hear the case, because Montgomery was outside the borders of his county, but eventually visited the town to try to deal with it there. The town's officials refused to co-operate, on the grounds that Montgomery was in the Welsh marches, but Joan de Middleton, backing the sheriff, proffered the evidence of Domesday Book, which showed that the place was in Shropshire and subject to the laws of England. In 1337, a Domesday extract was obtained from the treasurer and barons of the Exchequer, in which Montgomery was listed under the lands of Earl Roger in Shropshire; other references to the Book of Fees and to the Chancery rolls gave similar proof, and the sheriff was again ordered to hear the case. In a further writ he was to be instructed that he must execute all writs and summonses for Montgomery. Although it had recently been 'drawn to the law of Wales', Domesday Book and other records had proved that it was by right part of Shropshire.[100]

Mention has already been made of cases hinging on whether or not land was held in chief, that is to say, directly from the Crown. The escheators were vigilant in upholding royal rights, and on many occasions seized estates allegedly held in chief but granted out by their holders without permission. Domesday Book was regularly consulted in the resulting disputes, but its evidence often either proved inconclusive or had been superseded. In 1331, it was used in a case heard in the Exchequer of Pleas to determine whether the Crown had an interest in a messuage in High Wycombe, but it was the Book of Fees, rather than Domesday, which provided the information that it should be part of the honor of Wallingford.[101] In the 1340s, there was

36. *The Irish Exchequer in the fifteenth century. The chequered table was a large abacus used for accounting, as in its English equivalent.*

disagreement as to whether or not Birthorpe in Lincolnshire was part of the manor of Folkingham, and as to whether the lord of Folkingham had acted illegally in granting it away. Domesday was consulted, but it was on the strength of evidence drawn from other records that Birthorpe was found to be held by knight service and the escheator was ordered to remove his hand from it.[102]

Nor was Domesday always of much help in settling rights over services. In the 1330s, at a relatively early stage of his career, John de Molyns, that knight of the household with a thirst for money and power, inherited the manor of Ilmer in Buckinghamshire in fee tail, a tenure incompatible with its status as a manor held in chief from the Crown, as was shown in Domesday Book. In 1336, he was pardoned for this unorthodox acquisition, yet two years later he petitioned the Crown to give him custody of the royal goshawks, a responsibility which, he asserted, had belonged to the manor time out of mind. The treasurer and barons of the Exchequer were ordered to search Domesday Book and other records to see whether the profitable office of keeper of the royal goshawks indeed went with the manor. Domesday Book specified no such service, but enough evidence was obtained from other records to allow Molyns the position for which he had striven 'in consideration of his long and loyal service' to the king.[103]

In many of the examples discussed, Domesday's practical value was slight, and although on occasions it provided important evidence, very often it had little relevance or bearing on a case. Procedurally, however, it was a great success. In disputes involving ancient rights and tenures, Domesday Book was almost always specified as the first record to be searched for evidence. In writ after writ, the treasurer and chamberlains of the Exchequer were instructed to consult Domesday and other records, rolls and memoranda, and, as has been shown, if Domesday was omitted from the writ, the Exchequer officials might in their return firmly remind Chancery of its importance.[104] The fact that, as often as not, there was nothing of any use in Domesday's pages was irrelevant: the Conqueror's survey went unchallenged as the starting-point for all such inquiries. Nor did the passage of time change the procedures in any significant way, so that in 1700 – and, indeed, in 1900 – Domesday's evidence could still be called up by much the same means as in 1300 in the infrequently realized hope of resolving broadly similar kinds of case. Domesday's evidence as proof of ancient-demesne status was far more practically relevant in almost all cases, and its importance in this area may in part have sustained its reputation as proof of ancient rights. Yet, even in ancient-demesne cases, the problems of interpreting the survey sometimes left considerable leeway to the justices in deciding the outcome; and on occasions, too, particularly in the middle ages, Domesday could be overruled if expediency so dictated.

CHAPTER IV

The Ancient Demesne and
Domesday Book to 1833

Sir Edward Coke, writing in the early seventeenth century, gave a valuable account
of how ancient demesne was viewed in his day.

Certain it is that, as well before as after the Conquest, the king upon his ancient demesnes of
the Crown of England, had houses of husbandry, and stocks for the furnishing of necessary
provisions for his household: and the tenants of those manors did by their tenures manure,
till etc., and reap the corn upon the king's demesnes, mowed his meadows etc., repaired
the fences, and performed all necessary things belonging to husbandry upon the king's
demesnes: in respect of which services, and to the end they might apply the same the better,
they had many liberties and privileges, as that they should not be sued out of the court of that
manor, nor impanelled of any jury or inquest, nor appear at any other court, but only at the
court of the said manor, nor be contributory to the expenses of the knights of the shire which
serve at Parliament, nor pay any toll etc., which liberties and immunities appear to this day,
albeit the original cause thereof is ceased. Now all the manors which were in the hands of
Edward the Confessor before the Conquest, or in the hands of William the Conqueror, and
so appear in the book called Domesday, are accounted the ancient demesne of the Crown of
England, and had been the demesnes of the Crown long before.[1]

There are two main elements in this account: Coke the historian explaining the
origins of ancient demesne, and Coke the lawyer describing the privileges of its
tenants. The historical element, which impinges on the use of Domesday Book in
proving the tenure, is a matter of considerable complexity: the villeins' privileges are
far easier to explain. Tenants in ancient demesne did not have to attend the county or
hundred courts, to serve on juries, to pay taxes with the county, or to contribute to the
expenses of members of Parliament. They were free from paying tolls and customs,
but they could be taxed by the king at will.[2] Although unfree, they had, unlike others
of that status, immediate access to a royal court, not at Westminster but in their own
manors. The kind of freehold actions at first initiated by the writ of right, directed by
the king to the justices or to the sheriff, were, in the case of land in ancient demesne,
initiated by the little writ of right close. It was directed by the king to his bailiffs in the
manor, often bypassing the lord altogether.[3] Villein sokemen of the ancient demesne
were also subject only to fixed and usually nominal labour services: if any change was
imposed on them by their lords in manors granted out by the Crown, they could bring

a petition against their lord to the Crown. A writ of *monstraverunt* would then be issued by the king and the ensuing action would be heard by the royal justices. On manors retained by the Crown, the villeins could lodge a petition to the king against the exactions of his bailiffs.[4] The vitality of many ancient-demesne courts and the breadth of actions covered are shown by surviving court rolls, such as those of King's Ripton in Huntingdonshire and Basingstoke in Hampshire.[5]

Coke's view that ancient demesne was a special privileged tenure surviving from pre-Conquest times was generally accepted until the middle of the present century. A legal treatise traditionally ascribed to Bracton and written in the early years of Henry III seemed to provide corroborative evidence. It discussed the various kinds of tenant on the king's demesne lands and explained the privileged villeins there as the descendants of the free Anglo-Saxons who had been removed from their holdings by the Normans but were later allowed to return into villeinage.[6] Coke's exposition of that theory was coloured by his conviction that the common law was by definition immemorial custom, a view which was widely held in the seventeenth century.[7] In the nineteenth, Vinogradoff and Maitland expanded it, explaining that ancient-demesne rights originated in the protection afforded by the Anglo-Saxon kings to their free peasantry; the Crown, as a conservative force, preserved those privileges.[8]

In 1950, however, the whole theory of survival was overturned by R.S. Hoyt, whose account of the development of the royal demesne included an explanation of the origins of ancient demesne.[9] He noticed that, although tenure in ancient demesne was widely recognized after the 1250s, the legal treatise known as 'Glanville', written in Henry II's reign, gave it no explicit mention. From careful analysis of twelfth- and thirteenth-century legal records, Hoyt concluded that the privileged villein sokemen of the ancient demesne were not the direct successors of a free Anglo-Saxon peasantry but groups of ordinary villeins on royal manors who, by having access to the financial and judicial resources of a Crown which was anxious to spread its influence, won special privileges which set them apart from men on other manors.[10] His thesis has more recently been further developed, notably in M.K. McIntosh's studies of the manor of Havering in Essex[11] and in the work of the Soviet historian M.A. Barg,[12] but there are many problems and puzzles left to resolve.

It is therefore possible to offer only tentative answers to the questions as to why and how ancient-demesne tenure emerged during the late twelfth and thirteenth centuries. One of the most important factors in its development was the Crown's attitude to its ancient endowments. Henry II's administrators were well aware of the importance of royal resources, and sought to regain lands alienated in the previous reign and thus to raise more money from fixed farms and from rents. Those were, however, diminished in value by the inflation of the 1180s, so that the Crown shifted its interest towards the exploitation of tallage, a tax which could be levied at will both from current Crown demesne and from alienated royal lands. As has been noted, under Henry III there were further reviews of royal resources and experiments in ways of administering them. *Quo warranto* proceedings were used to recover the king's lost lands and franchises, and tallage continued to be levied on land currently and formerly royal. Decades of concerted interest in these matters by royal administrators culminated in 1257, when the king's councillors were required to swear that they would not allow any of the ancient demesne of the Crown to be alienated. A clear distinction was thereby drawn between the king's temporary feudal acquisitions and his ancient, traditional endowments.[13]

As the Crown increasingly exploited its demesne, so it began to extend legal and tenurial privileges to its tenants, including men on lands formerly held by the king. On some manors, the peasants probably had direct access to the royal courts in the late twelfth century, but in about 1200 they were excluded by the growing sophistication of legal procedures. Instead, they were allowed their own manorial courts under the aegis of the Crown.[14] Between the 1220s and the early 1240s, these privileges were gradually extended to the rest of the demesne, the Crown benefiting from the legal dues.[15] On certain manors, too, the level of labour services was fixed and protected by the king, at times (although not invariably) in conjunction with the granting of legal privileges. Some places where the king so intervened, such as Stoneleigh in Warwickshire, were in areas where land clearance was taking place and where all the lords were seeking to attract peasants to their lands by requiring only light labour services.[16] The Crown extended these and other privileges not only to manors which were of relatively more recent acquisition (for example, Stonesfield and Combe in the forest of Wychwood)[17] but also to some or all tenants on many manors of the ancient demesne. However obtained, the privilege of light labour services was of great practical importance to the tenants, because it left them with more time to cultivate their own lands. Moreover, ancient-demesne manorial courts were valued because they allowed groups of villeins direct access to royal justice.[18] The relatively oppressive levying by the Crown of tallages and, later, of lay subsidies must in many cases have seemed a small price to pay for the other privileges.

The complexities of the origins of ancient-demesne tenure are reflected in its later history, because its spread was far from uniform. The villeins of many ancient-demesne manors came to possess only some of the privileges to which they were entitled, or indeed, none at all. The advantages gained in one generation could be lost in the next by inertia or by adverse judgments. Privileged tenants were in the majority in some manors, but in many others were only a small group among the other classes of freemen, ordinary villeins, and other unfree people. The practical differences between villeins and ancient-demesne villein sokemen were often very slight, especially where ancient-demesne status was insecure. As villeinage developed into copyhold in the later middle ages, the distinction between that and ancient demesne tenure was further blurred, although enough persisted to allow their separate survival to the present century.[19]

A central issue in this study is how ancient demesne was defined. Under Henry III, several different criteria were adopted; in Edward I's reign, a listing as *terra regis*, the lands of the Conqueror, in Domesday Book emerged as the principal proof. By the sixteenth century, some authorities insisted that manors had to belong to the smaller group of lands held by Edward the Confessor in 1066 to qualify, and many historians have followed that definition. However, the balance of legal and historical opinion has subsequently favoured the interpretation of ancient demesne as *terra regis*, the Conqueror's lands. Whichever way it is explained, the ancient demesne accounted for a considerable proportion of all manors, as is illustrated in Maps 3–13. However, the maps do not show those places which had that status from time to time without the support of Domesday Book, and so prove that the definition by reference to Domesday was never clear-cut. In reality, particularly in the middle ages, Domesday's evidence was often ignored or overruled by the king's justices if political expediency, royal interest or advantages to the landlords so dictated.

Maps of the Ancient Demesne (pages 78–94)
The evidence for the following maps is drawn from Domesday Book. There are four categories of places: boroughs (as in A. Ballard, The Domesday Boroughs, *Oxford, 1904); lands held by both William the Conqueror and Edward the Confessor; lands held by the Conqueror; and lands held by the Confessor (the place-name identifications are from H.C. Darby and G.R. Versey,* Domesday Gazetteer, *Cambridge, 1977; from the Phillimore Domesday Series; and from the* VCH). *No source other than Domesday has been used, because the maps are drawn entirely from the point of view of those examining the evidence of the survey to determine whether or not a given place or piece of land was ancient demesne (information is given to cover both of the possible definitions — land listed as* terra regis *and held by the Conqueror, and land held by the Confessor). Domesday sometimes omits information about, for example, the identity of previous landholders, and the resulting picture is therefore not a complete guide to the pre-1066 holdings of Edward the Confessor. Some of the places on the maps are complete manors, others are parts of manors, or outlying portions or sokeland. Some* terra regis *sections include lands forfeited and held temporarily by the Crown, and these have not been included on the maps; whereas lands administered for the Crown by others but listed as* terra regis *have been brought in.*

Map 3. *The ancient demesne: Cornwall and Devonshire.*

C.
Hartland

Kilkhampton

Trevalga

Wer
Penheale

St Kew

Blisland

Caradon

Coswarth   Carworgie

C O R N W A L L

Pendrim

Towan

Probus

Connerton
Roseworthy

Binnerton

Helston

Winnianton

Braunton

Barnstaple

Tawstock

Bideford

North Molton

Langley

Molland

Blackpool

South Molton

Morebath

King's Nympton

Irishcombe

Bampton

Torrington

Langtree

Beaford

Ashreigney

Witheridge

Shebbear

Tiverton

Halberton

Hemyock

Iddesleigh

Winkleigh

Lapford

Monchard Bishop

Black Torrington

Down St Mary

Silverton

Northlew

North Tawton

Undercleave

Axminster

Okehampton

South Tawton

Kilmington

Broad Clyst

Whitford

Ash

Holcombe Burnell

Pinhoe

Exeter

Worford

Colyton

Lydford

Moretonhampstead

Alphington

Topsham

Colaton Raleigh

Axmouth

Exminster

Woodbury

East Budleigh

Kenton

Littleham

DEVONSHIRE

Spitchwick

Kingsteignton

Walkhampton

Bickington

Kingskerswell

Broadhempston

Little Hempston

King's Tamerton

Totnes

Sutton

Diptford

Langford

Ashprington

Plympton St Mary

Ermington

Farleigh

Yealmpton

Blackawton

West Alvington

Sherford

Chillington

Lands held by William the Conqueror and
■ Edward the Confessor

△ Lands held by William the Conqueror in 1086

▲ Lands held by Edward the Confessor in 1066

● Boroughs

Miles
0   10

Kilometres
0   16

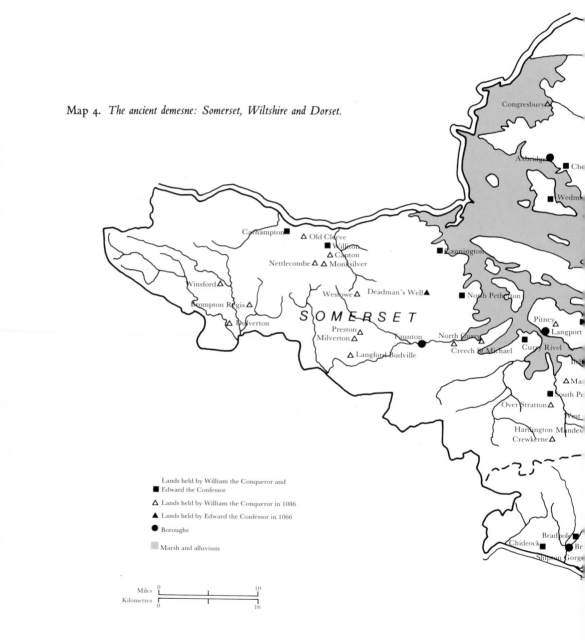

Map 4. *The ancient demesne: Somerset, Wiltshire and Dorset.*

Congresbury△

Axbridge■ Che

Wedm■

Carhampton■   △ Old Cleeve
                  ■ Williton
                  △ Capton
Nettlecombe△ △ Monksilver   ■ Cannington

Winsford△   Westowe△   △ Deadman's Well▲   ■ North Petherton

Brompton Regis△

△ Dulverton   S O M E R S E T   Pitney△
                                                                ● Langport
              Preston△   ■
              Milverton△   Taunton   North Curry△   Curry Rivel
                              ●   Creech St Michael
              △ Langford Budville   △ Ma
                                                          ■ South Pe
                                              Over Stratton△
                                                            West

                                              Hardington Mandev
                                              Crewkerne■

                                                        Bradpole
                                              Chideock■ ● Br
                                                    Shipton Gorge

     ■ Lands held by William the Conqueror and
       Edward the Confessor

     △ Lands held by William the Conqueror in 1086

     ▲ Lands held by Edward the Confessor in 1066

     ● Boroughs

     ■ Marsh and alluvium

     Miles   0   10
     Kilometres 0   16

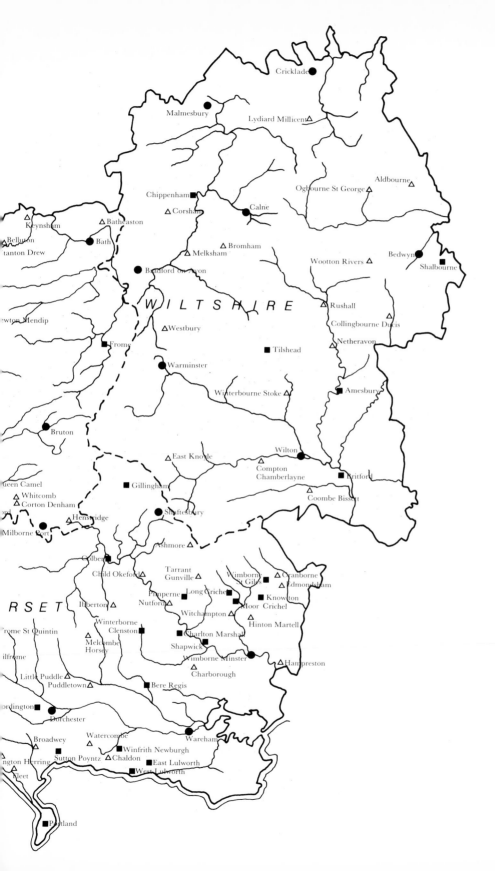

Cricklade •

Malmesbury •

Lydiard Millicent △

Chippenham ■   Oglbourne St George △   Aldbourne △

△ Corsham   Calne •

Keynsham △
Belluton △   △ Batheaston
Stanton Drew   • Bath   △ Melksham   △ Bromham   Wootton Rivers △   Bedwyn •
                                                                                                    Shalbourne •
                    • Bradford on Avon

W I L T S H I R E

Newton Mendip   △ Westbury   △ Rushall
                                            Collingbourne Ducis
          ■ Frome   ■ Tilshead   △ Netheravon

          • Warminster

          Winterbourne Stoke △   △ Amesbury

• Bruton

          △ East Knoyle   Wilton •
                              △ Compton
                              Chamberlayne   ■ Britford
Queen Camel
△ Whitcomb   ■ Gillingham   Coombe Bissett
△ Corton Denham
• Milborne Port   △ Hensridge   • Shaftesbury

                    △shmore   △ Ashmore

Colber   Tarrant   Wimborne △ Cranborne
Child Okeford   Gunville △   St Giles   △ Edmondsham
                              Long Crichel ■
          Ilberton △   Pimperne   Knowlton ■
                    Nutford   ■ Moor Crichel
                    Witchampton △
R S E T   Winterborne   Hinton Martell △
Frome St Quintin   Clenston ■   Charlton Marshall ■
          Melcombe   Shapwick △
          Horsey   Wimborne Minster •
Ilfrome
Little Puddle   Charborough △   △ Hampreston
Puddletown △   Bere Regis ■
Fordington ■   Charborough △
          • Dorchester

Broadwey   Watercombe   • Wareham
          ■ Winfrith Newburgh
Kington Herring ■ Sutton Poyntz   △ Chaldon   East Lulworth ■
Fleet   ■ West Lulworth

          ■ Portland

△ Littleworth
△ Great Faringdon
△ Great Coxwell
△ Little Coxwell
Sutton Courtenay
△ Steventon
■ Wallingford
Kingston Lisle
■ Charlton △
Sparsholt
■ Wantage
△ East Hendred
Shrivenham ■
Letcombe Regis ■ Betterton
△ Blewbury
△ Cholsey
△ Aston Tirrold

B E R K S H I R E

Little Fawley ■
△ Compton ■
△ Basildon △
△ Lambourn
Winterbourne △
Bucklebury △
Pangbourne ●
Reading ●
△ Earl
Remenham
△ Wargrave
Cook
■ Waltha
B
△ Eddington
Kintbury ■
Thatcham ■
Wokefield △
Shinfield △
Barkham △
Aldermaston ■
Swallowfield △
△ Finchampstead

△ Faccombe
■ Kingsclere

△ Upton
■ Hurstbourne Tarrant
Basingstoke ■
△ Odiham

H A M P S H I R E

Monxton △
Quarley △
△ Andover
△ Upper Clatford
△ Barton Stacey
Lasham △
Holybourne △
Anstey △
■ Neatham
△ Nether Wallop
Kings Worthy ■
Selborne △
△ Chiltley
Broughton ■
Kings Somborne
(Winchester) ●
Greatham △
East Dean ■

Rockbourne ■
■ Breamore
East Meon △
△ Mapledurham
Burgate ■
Meonstoke ■
△ Eyeworth
△ Soberton
Eling △
Southampton ●
Lyndhurst △
Portchester △
Wymering △
Cosham ■
Ringwood △
Titchfield ■
Stanswood ■
Hayling Island △
Bosham △
Holdenhurst △
Twynham ●

Whippingham △
△ Wootton
△ Puckpool
Kingwood △
△ Abington
Barnsley △
△ Nettlestone
Wilmingham △
△ Yellow
Shide
△ Arreton
3 8
△ Nunwell
Afton △
△ Freshwater
Bowcombe
1 △ 5 △ 4
△ Yaverland
Compton △
Merston ▲ 6
Sandown
Brook △
Shorwell
7 △
Scotlesford △
2
Dungewood △
△ Kingston
Sandford with Week
Atherfield △
△ 9 △ Luccombe
△ Walpen Stenbury
△ Niton

IOW

1	Haldley	6	Bathingbourne
2	Woolverton	7	Lessland
3	The Down	8	Kern
4	Knighton	9	Wroxall
5	Heasley	10	Adgestone

Lands held by William the Conqueror and Edward the Confessor

Lands held by William the Conqueror in 1086

Lands held by Edward the Confessor in 1066

Boroughs

Marsh and alluvium

Miles
Kilometres

Map 5. *The ancient demesne: Berkshire, Hampshire, Middlesex, Surrey and Sussex.*

Map 6.
The ancient demesne:
Essex and Kent.

Lands held by William the Conqueror and
■ Edward the Confessor

△ Lands held by William the Conqueror in 1086

▲ Lands held by Edward the Confessor in 1066

● Boroughs

Marsh and alluvium

Miles 0   10
Kilometres 0   16

ESSEX

KENT

Great Chesterford
Steeple
Newport
Great Sampford
Rickling
Finchingfield
Wethersfield
Lawford
Shalford
Birchanger
Lexden   Colchester
Stanway
Hatfield Broad Oak
Layer de la Haye   Layer Breton
Layer Marney
Brightlingsea
White Roding
Witham
Shellow Bowells
Writtle
Maldon
Fingrith Hall
Margaretting
Latchingdon
Woolston Hall
Havering atte Bower
North
Benfleet
Childerditch
South
Benfleet
North Ockendon
South
Ockendon
Dartford
Milton
Rochester
Seasalter
Faversham
Fordwich
Aylesford
Canterbury
Sandwich
Barham
Dover
Hythe
Romney

Map 7.
*The ancient demesne:
Herefordshire,
Worcestershire and
Gloucestershire.*

Leintwardine
Wigmore
Lye
Kymestrey
Brinfield
Upton
Yarpole
Ashton
Miles Hope
Loston
Stanford
Kingsland
Cholstrey
Street
Eaton
Stockton
Brockmanton
Radnor
Rushock
Eardisland
Lawton
Leominster
Edwyn Ralph
Stoke Prior
Humber
Rowden
Bromyard
Kington
Brierley
Marston Stannett
Breadward
Hopleys Green
Woonton
Welston
Eardisley
King's Pyon
Stanford
Suckley
Whitney
Clifford
Marden
HEREFORDSHIRE
Lugwardine
Hereford
Kingstone
Dewsall
Birch
Westwood
Much Marcle
Kilpeck
King's Caple
Pontrilas
Ashe Ingen
Baysham
Yatton
Dymock
Linton
Newent
Cleeve Aston Ingham
Howle Hill
Ashleworth
Sandhurst
Gloucester
Hempsted
Westbury on Severn
Down Hatherley

Hampley Franche Wannerton
Habberley
Clent
Wribbenhall
Sutton
Hurcott
Willingwick
Chadwick
Houndsfield
Ribbesford
Shurvenhill
Comble
Ashborough
Wythwood
Oldington
Woodcote Green
Timberhanger
Burcot
Wytnall
Cooksey Green
Grafton
Tutnall
Tynsall
Yardebigge
Droitwich
Feckenham
Martley
Hollow Court
Worcester
WORCESTERSHIRE
Pershore
Hanley Castle
Queenhill
Twyning Kemerton
Ashton under Hill
Pull Court
Pamington
Beckford
Bushley
Aston on Carrant
Eldersfield
Tewkesbury
Natton
Alderton
Northampton
Oxenton
Dixton
Southwick
Tredington
Stoke Orchard
Winchcombe
Boddington
Cheltenham
Guiting Power
Lower Slaughter
Great Barrington
Brookthorpe
Harescombe
Haresfield
Chedworth
Arlington
Monmouth Castle
Staunton
Arlingham
GLOUCESTERSHIRE
Bledisloe
Awre
Etloe
Purton
Lydney
Nass
Gossington
Hinton
Coaley
Woodchester
Cirencester
Fairford
Sharpness
Cam
Nympsfield
Hullasey
Tidenham
Berkeley
Uley
Avening
Down Ampney
Alkington
Dursley
Kingscote
Hill
Symonds Hall
Beverstone
Wotton under Edge
Ozleworth
Thornbury
Cromhall
Elberton
Olveston
Tockington
Almondsbury
Winterbourne
Wapley
Old Sodbury
Kingweston
Horfield
Bristol
Barton
Mangotsfield
Bedminster
Bitton
Marshfield

Collingham
Chickward
Walton
Kiddington
Bromsgrove
Mitton
Kidderminster

Lands held by William the Conqueror and
Edward the Confessor

Lands held by William the Conqueror in 1086

Lands held by Edward the Confessor in 1066

Boroughs

Marsh and alluvium

Miles 0   10

Kilometres 0   16

Map 8. *The ancient demesne: Warwickshire, Northamptonshire,*
Huntingdonshire, Cambridgeshire, Oxfordshire,
Buckinghamshire, Bedfordshire and Hertfordshire.

△ Duddington

King's Cliffe
...tton   △ Apethorpe   △ Nassington   ■ Botolph Bridge

△ Tansor

...anion   △ Stilton

...ngton   △ Brigstock   △ Barnwell

...edon   △ Islip   △ Great Gidding
                        ○ Little Gidding
                        ○ Steeple Gidding

HUNTINGDONSHIRE

...edon   ■ Keyston   ▲ Catworth   △ Alconbury
                        Huntingdon ●   ■ Hartford   △ Isleham
△ Higham Ferrers   △ Grafham   Brampton   ■   Soham
                        ■ Godmanchester   ▲ Fordham
                        △ Fen Drayton   ▲ Chippenham

△ Great Paxton
△ Little Paxton   △

CAMBRIDGESHIRE

Eynesbury   Chesterton ■   Little   ■ Cheveley
                        Wilbraham ■   △ Wooditton
△ Gransden   Cambridge ●   Great
                        Wilbraham ■
Kingston ■   △ Fulbourn
                        △ Combertom ■
Bedford ●   Haslingfield ■   ▲ Great Shelford
△ Chalton   Little Shelford ■
Potton △   ▲ Babraham
                        △ Little Abington
                        △ Great Abington

△ Pigott's Abington
BEDFORDSHIRE   △ Litlington

△ Ashwell

Westoning △   Hexton △ △   Wellbury Hitchin
...hton   Little Offley △   △ Great Wymondley
...zard   Great Offley △   Charlton △   △ Little Wymondley
Sewell △   Biscot ■   Wain Wood △ △   Temple Dinsley
Houghton Regis ■   Lea green △   △ Minsden
            Luton ●   △ King's Walden
            Wanden △   Flexmore △

Hertford ●
HERTFORDSHIRE   ● Stanstead

● Berkhamsted   ● St Albans   ▲ Bayford
            Little Berkhamsted   △ Bayford

Lands held by William the Conqueror and
■ Edward the Confessor

△ Lands held by William the Conqueror in 1086

▲ Lands held by Edward the Confessor in 1066

● Boroughs

○ Demesne forests held by William the Conqueror

░ Marsh and alluvium

Miles   0 ————————————— 10
Kilometres   0 ————————————— 16

Map 9.
The ancient demesne:
Lincolnshire and Rutland.

LINCOLNSHIRE

RUTLAND

Derby
Winterton
Thealby
Burton
upon Stather

Habrough
Newsham
Croxton
Kirmington
Little Limber
Keelby
Great Limber

Scunthorpe
Brumby
Ashby
Maddlethorpe
Bottesford

Somerby
Somby
Searby
Grasby
Clixby
Fonaby
Hundon

Cadney
Howsham

Hibaldstow
North Kelsey
Caistor

Redbourne
Kirton in
Lindsey
South Kelsey
Holton le Moor

Northorpe
Grayingham
Stainton
Waddingham
Snitterby

Grainthorpe
Yarburgh
Somercotes
Skidbrooke
Saltfleetby

Blyton
Pilham
Aisby
Corringham
Hemswell
Harpswell
Glentworth

Alvingham
Grimoldby
Louth
Manby

Springthorpe
Somerby
Heapham

Welton le Wold
Gayton le Wold

Saxby

Swinthorpe
Wickenby

T O R K S E Y

Nettleham

West Ashby
Low Toynton
High Toynton
Langton
Thimbleby
Langton
Horncastle
Scrivelsby
Roughton
Wood Enderby
Moorby
Halthan
Wilksby
Mareham le Fen
Fulsby

Lincoln

Thorpe on the Hill

Bassingham
Coleby
Boothby Graffoe
Coningsby
Wellingore

South Kyme
Evedon
Ewerby Thorpe
Kirkby la Thorpe
Howell
Quarrington
Heckington

Barkston
Belton
Welby
Great Gonerby
Londonthorpe
Harrowby
Braceby
Grantham
Dunsthorpe
Sapperton
Spitlegate
Harlaxton
Denton
Great Ponton

South Stoke
Skillington

Holbeach
Lutton
Whaplode
Gedney
Fleet

Tydd St Mary

Greetham
Cottesmore

Oakham
Great
Casterton
Little Casterton
Hambleton
Stamford

Ketton
North Luffenham
Ridlington
South
Luffenham
Sculthorp
Glaston
Tixover
Bisbrooke
Morcott
Barrowden
Thorpe by Water
Seaton

Lands held by William the Conqueror and
■ Edward the Confessor

△ Lands held by William the Conqueror in 1086

● Boroughs

Marsh and alluvium

Miles 0   10
Kilometres 0   16

1 Great Walsingham 7 Hemblington 13 Hassingham
2 Little Walsingham 8 North Burlingham 14 Buckenham
3 Hindringham 9 Ormesby St Michael 15 Cantley
4 Little Plumstead 10 Ormesby St Margaret 16 Surlingham
5 Great Plumstead 11 Moulton St Mary 17 Yelverton
6 South Walsham 12 Freethorpe

Holme next the Sea
Holkham Wells next the Sea Morston Cley next the Sea
Burnham Overy Warham Stiffkey Blakeney Glandford
Wighton Bayfield
Quarles Field Dalling Holt
Southmere Egmere Bale Sharrington Hempstead East Beckham
Stanhoe Houghton St Giles Great Snoring Stody Hunworth Matlaske
West Barsham Gunthorpe Little Barningham Little Wickmere
East Barsham Thursford Briston Mannington Colby Happisburgh
Little Snoring Alethorpe Thorning Saxthorpe North Walsham
Thorpland Fakenham Oulton Blickling Felmingham Kessingham
Dunton Pudding Norton Stibbard Sall Crackford Hempstead
Helhoughton Aylsham Palling
West Raynham Marsham Scottow
Little Massingham East Raynham Whitwell Hevingham Easton
Great Massingham Weasenham St Peter Horningtoft Brandiston Stratton Strawless Winterton
Woodton Weasenham All Saints Witchingham Felthorpe Belaugh Martham
Rougham Mileham Wroxham Rollesby
East Winch Bittering Woodbastwick
South Acre NORFOLK Beeston St Andrew Ranworth Clippesby Burgh St Margaret
Palgrave Sparle Taverham Rackheath Upton Thrigby
North Pickenham Shipdham Sprowston Panxworth Fishley Runham
Cockley Cley Holme Hale Bowthorpe Norwich Witton Acle Yarmouth
South Pickenham Swathing Runhall Earlham Newton Brundall
Saham Toney Cranworth Plockthorpe Eaton Trowse Caister Caistor
Woodrising Kimberley Framingham Pigot Bedon Rockland St Mary Wickhampton Halvergate
Griston Manson Framingham Earl Holverston Reedham Browston Belton
Easton Little Ellingham Crownthorpe Stoke Holy Cross Poringland Limpenhoe Fritton
Illingham Shotesham All Saints Howe Sisland Herringfleet Somerleyton
Stow Bedon Saxlingham Shotesham St Mary Mundham Aldeby Corton
Buckenham Breckles Saxlingham Nethergate Woodton Raveningham Gillingham Lowestoft
Carleton Rode Bedingham Beccles Barnby
Ashby Worlington Kirby Pakefield
Roudham Quidenham Tivetshall St Margaret Alburgh Ringsfield Weston Mutford Rushmere
Kenninghall Winfarthing Tivetshall St Mary Kessingland
Silverstone East Harling Shelfhanger Gissing Rockenhall
Thetford West Harling Fersfield Burston Starston
Garboldisham Shimpling
Gasthorpe Bressingham Diss
Brome Easton Bavants
Gislingham Eye Blythburgh
Sticklingland Dunwich
SUFFOLK Darsham
Exning
Barrow
Badmondisfield Thorney Stonham
Olden
Hemingstone
Great Blakenham
Somersham Little Blakenham
Clare Bramford Rushmere St Andrew
Sudbury Ipswich
Bentley Shotley
East Bergholt Harkstead

■ Lands held by William the Conqueror and Edward the Confessor
△ Lands held by William the Conqueror in 1086
● Boroughs
▨ Marsh and alluvium

Miles 0 ——————— 10
Kilometres 0 ——————— 16

Map 10. *The ancient demesne: Norfolk and Suffolk.*

Map 11. *The ancient demesne: Cheshire, Derbyshire, Nottinghamshire, Shropshire, Staffordshire and Leicestershire.*

Map 12. *The ancient demesne: Yorkshire.*

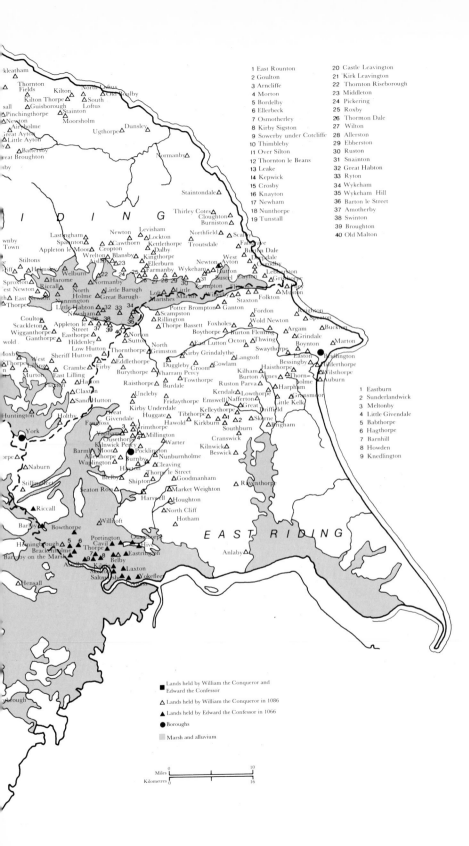

1 East Rounton
2 Goulton
3 Arncliffe
4 Morton
5 Bordelby
6 Ellerbeck
7 Osmotherley
8 Kirby Sigston
9 Sowerby under Cotcliffe
10 Thimbleby
11 Over Silton
12 Thornton le Beans
13 Leake
14 Kepwick
15 Crosby
16 Knayton
17 Newham
18 Nunthorpe
19 Tunstall
20 Castle Leavington
21 Kirk Leavington
22 Thornton Riseborough
23 Middleton
24 Pickering
25 Roxby
26 Thornton Dale
27 Wilton
28 Allerston
29 Ebberston
30 Ruston
31 Snainton
32 Great Habton
33 Ryton
34 Wykeham
35 Wykeham Hill
36 Barton le Street
37 Amotherby
38 Swinton
39 Broughton
40 Old Malton

1 Eastburn
2 Sunderlandwick
3 Meltonby
4 Little Givendale
5 Babthorpe
6 Hagthorpe
7 Barnhill
8 Howden
9 Knedlington

■ Lands held by William the Conqueror and Edward the Confessor

△ Lands held by William the Conqueror in 1086

▲ Lands held by Edward the Confessor in 1066

● Boroughs

▨ Marsh and alluvium

Miles 0 10
Kilometres 0 16

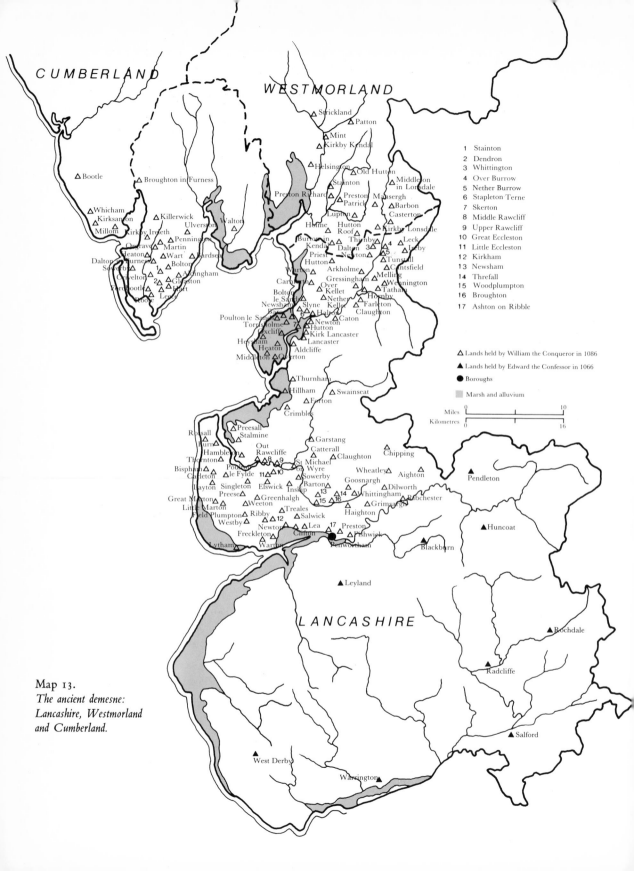

CUMBERLAND

WESTMORLAND

△ Strickland
△ Patton
△ Mint
△ Kirkby Kendal
△ Helsington
△ Old Hutton
△ Stainton
△ Middleton
in Lonsdale
△ Preston Richard
△ Preston Mansergh
Patrick
△ Barbon
△ Lupton
△ Casterton
△ Bootle
△ Broughton in Furness
△ Holme
△ Hutton
Roof
△ Kirkby Lonsdale
△ Whicham
△ Killerwick
△ Walton
△ Burton in
Kendal
△ Thirnby
△ Dalton 3
△ Leck
△ Ireby
△ Kirksanton
△ Ulverston
△ Priest
Newton
4
△ 5
△ Tunstall
△ Millom
△ Pennington
△ Kirkby Ireleth
△ Warton
△ Priest
Hutton
△ Gantsfield
△ Wart
△ Cardsea
△ Arkholme
△ Melling
△ Osgrave
△ Martin
△ Carnforth
△ Gressingham
△ Wennington
△ Dalton in Furness
△ Bolton
△ Aldingham
△ Over
Kellet
△ Tatham
△ Sowerby
△ Conyston
△ Gleaston
△ Bolton
le Sands
△ Nether
Kellet
△ Hornby
△ Yardbooth
△ Leece
△ Newsham
△ Slyne
△ Farleton
△ Claughton
△ Roos
△ Halton
△ Caton
△ Poulton le Sands
△ Torrisholme
△ Newton
△ Oxcliff
△ Hutton
△ Kirk Lancaster
△ Heysham
△ Lancaster
△ Heaton
△ Aldcliffe
△ Middleton
△ Overton
△ Thurnham
△ Hillham
△ Swainseat
△ Forton
△ Crimbles
△ Rossall
△ Preesall
△ Stalmine
△ Garstang
△ Burn
△ Out
Rawcliffe
△ Catterall
△ Hambleton
8
9
△ Claughton
△ Chipping
△ Thornton
△ St Michael
on Wyre
△ Bispham
△ Poulton
le Fylde
11
△ 10
△ Wheatley
△ Aighton
△ Carleton
△ Sowerby
△ Barton
△ Goosnargh
△ Layton
△ Singleton
△ Elswick
△ Inskip
△ Dilworth
△ Ribchester
△ Great Marton
△ Preese
△ Greenhalgh
13
△ 14
△ Whittingham
△ Little Marton
△ Weeton
△ 15
△ 16
△ Grimsargh
△ Field Plumpton
△ Treales
△ Salwick
△ Haighton
△ Westby
△ Ribby
12
△ Newton
△ Lea
17
△ Preston
△ Freckleton
△ Fishwick
△ Lytham
△ Warton
△ Clifton
● Penwortham

1 Stainton
2 Dendron
3 Whittington
4 Over Burrow
5 Nether Burrow
6 Stapleton Terne
7 Skerton
8 Middle Rawcliff
9 Upper Rawcliff
10 Great Eccleston
11 Little Eccleston
12 Kirkham
13 Newsham
14 Threfall
15 Woodplumpton
16 Broughton
17 Ashton on Ribble

△ Lands held by William the Conqueror in 1086
▲ Lands held by Edward the Confessor in 1066
● Boroughs
▨ Marsh and alluvium

Miles 0 ——————————— 10
Kilometres 0 ——————————— 16

▲ Pendleton

▲ Huncoat

▲ Blackburn

▲ Leyland

LANCASHIRE

▲ Rochdale

▲ Radcliffe

Map 13.
The ancient demesne:
Lancashire, Westmorland
and Cumberland.

△ West Derby

△ Warrington ▲

▲ Salford

During the reign of Edward I, a major royal stocktaking took place, which, with its related legal processes, brought Domesday Book to its preeminent place as proof of ancient demesne. In 1274–75, the Crown used commissioners to carry out an extensive inquiry into its lands and franchises. Preliminary, non-binding verdicts were taken from juries, and the results were written down and returned to Westminster. The lists of lands which emerged were of immediate value, but the franchise claims needed further proof. Legal proceedings to that end were therefore held in Parliament; however, the amount of business was overwhelming and in 1278 responsibility for verification returned to the justices in eyre. They continued the campaign, and included some cases in which rights to land were tested, yet the legal principles underlying *quo warranto* remained uncertain. That is demonstrated by questions on the matter submitted in 1285 to Ralph de Hengham, chief justice of the court of King's Bench, and by the answers he gave. *Quo warranto* writs were generally accepted as a valid way for the Crown to recover franchises, but Hengham was asked if they could properly be employed similarly to claim title to land. He replied that they could; although the Crown had recently used writs of common form, which took no account of evidence from before 1189, the limit of legal memory, to regain its recent possessions, it had employed *quo warranto* to take back ancient-demesne lands. The validity of such *quo warranto* writs, he added, depended entirely on the appearance of the manors as Crown land in Domesday Book. Hengham, in fact, rationalized previous practices in the royal courts, but his emphasis on Domesday as key evidence in certain *quo warranto* processes is of considerable value and interest, and is supported by certain cases brought at about that time. In 1293, however, the Crown's use of *quo warranto* in land claims was discontinued, as the result of strong opposition from landholders; any tenant who could demonstrate continuous possession by himself and by his predecessors since 1189 was subsequently safe from any action by the Crown.[20] The king's ability to recover ancient-demesne manors was thereby curtailed.

Meanwhile, in 1279, the stocktaking had continued with another royal inquiry into the lands and rights of the king and of other lords. Its scope and scale were almost on a par with the Domesday survey, and it is unfortunate that many of the hundred rolls in which its findings were recorded have been lost.[21] In it, as in the 1274–75 inquisitions, title to land was evidenced by the verdict of a jury. That process favoured the Crown, because many groups of tenants serving on juries were anxious to obtain an ancient-demesne ranking for their manors. They did not, however, merely follow the definition of ancient demesne as lands possessed by Edward the Confessor in 1066 or by William the Conqueror in 1086, but successfully claimed that status for some places which had been held by the Anglo-Saxon and Danish predecessors of the Confessor[22] or by the Norman and Angevin successors of the

Conqueror.[23] The peasants wanted to establish their ancient demesne rights in order to claim the privileges which went with them, in particular, freedom from the burdensome labour services which were increasingly being imposed upon them.[24] Their interests, therefore, were in conflict with those of their landlords, but coincided with those of the king as he actively sought to expand the ancient demesne.

Such peasant claims did not often stand up convincingly when tested in the courts, because the justices tended to uphold the rights of the lords. From 1274, and increasingly from about 1279, perhaps in reaction to the hundred rolls inquiry, they began consistently to adopt the Domesday definition of ancient demesne and its privileges, which they used to bring judgments against villeins seeking to better their lot. Their proof of ancient demesne was a mention in Domesday Book as royal land, rather than an acceptance of former ownership by any king. Many manors potentially included by the wider definition were thereby excluded. Thus in 1274, in an action over services between the prior of St Swithun's, Winchester, and his tenants at Havant, Domesday Book was consulted. The manor was found not to be ancient demesne and the claims of the peasants to lighter labour dues were rejected.[25] Similarly, in 1279, the tenants of Langar in Nottinghamshire claimed ancient demesne privileges, but did not want to have their case tried by Domesday Book, which had clearly gained an unfavourable reputation among the informed peasantry. It was nevertheless consulted and showed their claim to be false.[26] When Domesday appeared to support villein interests, further legal obstacles and quibbles were sometimes raised to prevent them from being secured. Also in 1279, the tenants of Tavistock brought an action over services against their lord, Geoffrey de Camville, and it was agreed in court that, according to Domesday, Tavistock was ancient demesne. Nevertheless, the tenants were judged to be villeins rather than privileged villein sokemen, because Domesday mentioned only the former and not the latter.[27]

Barg considers that, in the late thirteenth century, peasants managed to prove ancient demesne status only in exceptional circumstances. He sees the enigmatic wording in Domesday as a useful weapon for the justices, who used 'the entire weight of the formalism and casuistry of the medieval court proceedings and the entire complexity of the Domesday entries' to favour the landlords.[28] There is no doubt that the peasants did badly in the courts, but they had made gains in the hundred rolls inquiry, and the justices may in part have been attempting to sort out the consequent confusion about tenures. Moreover, a look at the wider context of the unsuccessful cases suggests that the peasants sometimes made *de facto* gains from their resistance. In the 1270s and 1280s, the abbey of Halesowen in Worcestershire was involved in disputes over services with its tenants at Hales. There were violent confrontations and an appeal to Domesday, which showed that the manor was not ancient demesne.[29] Nevertheless, by their opposition, the villeins succeeded in bringing about some reduction in their rents and services.[30] At Halesowen's daughter-house of Titchfield, the peasants reacted against the imposition of heavy services by having a writ of *monstraverunt* brought against the abbot in 1271. Domesday Book was consulted and showed that Titchfield, as an outlier of Meonstoke, was ancient demesne.[31] However, the customs at Meonstoke were far heavier than those at Titchfield, and the justices found against the men of Titchfield and amerced them heavily. In 1276, the tenants adduced a new argument, that the customs of royal sokemen should be fixed. This plea was accepted, and a compromise was reached with the abbot.[32]

An adverse judgment passed in the 1270s could be reversed later. The practice of accepting the older and wider definition of a manor as ancient demesne, namely that it had once been, or currently was, royal, was still on occasions followed into the fifteenth century. Once a manor had gained that status, even if it was not part of the *terra regis* in Domesday Book, it was normally allowed to enjoy the concomitant rights. As a result, the more persistent groups of tenants who could prove royal ownership of their manor at some distant time in the past might benefit in the end, if they lodged their case at a time when the Crown and justices were seeking to extend the ancient demesne. But there is another side to the story. In the first half of the fourteenth century, some groups of tenants fought equally hard to escape ancient-demesne status, because of the heavier taxes which went with it.

There were two main kinds of tax which could be raised from ancient-demesne lands in the fourteenth century: tallage and lay subsidies. Tallage, levied by the Crown on its boroughs and ancient-demesne manors, had been raised fairly frequently under Henry III, but gradually fell into disrepute and disuse thereafter. Tallages were collected in 1304 and 1312 and, because the old assessments had become unworkable in many areas, a new basis was adopted: a percentage was raised on revenues and movable goods as on non-demesne lands. That provoked some opposition, and when in 1332 Edward III once more tried to levy tallage, he was met with concerted demands in Parliament to return to the basis of assessment used by his ancestors. He therefore withdrew his demands and an aid was granted instead.[33]

In 1304 and 1312, the king, following earlier custom, had permitted lords to raise tallages, at the same rate as the royal tallage, on ancient-demesne manors which had been granted with that right attached. A number of communities resisted the royal or seigneurial demands, on the grounds that they were not of the ancient demesne and therefore not liable for tallage. In 1323, for example, the tenants of Queen Isabella on the manors of Christchurch, Ringwood, Westover, Bourton and Donnington petitioned the Crown that, although these places were not ancient demesne, the inhabitants had in 1313 been unjustly assessed for tallage by John Morice; their refusal to pay had led to their being cited in court. In 1325, Edward II ordered the

Exchequer officials to search Domesday Book and other records, and if the places were indeed found not to be ancient demesne, to exonerate those tenants from blame and to free them from their debts. Christchurch, Westover, Bourton and Donnington fitted that category and benefited accordingly, but Ringwood had been listed as *terra regis* and the sum of eleven marks was declared as its still outstanding debt.[34] Although tallage was never again to be levied after the failed attempt of 1332, the Crown tried to maintain its right to tallage on some alienated ancient demesne. In 1342, the barons of the Exchequer heard a case in a long-running dispute between the Crown and the abbey of Cirencester about whether the king or the abbot should tallage the town. Domesday showed that Cirencester was ancient demesne, but because other, later, evidence which favoured the abbot was found, the case eventually went in his favour.[35]

Aids levied on movables had been popular with the Crown at the time of Henry III and emerged as a key element in public finance under his successors. They were granted by Parliament to meet a specific need, rather than being raised at the sovereign's will, and could cause considerable friction between the two, as in the 1290s and in 1340–41, when the king needed money for wars with the French.[36] Nevertheless, these levies, known from the fourteenth century as lay subsidies, developed into a well-established system of national taxation. That system brought about the gradual assimilation of the royal demesne into the rest of the realm for fiscal purposes, but the differences between royal and other lands were sustained by the assessment of the former at a higher level. In 1294, the counties paid a tenth, the boroughs, which were royal, a sixth; in 1306, the counties a thirtieth, the boroughs and the rural royal-demesne manors a twentieth. Under Edward II, much of the rural royal demesne was taxed with the counties, leaving the ancient demesne and the boroughs paying at a higher rate. After 1334, the standard rates of assessment were fixed at one fifteenth for the counties and one tenth for the boroughs and ancient demesne.[37]

The boroughs were represented in Parliament by two knights each, but the rural ancient-demesne tenants were, as already noticed, exempted from attending the county courts where the knights of the shire were elected. They therefore had no direct representation in Parliament, although the Crown was careful to associate them with the shire at large for the purposes of consent to taxation.[38] It was, however, financial rather than political motives which led the men of numerous manors to try to escape the higher assessment as ancient demesne. That happened increasingly after 1316, when the Crown took careful stock of the ancient demesne and made a survey to extend the list of manors liable to pay at the higher rate[39]; it also further increased the numbers by including ancient-demesne manors granted out by the king during his own lifetime.[40] Thus, in 1319, the men of Banstead in Surrey successfully cited

Domesday Book to prove that their manor was not *terra regis* and therefore not ancient demesne. They thus avoided paying tax at the higher rate.[41]

A similar case which began in the 1340s took almost thirty years to resolve. In February 1344, a writ was issued to the Exchequer ordering Domesday Book and other rolls and memoranda to be searched to establish whether or not Oakham, Langham and Egleston in Rutland had rightfully been assessed for subsidies as ancient demesne. The tenants claimed that they had been unjustly assessed and unduly oppressed by the tallages of 1304 and 1312 and by Edward II's four lay subsidies, blaming the malice of Gilbert de Holm and John Bassett, their assessors. The Domesday entry for Oakham indicated that it had been *terra regis* in 1086, but lacked a clear heading and may therefore have been ambiguous. Langham and Egleston were not mentioned at all. The Domesday extract for Oakham was considered by the royal administration and it was decided that the manor was ancient demesne, and also that Langham and Egleston had since become attached to it as outliers. The Exchequer rolls showed that the tenants of all three places had claimed ancient-demesne status during the reigns of Edward I and Edward II and that they had been taxed accordingly at a higher rate. It was therefore decided not to discharge them from their debts.[42] Soon after that, the tenants claimed that, although Langham and Egleston were indeed part of the soke of Oakham, none of the three was ancient demesne: the tenants had always pleaded before the justices of assize and, until recently, had been assessed for taxation with the shire.[43] The matter continued on its slow and inconclusive passage for many years, until finally in 1372 the men of all three manors succeeded in gaining exemption from paying their taxes at a higher rate, although they thereby lost their ancient-demesne privileges.[44]

In 1377, 1379 and 1381, a novel levy was made on each person at a flat rate: the poll tax. The strong opposition it aroused is often seen as a major contributory factor to the outbreak of the Peasants' Revolt in 1381.[45] It is possible that, initially, ancient-demesne tenants believed that they would be exempt from paying it; if that was so, it might have increased the large numbers of Domesday exemplifications requested in 1377 and immediately after.[46] The major factor in those requests was, however, a more longstanding grievance, that of oppressive labour services, an issue which came to a head in that year.

In the first half of the fourteenth century, when some peasant communities were trying to escape ancient-demesne status and the heavier taxation which accompanied it, others still continued to claim it in order to avoid increased labour services, in much the same way as in the preceding thirty years. Relations between landlords and tenants remained consistently strained on many manors, and cases were often brought to court which hinged on ancient-demesne status being confirmed or denied. One such dispute arose between the Norman abbey of Bec and its tenants at Ogbourne St George and Ogbourne St Andrew in Wiltshire and was to run on for many decades. Before 1309, four tenants of the abbot's proctor at Ogbourne brought a writ against him; the proctor, however, refused to answer, because they were his villeins. In 1312, more writs were brought and backed up with claims that the villeins were rightfully tenants of ancient demesne and that the abbot of Bec had, through the proctor, imposed burdensome labour duties upon them. Domesday Book was consulted and it was found that, although one Ogbourne manor (Ogbourne St George) had been in royal hands in 1086, the other (Ogbourne St Andrew) had been held by Miles Crispin. Some at least of the tenants had a good claim, but there was difficulty at that time in ascertaining which Domesday Ogbourne was which. In 1315, the case was due to be heard again, but went against the tenants by default; meanwhile the abbot had confiscated some of their lands.[47] In 1327, the villeins erupted into open revolt and, although they had won the support of certain local lesser gentry, they were treated harshly by the abbot. They brought another ancient-demesne lawsuit in 1332 and purchased another Domesday exemplification and initiated further legal action in 1341, again to no avail. Further unsuccessful lawsuits and resistance to the abbot's proctor were to follow in 1389 and in 1416, when the exemplification of 1341 was reissued.[48] The determination with which the peasants pursued their case over more than a century is striking, and so too is their longlasting faith in Domesday Book.

In the middle years of the fourteenth century, the Black Death produced a shortage of labour. The Statute of Labourers was passed in 1351 to restrict wages, to enforce labour services and to circumscribe the mobility of labour. A steady stream of exemplifications from Domesday Book made in the 1350s and 60s, many at the request of the tenants of the manors, shows that numerous groups of peasants were trying to resist the new demands by claiming ancient-demesne status.[49]

In 1381, the combination of peasant resentment against their landowners and against the harsh services which they imposed, dislike of royal government as it was perceived, and dissatisfaction with the ways in which the law was interpreted by the justices finally brought about the Peasants' Revolt.[50] A foretaste of this resistance came in 1377 from groups of tenants mainly on the estates of ecclesiastical landlords in Hampshire, Wiltshire and Surrey,[51] for whom Domesday Book was the symbol of liberation from onerous labour services. The nature of their revolt is explained in a petition presented by the Commons in Parliament in that year:

To our lord the king and the council of Parliament, the Commons of the realm show that in many parts of the kingdom of England the villeins and tenants of land in villeinage, who owe services and customs to the lords for various reasons and within various lordships, both ecclesiastical and secular, have (through the advice, procurement, maintenance and abetting

37. *John Ball and Wat Tyler leading the Peasants' Revolt of 1381.*

of certain persons) purchased in the king's court for their own profit exemplifications from the book of Domesday – concerning those manors and vills where these villeins and tenants live. By colour of these exemplifications, and through misunderstanding them, as well as the malicious interpretation made of them by the said councillors, procurers, maintainers and abettors, they have withdrawn and still withdraw the customs and services due to their lords, holding that they are completely discharged of all manner of service due both from their persons and their holdings. ... They threaten to kill their lords' servants if these make distraint upon them for their customs and services. ... Accordingly the said lords lose and have lost much profit from their lordships, to the great prejudice and destruction of their inheritances and estates. Moreover in many parts of the realm the corn lies unharvested for this reason. ... Therefore let it please our lord king and his Council to ordain a due and speedy remedy, directed against the said councillors, procurers, maintainers, and abettors as well as the said villeins and tenants and especially those who have now come to court.

The reply provides a valuable official comment about the significance of the Domesday extracts:

As regards the exemplifications made and granted in Chancery, it is declared in Parliament that these neither can nor ought to have any value or relevance to the question of personal freedom; nor can they be used to change the traditional terms of tenure and its customs or to the prejudice of the lords' rights to have their services and customs as they used to be in the past. If they wish, the lords may have letters patent under the great seal recording this declaration. As for the rest of this article, the lords who feel themselves aggrieved shall have special commissions of inquiry appointed under the great seal and directed either to the justices of the peace or to other suitable persons. These commissions shall investigate all such rebels, their councillors, procurers, maintainers and abettors. Those indicted before the commissioners, for either past or future offences, shall be imprisoned. ... And if such rebellious tenants are attainted of the offences mentioned above, they shall not be released until they have made a fine with the king and have the consent of their lords.[52]

The truth of the Commons' statement about the exemplifications purchased by groups of peasants in 1377 is evident from the considerable numbers which have survived for that year, a contrast with the years immediately before and immediately after.[53] A cartographical representation of the manors and their Domesday landlords, moreover, shows the spread of the movement from one estate to another (Map 14). The exemplifications purchased late in 1376 by Surrey tenants of the bishop of Chichester and those of the college at Lambeth may have heralded the movement; then, in March and April 1377, the men of the bishop of Winchester on one Hampshire and five Surrey manors all put in similar requests, probably concerted. Neighbouring peasants on the estates of other mainly ecclesiastical landlords followed suit. In April, one Hampshire manor of Hyde Abbey, Winchester, and four Surrey manors of Chertsey Abbey were so involved. In July and August, the tenants of eighteen manors in Wiltshire did likewise; their landlords included the king, the bishop of Salisbury, and the abbeys of Wilton, Shaftesbury, Romsey and Amesbury.[54] However, by the end of August, the unusually high number of exemplifications requested had returned to a more normal level.

The chronological and geographical pattern of the evidence and, above all, the Commons' petition make it clear that this was an organized movement. The identity of one of its 'maintainers and abettors' is known: he was John Godefray, who appeared before the justices of the peace at Melksham in the 1380s, accused of persuading unfree tenants in Wiltshire that, if they purchased exemplifications from Domesday Book, they would be free men, all to the detriment of the lords of the county. Godefray already had a record of conspiracy and of breach of the peace; with a fellow confederate, John Donham, a clerk, he had *inter alia* altered the date on a notarial instrument which had been produced by the precentor of Salisbury Cathedral in a dispute with the parishioners of Westbury, and, with his brother, he had attacked the property of the prioress of Dartford at Norton Bavant.[55]

It is unfortunate that none of the records of the commissioners sent out to suppress the rebellious peasants in 1377 and 1378 has survived, particularly because the commissions which initiated their activities show that the unrest had spread well beyond its main centres in Wiltshire and Surrey.[56] In September 1377, the warden of the college of Ottery St Mary in Devon petitioned the Crown about such a problem on his estates and it was ruled that he should not be deprived of labour services on the pretext of a Domesday exemplication.[57] A similar petition by the abbot of Chertsey secured a commission of oyer and terminer against his tenants at Thorpe, Egham and Chobham the following spring.[58] The abbot had meanwhile made certain of his

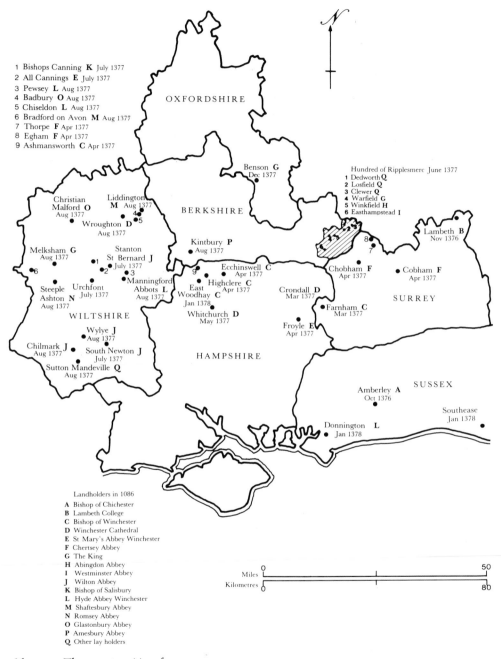

1 Bishops Canning **K** July 1377
2 All Cannings **E** July 1377
3 Pewsey **L** Aug 1377
4 Badbury **O** Aug 1377
5 Chiseldon **L** Aug 1377
6 Bradford on Avon **M** Aug 1377
7 Thorpe **F** Apr 1377
8 Egham **F** Apr 1377
9 Ashmansworth **C** Apr 1377

OXFORDSHIRE

N

Benson **G**
Dec 1377

Hundred of Ripplesmerc June 1377
1 Dedworth **Q**
2 Losfield **Q**
3 Clewer **Q**
4 Warfield **G**
5 Winkfield **H**
6 Easthampstead **I**

Christian
Malford **O**
Aug 1377

Liddington
M Aug 1377

BERKSHIRE

Lambeth **B**
Nov 1376

Wroughton **D** 5
Aug 1377

Melksham **G**
Aug 1377

Kintbury **P**
Aug 1377

Ecchinswell **C**
Apr 1377

Chobham **F**
Apr 1377

Cobham **F**
Apr 1377

Stanton
St Bernard **J**
July 1377

Highclere **C**
Apr 1377

Steeple
Ashton **N**
Aug 1377

Urchfont
July 1377

Manningford
Abbots **L**
Aug 1377

East
Woodhay **C**
Jan 1378

Crondall **D**
Mar 1377

SURREY

WILTSHIRE

Whitchurch **D**
May 1377

Farnham **C**
Mar 1377

Wylye **J**
Aug 1377

Froyle **E**
Apr 1377

Chilmark **J**
Aug 1377

South Newton **J**
July 1377

HAMPSHIRE

Sutton Mandeville **Q**
Aug 1377

SUSSEX

Amberley **A**
Oct 1376

Southease
Jan 1378

Donnington **L**
Jan 1378

Landholders in 1086
A Bishop of Chichester
B Lambeth College
C Bishop of Winchester
D Winchester Cathedral
E St Mary's Abbey Winchester
F Chertsey Abbey
G The King
H Abingdon Abbey
I Westminster Abbey
J Wilton Abbey
K Bishop of Salisbury
L Hyde Abbey Winchester
M Shaftesbury Abbey
N Romsey Abbey
O Glastonbury Abbey
P Amesbury Abbey
Q Other lay holders

Miles 0   50
Kilometres 0   80

Map 14. *The peasant uprising of 1377.*

own ground by purchasing a Domesday exemplification listing Chertsey's 1086 lands in Surrey and Berkshire.[59] In May, analogous commissions were issued in favour of the abbess of Shaftesbury concerning lands not only in Wiltshire but also in Dorset; of the prior of Bath for his manors of Bath and Bath Easton; and of Richard de Molyns and his wife for Aston Bampton in Oxfordshire.[60] The effectiveness of the repressive action by the commissioners is demonstrated by the general lack of participation by the men of these counties in the revolt of 1381.[61]

What does the peasant movement of 1377 tell about the attitudes of the protagonists to ancient demesne and to Domesday Book? Of all the manors whose tenants took action in 1377–78, only three (Melksham, Benson and Warfield) satisfied the strict definition of ancient demesne: a listing as royal land in Domesday Book. If an older and wider criterion, possession by a pre-Conquest king, were applied, many more manors would have been eligible. Among them were Farnham, granted to Winchester in the 680s by King Caedwalla; Steeple Ashton, a gift from King Edward to Romsey Abbey in the late ninth century; and Easthampstead, given by Edward the Confessor to Westminster Abbey. Moreover, the tenants of Crondall, granted by King Edgar to St Swithun's, Winchester, in 972 and listed in Domesday Book under that abbey's lands, had struggled for its recognition as ancient demesne since the late thirteenth century and had been allowed certain of the privileges in 1364.[62] The peasants' case in claiming ancient demesne had some validity, but its acceptance was entirely at the discretion of the Crown and in 1377 the opposition of the landlords and the Commons was too great.

If most of the manors were ancient demesne according only to older and, by that time, comparatively rarely accepted definitions, it is strange and striking that the peasants imagined their cause would be helped by exemplifications from Domesday Book. After all, most of the estates were not found among the royal lands in 1086. The most likely explanation is that they relied on their long folk-memories and that neither they nor their abettors had any precise knowledge of what Domesday contained. They equated it, rather, with the Day of Judgment, when the rich would be humbled and they would be freed.[63] It was an almost talismanic symbol of liberation from servitude and oppression.

Although the resistance of 1377 is the only example of concerted action with Domesday exemplifications as the justification, there are many other examples of tenants obtaining such documents in an attempt to escape onerous duties after 1377 as well as before. The burgesses of St Albans struggled long and hard against their abbots, obtaining a Domesday exemplification in the 1320s to lay claim to their rights and wreaking considerable damage on the abbey's property in 1381.[64] Likewise, in February 1393, the tenants of Abingdon Abbey on the manors of Winkfield, Hurst and Whistley in Berkshire, under the leadership of Stephen

38. *Fourteenth-century window from Fairford church, Gloucestershire, depicting the Last Judgment.*

Saward and Thomas Somerton, requested a Domesday exemplification for the hundred of Ripplesmere.[65] Although it showed that Winkfield had belonged to the abbey in 1086, they withdrew their services on the grounds that the manor was ancient demesne. In May, the abbot obtained an oyer and terminer commission in his favour, but the peasants of Winkfield struck back, arguing that since 1348 Winkfield had been part of the manor of Windsor and therefore Crown demesne (although not ancient demesne). Their services — but not those of the other manors — were judged excessive, yet it is not clear how firmly that verdict was enforced.[66]

The early fifteenth century saw a similar pattern of demand for Domesday exemplifications; a significant proportion of the manors involved were not listed as royal lands in 1086. Some such exemplifications, like the one requested by Thorpe, Egham, Cobham and Chobham in 1403, mark the continuation of an earlier struggle;[67] others may represent new disputes. As the century progressed, the purchase of Chancery exemplifications from Domesday Book by groups of tenants attempting to escape labour services became rarer. More and more of the letters patent and certificates were produced for groups of burgesses or for the Crown in response to petitions, the object being a grant of freedom from tolls and other dues.

Freedom from tolls, the paying of duty on local trade, was a privilege allowed by the Crown to many tenants of the royal demesne in the twelfth century,[68] and had become one of the privileges of ancient demesne by the late thirteenth.[69] But not for another hundred years did it emerge as one of the principal reasons for seeking ancient-demesne status. A case heard in King's Bench in 1388 gives an indication of its value. The mayor of Totnes had had a certain John Tanner imprisoned and his goods seized for not paying the tolls due in this ancient-demesne market town. Tanner argued that, as an ancient-demesne tenant himself, coming as he did from Ashburton, he was exempt from paying tolls throughout the land. The cause proved inconclusive, the uncertainty arising largely from problems with identifying Tanner's town of origin. When discussing the case, one of the justices questioned whether, in fact, Tanner came from the Domesday 'Aisbertona' (Ashprington), a royal holding, or from 'Esse Bretona' (Ashburton), a manor of the bishop of Exeter (this problem of identification has equally exercised twentieth-century scholars). Nevertheless, they all agreed that ancient-demesne tenants should be exempt from paying tolls throughout England.[70]

Such an exemption not only covered tolls, but was also gradually extended to stallage (payment for a market stall), cheminage (cart-toll), pontage (for bridge repairs), pavage (for repairing streets), picage (for breaking the ground to build a stall), murage (for repairing walls), lastage (export duty) and passage (ferry tolls), which were usually listed in charters in that order. Members of trading communities would benefit considerably by such wide-ranging exemptions. Urban fortunes fluctuated from the fourteenth to the seventeenth centuries, but there was consistent competition for an expanding market between all towns which had commercial activities, whether old or newly established. Many became involved in trading disputes with their neighbours, in which the successful claiming of ancient-demesne status was an important weapon. The borough of Godmanchester is a good example of a place which consolidated its ancient-demesne status and which struggled to maintain its privileges as a way of upholding its prosperity.

39. Sixteenth-century map of Godmanchester, Huntingdonshire.

Godmanchester's communal life in the middle ages has recently been subjected to detailed scrutiny,[71] but the significance of its ancient-demesne status has been overlooked. In 1212, King John issued the town with a charter stating that its burgesses were to hold it in fee farm for £120 a year, and the document was confirmed by several subsequent monarchs.[72] From the thirteenth century onwards, the tenants vigorously pursued all possible privileges. In 1279, an inquiry established that Godmanchester was royal demesne and, seven years later, its men tried to claim certain judicial rights, which they were allowed only in return for annual payments.[73] In 1283, they were successful in asserting that all the tenements in the town were held in ancient demesne and that no royal writ was valid there except for the little writ of right close.[74] The town's court rolls bear witness to a flourishing ancient-demesne court in the later middle ages,[75] and the lay subsidy returns for the later fourteenth century place Godmanchester among the ancient-demesne towns and manors paying taxes at a higher rate. Its total contribution in 1334 was £14 5s. 4d.[76] In 1361–62, its ancient-demesne status was, by contrast, used against the escheator to prevent him from interfering in the town's affairs on behalf of the king.[77]

Economic pressure from its close neighbour Huntingdon built up during the fourteenth century. In 1365, Edward III ordered the bailiffs of Huntingdon to cease their oppressive levying of tolls from Godmanchester men, who, as tenants of the ancient demesne, should be exempt from paying.[78] In 1381, Richard II granted them two charters, one reciting their privileges, including the right to take the goods of felons and fugitives, the other confirming their exemption from tolls as ancient-demesne tenants.[79] After a disastrous flood, the men of Godmanchester again appealed to the Crown in 1392 for a clearer statement of their liberties.[80] Only in return for a payment of £40 at the hanaper were their privileges extended to include infangtheof and outfangtheof (the proceeds of certain minor offences) and the forfeited goods of outlaws and abjurors of the realm, as well as of felons and fugitives. The freedom from tolls was again confirmed and extended.[81]

By the 1420s, the burgesses of Godmanchester felt a further need to renew their privileges, presumably again in response to economic pressure from Huntingdon. The royal administration by that time required a full Domesday exemplification to be produced by the beneficiary before a confirmation of ancient demesne privileges could be made. In 1424, therefore, the burgesses bought an exemplification of their Domesday entry from Chancery.[82] Having produced it there once more in January 1427, they were issued with a full and solemn statement of their freedom from tolls.[83] In 1431, the more important charter of 1392 was again confirmed and enrolled on the Exchequer memoranda roll, an indication of the fiscal aspects of such exemptions.[84] By 1464, Godmanchester had become part of the Duchy of Lancaster, but its burgesses still continued to uphold their rights and privileges. The principal 1392 charter was confirmed successively by Henry VII, Edward VI, Mary and Elizabeth I, and in 1604 James I, in a remarkably verbose document, finally constituted it a free borough.[85] Godmanchester's disputations with its neighbours also continued: in 1673, its men claimed, as ancient-demesne tenants, freedom from toll at the market at St Neots.[86]

Although many of the Godmanchester charters lack immediate context, the burgesses' longstanding commitment to preserving and extending their ancient-demesne privileges is evident from the content. What also emerges is the degree of success which this urban community enjoyed; its prosperity was to a considerable degree founded upon its privileges. Many other exemplifications were made by Chancery in the fifteenth century for groups of burgesses and tenants seeking similar rights, such as the exemplification issued in 1480 to the inhabitants of Chesterfield, Boythorpe, Whittington, Brimington, Tapton and Aston in Derbyshire, which was used not only to establish freedom from toll and from the other dues, but also to confirm their exemption from the expense of sending knights to Parliament and from serving on juries or appearing at assizes.[87] After a hiatus in the early sixteenth century, exemplifications were again produced in considerable numbers after 1568. Markets were, at that time, expanding rapidly in numbers and importance; and there was a revived interest in obsolescent tolls, and in the resurrection of moribund exemptions and customs, including the economic privileges of ancient demesne.[88] Thus, similar exemplifications were made for the inhabitants of Lowestoft in Suffolk and for those of Bromsgrove in Worcestershire, leading to the issuing of charters of exemption from toll in 1573 and 1577 respectively.[89] In the course of a case heard in King's Bench in 1586, in which the claim was made that Leicester was an ancient-demesne town and should be discharged from paying tolls, the judge opined that, not only the tenants in ancient demesne there, but all the inhabitants should enjoy the privilege.[90]

Although the economic privileges of ancient demesne were often obtained in the spirit of urban competition, important trading centres might also on occasion form alliances to their mutual benefit. In 1485, the mayors and men of Lincoln and Nottingham signed a solemn agreement stating that, because many disputes had recently arisen over tolls and other royal customs claimed by both, the two sides had now come together to settle their differences. They had found from the evidence of several Domesday exemplifications that both sets of burgesses were entitled to ancient-demesne status and to the concomitant freedom from tolls and dues. Each side therefore agreed to observe the privileges of the other and stated that

the mayors, aldermen, justices of the peace, sheriffs, citizens, enfranchised men and burgesses inhabiting the city and town aforesaid . . . shall be exonerated and quit towards each other of all tolls and charges owed or claimed between them from the beginning of the world until the making of these [records].[91]

Traditions and knowledge of ancient-demesne tenure were kept alive by the manorial courts and by the manorial customs which regulated their procedures. The preservation of those customs was a matter of pride as well as of practicality and, in some ancient-demesne manors, they were copied many times, even as late as the nineteenth century. Their antiquity was often stressed to emphasize their legitimacy. Thus, the customs of Clipstone in Nottinghamshire, as copied into a memorandum book in 1554, begin: 'It is to be had remembrance that in the book of Domesday of the county of Nottingham made at London in the time of King Henry I, the seventh year of his reign, are contained the customs of the manor of Clipstone.'[92] The tenants are said to be freeholders and the manor to be of the ancient demesne of the Crown of England. The erroneous reference to Domesday is of particular interest. Clipstone was not listed as *terra regis* in Domesday Book, but had escheated to the Crown in the reign of Henry I as part of the honor of Tickhill. It was within the boundaries of Sherwood Forest and a favoured residence of medieval kings,[93] and by 1337 its tenants had claimed and gained ancient-demesne status,[94] the privileges of which they retained into the eighteenth century.[95] It is striking that they attributed Domesday to Henry I's reign, the very time when their manor came into the Crown's hands, and believed that their customs were enshrined in it. The tenants of nearby Warsop, part of which was royal, and another part of which had passed to Henry I with the honor of Tickhill, made almost identical claims in their customs. As with Clipstone, some of Warsop's tenants later established their rights to the legal privileges of ancient demesne.[96]

Although such customs prevailed for centuries, the nature of the tenancies which they regulated underwent gradual change as villeinage was transformed into copyhold. In the fourteenth century, the Black Death had decimated the labour force, labour services were increasingly commuted into rents, and lords came to rely more on hired than on tied labour to cultivate their lands. The social standing of the villeins apparently improved, and by 1500 they were commonly known as copyholders, the name deriving from the arrangements by which their land was transferred. The donor would surrender his holding to the lord of the manor, who would then regrant it to another, the transaction being recorded on the court roll for easy future reference. Such lands were said to be held by copy of court roll at the will of the lord. As early as the fifteenth century, the equitable jurisdiction of Chancery was extended to cover such tenants, and by 1600 the courts of Exchequer, King's Bench and Common Pleas were also prepared to defend the rights of copyholders, the justification being the protection of their manorial customs. When in 1660 almost all feudal tenures were abolished, copyhold, as an unfree tenure, survived unscathed, as did ancient demesne, which, although more privileged, had many features in common with it.

The nature of ancient-demesne tenure in the seventeenth and eighteenth centuries was lucidly explained by Blackstone in the late 1750s. He drew a clear distinction between tenants holding by copy of court roll at the will of the lord, who were the descendants of villeins, and those holding by copy of court roll according to the customs of the manor, who were the successors of ancient-demesne sokemen. The proof of ancient demesne was in Domesday Book; the tenants on such lands were neither freemen nor copyholders, but halfway between. Their bodies were free and their interest in their land was freehold, because, provided that they paid their dues and fines to their lord, he could not remove them from it. But their tenure was base, because, if they failed to pay, they could be ejected from their land; and they could not bring real actions in the royal courts. Rather than going to Westminster, they had to use the manorial court to effect land transfers. Nor did they make any contribution towards the expenses of the knights of the shire, whom they therefore had no right to elect.[97]

Blackstone's tract was written to determine whether or not such tenants could vote. In the eighteenth century, there was considerable confusion about their status and many of them saw no distinction between their personal and their tenurial standing, regarding themselves as free men. They might well be prosperous and substantial figures in local society, and the decay and disappearance of certain manorial courts in this period removed for some the body which should have preserved their tenurial arrangements. Thus, many ancient-demesne tenants were either ignorant of their exclusion from voting in parliamentary elections, or were prepared to ignore it. Statutes enacted in the fifteenth century had restricted that right to freeholders, but by the eighteenth, many ancient-demesne tenants, particularly on the manor of Woodstock in Oxfordshire, and in Herefordshire, Gloucestershire and parts of South Wales, nevertheless voted at elections.[98] However, the attention of Parliament was drawn to that anomaly by the notorious disputed election in Oxfordshire of 1754, when, as the result of rigging and other dubious practices, four members were returned to Parliament instead of two.[99] That was why Blackstone was commissioned to investigate the matter, and his recommendations barring all copyholders, including ancient-demesne tenants, from voting were enacted as legislation in 1758. It was not until 1832 that the wealthier copyholders were to be enfranchised.

The distinction between the freedom of their persons and the servile nature of their tenures was one which had early been lost sight of by the tenants of many ancient-demesne manors, who had for centuries regarded themeselves as free. Indeed, the mythical as well as the procedural side of ancient-demesne tenure survived in some places from the thirteenth to the nineteenth centuries. Records of the royal manor of Mansfield in Nottinghamshire give an excellent illustration of this continuity of institutions, both as operated and as perceived by their tenants.[100] Its thirteenth-century custumal, the earliest surviving copy of which dates from the sixteenth century, stressed that the tenants of Mansfield, all of whom held in ancient demesne, were 'free of blood' and that their legal privileges stretched back to the Norman Conquest. Their lands, too, were described as freehold.[101] Although the document undoubtedly exaggerated the antiquity of their privileges, it was only by a mere two hundred years or so. A Domesday outlier of Mansfield, Skegby (and thus by implication Mansfield itself) had in 1274 been described as ancient demesne in the hundred rolls,[102] and in the entry of a case heard in King's Bench between 1301 and 1303, the Mansfield procedures for land actions, including fictitious ones, using the little writ of right close, are described.[103] An isolated manorial court roll surviving from 1316 shows those processes in operation.[104]

In 1592, the tenants still considered themselves to be freeholders with lands in ancient demesne according to the custom of the manor, and with an entitlement to use the writ of right close.[105] The importance of their status to them was shown when, shortly afterwards, Mansfield came up for sale. When royal commissioners were appointed to dispose of Crown lands, the ancient demesne was excluded, but Gilbert Talbot, earl of Shrewsbury, first prevented his half-brother William Cavendish from buying Mansfield by encouraging the tenants to petition against its sale, and then, in 1601, secured it for himself by deceiving the commissioners. The tenants petitioned again, stressing their ancient-demesne status, as shown in Domesday Book, and expressing serious concern that they would lose their court and its privileges.[106] Their fears proved unfounded, because the earl and his successors preserved the manorial court and its customs for another two centuries.

The Mansfield court books of the seventeenth and eighteenth centuries contain many examples of the use of the writ of right close to effect land sales and transfers. The kind of collusive actions brought in the court of Common Pleas to transfer freehold land, and recorded by fines and recoveries, were at Mansfield and at other ancient-demesne manors effected, in theory at least, by the use of the writ of right close in the manorial court. In practice, the relative expense and complexity of the process probably restricted its use on many manors to transfers of particular importance, minor land transactions being recorded by deeds which were enrolled on the court roll. An action known as ejectment was available to freeholders and, from the late sixteenth century, to copyholders to defend their title to land, but, as much case law showed, could not be used by ancient-demesne tenants. Such causes presumably had in their case to be initiated by the writ of right close.[107]

A comparatively large number of fines and recoveries based on the writ of right close were brought at Mansfield in the late seventeenth century; and a register of searches kept by the deputy chamberlains of the Exchequer shows that Domesday Book was consulted in 1685 and in 1689 in verification of Mansfield's ancient-demesne status.[108] After 1733, the records of the Mansfield court, like others, were written in English instead of Latin, but the procedures remained the same. The latest land transfer using the writ of right close was in 1809;[109] the next major land action, in 1813, was completed by two fines and recoveries levied in the court of Common Pleas.[110]

The writ of right close was similarly used on other ancient-demesne manors into the nineteenth century. The ancient royal manor of Basingstoke in Hampshire[111] contained tenants holding in a variety of different ways, among them an important group in ancient demesne. In the middle ages, their court, known as 'the court of the proved men of the manor or hundred of Basingstoke', was held by their elected bailiffs according to the custom of the manor,[112] and on infrequent occasions heard actions or registered concords initiated by the little writ of right close.[113] From 1622 to 1641, the court represented the bailiffs and burgesses of Basingstoke, and after 1641, the mayor, aldermen and burgesses, as the town's status changed. The form of land conveyances, however, remained the same, and they were always made according to the customs of the manor. A number of fines and recoveries, and the relevant proceedings in court, have survived for the years 1538 to 1819. If they represent the majority of the actions which took place, the court's activities reached a modest peak

40. *View of the eighteenth-century Moot Hall at Mansfield, Nottinghamshire. The ancient-demesne court was held here.*

in the seventeenth century. Although it apparently fell into disuse after 1819, it was to escape formal abolition until 1977.[114]

At Havering in Essex, too, the writ of right close was in use to effect land transfers until at least the first decade of the nineteenth century.[115] It was, however, employed only for land held directly from the Crown, not for subtenancies, and even so was not invoked unless a new tenant wished for a particularly secure title to the land.[116] On smaller manors, or ones where the hold on ancient demesne was more tenuous, the use of the writ died out somewhat earlier. The last such conveyance in the rectory manor court at Mansfield was in 1753; at Warsop, it was in 1785; and at Clipstone, in 1791.[117]

These land-transfer practices were increasingly disliked in official and judicial circles. The Commissioners on Real Property, reporting in 1829, described the problems which arose when holders of land in ancient demesne transferred it to others, in ignorance about its status, by fines and recoveries levied in Common Pleas. The land thereby became freehold until the lords of the manor reversed the action, but the tenants were meanwhile unable to claim any protection from them and the land was therefore unsalable.[118] In another report, of 1832, they showed that tenants in ancient demesne 'were made subject to certain restraints and entitled to certain immunities, which produce serious inconveniences at the present day. They were forbidden to bring or defend any action except in the lord's court.' After reviewing all the evidence, the commissioners recommended that ancient-demesne tenure should be abolished as soon as possible.[119]

In the central courts, too, ancient-demesne cases were treated with a growing hostility. Whereas in 1601 a judge had praised ancient-demesne courts and suggested that they should hear most relevant actions in the first instance,[120] in 1760 his successors were frustrated by the necessity to use Domesday Book to prove whether or not a manor was ancient demesne, but a jury to determine if certain land was a parcel of that manor. One judge criticized ancient-demesne courts as 'putting people out of the protection of the law, and fitter to be totally destroyed, than favoured and assisted'. Another found that they had 'a strange, wild jurisdiction, where the jurors are judges of both law and fact, and ignorant country fellows are to determine the nicest points of law'.[121] In 1833, as part of a slow and cautious reform of the land laws, fines and recoveries were abolished by statute.[122] With them went the writ of right close, but tenure in ancient demesne was allowed to continue. Its practical applications were considerably reduced, but it was subsequently brought up in court to vex and perplex the judiciary on a number of occasions, most recently in 1960.[123]

CHAPTER V

Domesday Book in Antiquarian and Historical Writing, 1570–1800

The reign of Elizabeth I saw the beginnings of serious scholarly research into Domesday Book. Arthur Agarde, one of the deputy chamberlains of the Exchequer from 1570 to 1615, explored the Domesday text himself and also disseminated his knowledge to other scholars and antiquarians. His colleagues and many of his successors in the seventeenth century similarly offered advice, but unremitting security and complex bureaucracy still seemed to surround the original Domesday record. Thus, Sir Henry Spelman, writing in 1626, said that it was kept in the Treasury of Receipt behind three locks; one key was held by the chamberlain, the other two by his deputies. Only for an initial fee of 6s. 8d. could even an inspection be made, and, on top of that, transcripts were charged at the rate of fourpence a line.[1] Its consultation could therefore be an unnerving and expensive experience, as George Owen, a local antiquarian from Henllys in Pembrokeshire discovered when, on 29 May 1589, he arrived at the Exchequer of Receipt in search of material for his history of the lordship of Cemaes.

I searched in the Exchequer the book of Domesday which remaineth with Mr Agard and Mr Fenton in the tellers' office, for the lordship of Kemes and for the name of Martyn; but I could find nothing. The book is very ancient and hard to be read, and who so findeth anything must pay for the copy of every line 4d., for it must be exemplified in the self same correctness as it is written in the book, which is strange, and hard for any man to read.

With the help of the deputy chamberlains, however, he began to make some progress.

There are something of diverse lordships in the marches in the said book of Domesday as of Harding Castle and Rutland which I saw. Also Mr Fenton told me he had much for the lordship of Gower and told me he knew it was Beauchamp's land.[2]

A visible manifestation of the care with which Domesday was protected is the chest in which it was traditionally kept from the seventeenth century, and which still survives. Probably constructed in the fifteenth century, it was adapted to contain Domesday at a later date. It is made of wood clad with iron inside and out, and reinforced with iron straps. The contents are protected from theft by four strap hinges,

41. *The chest in which Domesday Book was kept in the seventeenth and eighteenth centuries.*

by two massive iron flanges to prevent it being forced from the side, and by the three locks which were mentioned in many discussions of Domesday from the seventeenth century onwards.[3] Despite the special security surrounding Domesday, it was, however, little more difficult for a record scholar to obtain access to it than for him to inspect other documents.[4] Unlike all others, Domesday extracts were made in a quasi-eleventh-century hand, but the charges for them were lower than for those from other records.[5] The majority of deputy chamberlains in the late sixteenth and seventeenth centuries were, moreover, glad to provide help and advice as well as copies for serious researchers.

For the would-be student of Domesday, it was therefore essential to obtain an introduction to one of the deputy chamberlains through an established user of the records. In 1637, for example, Sir Christopher Hatton wrote to Sir Simon Archer in London, asking him to help the young William Dugdale to gain access to Domesday Book and to other sources to further his historical work.[6] Once the contact had been made, the scholar could have expected to have considerable help and guidance. At the end of the seventeenth century, two places at the record table in the Tally Court were permanently reserved for readers,[7] some of whom studied Domesday. However, not all deputy chamberlains were co-operative, particularly with less knowledgeable searchers. In 1649, Scipio le Squyer, who combined the duties of chamberlain and deputy during the Civil War, refused to allow Peter Leycester to compare with the original a Domesday transcript which le Squyer had made for him. William Dugdale, by then well versed in Domesday, agreed with le Squyer that Leycester was not a serious scholar, but generously performed the task on his behalf.[8] Ironically, the transcript was later to be published in Leycester's history of Cheshire and was well received.[9]

Arthur Agarde, one of Domesday's most able custodians, was born in 1540 and was trained as a lawyer. Through him, the office of deputy chamberlain gained an archival and scholarly quality which it had not had before.[10] He worked on the records in his care, sorting, annotating, calendaring and listing them; some of his abstracts of plea-roll entries are still of value today.[11] He compiled a catalogue of the records in the four treasuries of the Exchequer, which became an invaluable guide for searchers, but is also a telling reminder of the difficulties confronting the record keepers of his day. To Agarde, the principal enemies of the archive were fire, water, rats and mice, and the misplacing or, worst of all, removing of records. His modern successors would find little to disagree with in this analysis.

In his catalogue, Agarde described the documents at the treasury of the Court of Receipt, among which were

two of the most ancientest books of record in the realm, made in William the Conqueror's time (called Domesday), in the twentieth year of his reign, the one book in quarto containing the description of Essex, Norfolk and Suffolk, and the other in folio, the like for all the shires in England, from Cornwall to the river of Tyne.[12]

Domesday Book also has a prominent place in a repertory of records in the Exchequer and other repositories, edited and printed after Agarde's death from the notes which he had made. It contains comments on the need for the deputy chamberlains to have good knowledge of Latin and French, 'and especially, to understand the records'. There follows an instruction, which is still rigorously upheld by Domesday's custodians (see Plate 32), that researchers must, among other things, avoid touching the manuscript with their bare hands and 'blotting' (i.e., smudging) it.[13] An interesting editorial comment in the same volume describes 'a book of Domesday, made by Master Arthur Agarde . . ., remaining in the Treasury, which, if you peruse it, will ready the searcher much, both for the reading, and for the somewhat better understanding thereof'.[14] This, the earliest finding aid to be produced by a record keeper, still survives. Now in the Bodleian Library, it contains a valuable annotated glossary and notes about Domesday, including extracts from other records which bore upon its historical context.[15] It was to be of considerable value to future readers and to the deputy chamberlains alike.

Agarde did not, however, confine himself to the Receipt of the Exchequer. He was a friend and associate of the leading scholars of his day, and when, in the 1580s, the first Society of Antiquaries was formed, he was one of its leading members. In 1599, he read a paper to the society in which he discussed the origins of measurements of land, referring particularly to Domesday Book and showing the fruits of years of research in the records.[16] Measurement had probably been a longstanding preoccupation with Agarde; in an important treatise on Domesday written before 1599, he devoted much space to it. Anticipating the conclusions of many far later historians, he linked the record with the levying of Danegeld by the Conqueror, quoted the passage from the *Dialogus* to show how the survey was named, and demonstrated that the compilation of Domesday could be explained by reference to the *Inquisitio Eliensis* where the questions asked by the commissioners were set down.[17] The *Inquisitio Eliensis* was in the library of Sir Robert Cotton, one of Agarde's fellow Antiquaries, who shared some of Agarde's intense interest in Domesday Book. Cotton's studies of parish histories, for example, always begin with the Conqueror's survey.[18] Similarly, Sir Henry Spelman, another member, made considerable use of Domesday and showed familiarity with its context and content.[19] Agarde therefore not only began the process of critical assessment of Domesday Book, but, as already indicated, also shared his knowledge with other scholars of the day.

Unlike modern record keepers, Agarde had no hesitation in making annotations and glosses, sometimes copious, in the records in his charge, and Domesday was no exception. His handwriting appears in a few places in Little Domesday and with some frequency in Great Domesday, both on the preliminary folios and in the text.[20] He counted the folios (incorrectly), and he annotated the book not only with passages from the *grand coustumier de Normandie* about parage tenure, but also with memoranda about farms, service, tenure, landholders and measurements of land; with explanations of how to extend some of the abbreviations into correct Latin; with cross-references to the Black Book of the Exchequer and other records; and with his own name as a mark of authorship. The page reproduced in Plate 42 shows the variety of hands which he could use (although parts of it were written later). At the bottom are Agarde's name latinized (*Acardus*), and a memorandum written upside down about the loan of the Black Book of the Exchequer to Sir Walter Mildmay and its return in 1571.[21] Plate 43 contains a sentence written by Agarde at the head of a column of text.[22] He used the Domesday lettering which he had practised in making extracts for legal and antiquarian purposes.[23] It was that task which had given him his close acquaintance with Domesday Book and which had enabled him to make his lasting contribution to Domesday studies.

The political climate of Stuart England proved unfavourable to the Society of Antiquaries, which was forced to disband in about 1607, but its members continued with their scholarly work and influenced younger enthusiasts. Those successors of Agarde who took over his duties of searching and copying Domesday were not of his calibre as record scholars, but were willing to allow bona fide searchers to peruse the volumes and prepared to make extracts which were clear, reasonably accurate and in the Domesday script. John Bradshaw, deputy chamberlain from 1613 to 1633, employed the same antique style of lettering for writing out the passage from the

Dialogus which describes Domesday Book. He copied it into Domesday's preliminary pages,[24] the inappropriateness of using an eleventh-century script for material written almost a century later clearly having escaped him.

One of the more distinguished antiquarians whom Bradshaw accommodated at the Treasury of Receipt was Sir Simonds D'Ewes.[25] A puritan gentleman with a training at the bar, D'Ewes first became interested in antiquities in the 1620s, and an advantageous marriage in 1626 enabled him to relinquish his legal career and concentrate on his studies. A friend and associate of Cotton, Spelman and Dugdale, he corresponded on a wide range of antiquarian matters and built up a library of which he was very proud. His autobiography reveals him as pompous and pedantic, and demonstrates his obsession with research into archival sources. Among his greatest interests was Domesday Book, which he first saw in 1630. After some preliminary skirmishes with it in that year, in October 1631

I began my search in that august and rare record called Domesday in the Tally Office of the Exchequer, which I continued until I had extracted a large volume of it of all the shires, excepting Norfolk only, and part of Suffolk: of which I gathered a great part out of an exact transcript written out of the second tome of Domesday, in the character thereof, in November ensuing, a great part of which month I spent each morning at the same Tally Office in Westminster, as I had often done in October foregoing, to view and search in the very autograph itself of Domesday aforesaid.[26]

By the end of 1632, D'Ewes had finished his study of Great Domesday.

I had taken short notes of all the shires there so far only as concerned families, history, and some other observations, excepting Cambridgeshire, of which county I had taken all the peculiar quantities and contents of the acres of each town and village . . ., intending, if God permit, to publish it.[27]

Soon afterwards, he had to leave London because he was threatened with prosecution under a proclamation forbidding the gentry to stay in the capital during the Long Vacation, which he had infringed for the sake of his studies. 'I resolved for a remove, being much troubled, not only with my separation from records, but with my wife's being great with child.'[28] To console him for being unable to complete his work on Little Domesday, Bradshaw lent him a transcript of the Norfolk folios which he had made for Thomas Howard, earl of Arundel and Surrey; but by 1637, D'Ewes was again able to make notes, this time about Suffolk, from the manuscript itself.[29]

D'Ewes's notes from Domesday, preserved in the Harleian Library, contain a summary of Domesday's contents and a commentary. They were elegantly bound up

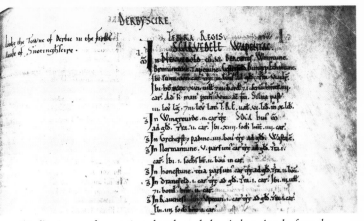

42. (*Left*) *A page of annotations, largely made by Arthur Agarde, from the preliminary section of Great Domesday.*

43. (*Above*) *A useful annotation by Arthur Agarde in Domesday's text. The reader is referred to the Nottinghamshire section for information about Derby.*

44. (*Below left*) *Title-page of Sir Simonds D'Ewes's Domesday collections.*

45. (*Below right*) *A page from D'Ewes's Domesday collections.*

Excerptiones

ex utroque.

Tomo ſiue Volumine

appellato.

DOMESDEI

auguſtiſſimo

Et omnium antiquiſſimo in Archiuis

Regni Angliæ cimeliorum Recordo a Domino

Simonds D'Ewes

De Stowhall in agro Suffolcienſi equite

durato et Baronetto propriâ

ſuâ manu et incredi-

bili pene induſtriâ

ſelecta.

by a Mr Paybody in August 1643, at the cost of 3s. 6d.[30] The title-page reproduced in Plate 44 is typical of D'Ewes's work, introducing in a most grandiose fashion his Domesday collection, which is said to have been selected with great diligence and industry.[31] The introduction mentions the help, particularly in waiving the fees, which the deputy chamberlain, Bradshaw, and le Squyer (his colleague since 1620) had given to D'Ewes. As the next plate shows, D'Ewes used a pseudo-Domesday script for some major headings and an ordinary hand for the rest of the text.[32]

Although his work was never published, D'Ewes had a considerable under-standing of Domesday and its contents, which, if he is to be believed, he put to an unusual, even absurd, use when in 1631 he addressed his tenants before a session of the manorial court at Lavenham in Suffolk. He described Domesday Book to them at length, and, to demonstrate the antiquity of their villein tenure, assured them that

therein it appears plainly that ... in the time of Edward the Confessor ... there were such manors or seignories as there are at this day, consisting of demesnes and services, containing under them [free tenants, villeins, cottars and slaves].

He then reminded them of their consequent duties and obligations to him as their landlord, which, in view of their bitter legal disputes with his father, must have left them unimpressed.[33] D'Ewes's pompous conceits have their amusing side, but his enthusiasm and diligence in antiquarian pursuits are undeniable; and he left a valuable contribution to scholarship with his journals of Queen Elizabeth I's Parliaments, which were printed after his death. That edition reflects his interest in parliamentary liberties, a matter of which he gained considerable first-hand knowledge as member of Parliament for Sudbury during the Civil War.

A scholar of far greater stature, who shared many of D'Ewes's interests, was William Dugdale.[34] Instructed in antiquities from an early age, he settled in Warwickshire in 1626 and was drawn into local antiquarian circles. In 1638, he was introduced to Spelman, who suggested that he should work with the Yorkshire scholar Roger Dodsworth on his vast collection of monastic records. That was the starting-point of Dugdale's historical career. By the time of his death in 1686, he had built extensively on the collections of Dodsworth and of others to produce major and highly praised surveys of the religious houses and the baronage of England, a history of Warwickshire parishes, and a description of St Paul's Cathedral. Among yet other works, he had written a much criticized account of the Civil War, in which he took a staunchly royalist viewpoint. As an overt supporter of the king, he had been proscribed by the parliamentarians in the 1640s, but had managed to profit from

46. Sir William Dugdale with his manuscripts.

adversity by visiting France in order to collect charters for his *Monasticon*. As a herald, and later as Garter King of Arms, he lost few opportunities to inspect antiquities and manuscripts during his official visitations.

At the beginning of his *Antiquities of Warwickshire*, Dugdale says that 'I shall now, by the guidance of that incomparable record, Domesday Book, show what hundreds there were in this county at the Norman Conquest',[35] and proceeds to list them. The parish histories of which the book is composed use and discuss Domesday material, including place-names, measurements of land and tenures. In writing this work, Dugdale relied on the collection of transcripts which he had taken from 1639 onwards from records in the Exchequer and the Tower of London and from others in private hands. Among them was a Domesday transcript for Warwickshire, its heading in mock-Domesday script, which was carefully copied from the original.[36] Dugdale's acquaintance with Domesday and its custodians was therefore close. In a letter of 1650 to William Vernon, he commented:

I perceive that you imagine your copy of Domesday not perfect, but did you know so much as I you would not impute the fault to Mr Squyer, for I carefully examined it with him. The truth is that the errors which are, were in the Norman transcribers of that survey from the originals which were brought in out of the several counties.[37]

His critical approach was matched by an understanding of Domesday's importance as evidence about the Conqueror's reign. In an unpublished tract of about 1681,[38] he used it to show that William I dispossessed the Anglo-Saxons after the Conquest.[39] His assertions were based on sound study: his *Baronage of England* (1675) included a full list of the estates of King Harold which he had extracted from Domesday,[40] a matter still of interest to historians today.

Not all those who expressed interest in Domesday Book were as fully appraised of its contents as was Dugdale. In 1661, Samuel Pepys met Edward Fauconberge, a deputy chamberlain, in a public house and asked him 'to look whether he could, out of Domesday Book, give me anything concerning the sea, and the dominion thereof, which he says he will look after'.[41] Fauconberge, a record keeper of some ability, who made Domesday abstracts and who added the foliation numbers to both volumes[42] treated Pepys's misplaced enthusiasm with courtesy. Some twenty years later, Pepys again pursued the matter with his friend Dr Thomas Gale, who possessed some extracts from Domesday. Gale told Pepys that the book included neither London nor several entire counties, and that its evidence had serious limitations; and Pepys concluded, in some disgust, that Domesday 'appears contrary to the perpetual and vulgar acceptation of it, to be no true general survey of England, but a very imperfect one'.[43] Pepys's first impressions of Domesday Book are revealing. He was a man of antiquarian interests and a collector of printed books, as well as being an expert on naval affairs, but he knew of the survey only from its misleading and exaggerated popular reputation. It seems that, in his time, Domesday was understood by only a few within the scholarly élite.[44]

Throughout the seventeenth and eighteenth centuries, most of the popular historians followed the approach to the Norman Conquest taken by medieval chroniclers and their Tudor successors. William the Conqueror was portrayed as having subjected the English and brought great changes to their society and government, and Domesday Book as having marked those changes. For example, the description in John Hayward's history of the first three Norman kings of England, published in 1613, is very much in the tradition of writers from Henry of Huntingdon to John Stow,[45] as is the corresponding passage in the influential chronicle of John Speed, published in 1611. In his description of Domesday, Speed also echoed the anti-Norman hostility of chroniclers such as Matthew Paris in his assertion that 'the English grievously groaned under their miserable estate'; the Conqueror strove to bring the English name to ruin and it was shameful to be called an Englishman in his day.[46] The idea of Anglo-Saxon subjection similarly emerged in William Howell's perennially popular history, first published in 1679,[47] and was to remain a basic tenet in many other works of a similar kind. It was taken up in a more sophisticated guise by the Levellers, who believed in the antiquity of English law and government, but saw it as having been disrupted and perverted by the Conqueror and by all his successors; their aim was to return to the golden age of

Saxon liberty. Thus the Leveller leader, John Lilburne, read and cited the works of Speed. His pamphlet *Regall Tyranny Discovered*, issued in 1647, portrays the Conqueror as a bloody tyrant who dispossessed and oppressed the conquered Saxons.[48]

At a higher level, however, the most commonly held view of the Norman Conquest in the seventeenth century was that it marked a legitimate transfer of power from the Saxon to the Norman kings, the reign of Harold marking a temporary usurpation of power. The underlying assumption was that the English common law reached back to time immemorial. It was the only law which the kingdom had ever had, and William the Conqueror, by confirming the customs of Edward the Confessor, had allowed it to continue unbroken. The most influential exponent of this view was Sir Edward Coke, who, faced with Stuart tendencies towards absolutism, made a powerful case for an ancient constitution in his many legal tracts and commentaries.[49] That assumption, a forerunner of the Whig view of history, was held almost universally in legal and administrative circles in the seventeenth century, even by many of the monarchy's most ardent supporters. Because of the supposed antiquity of the constitution, the earliest possible examples were widely felt to be of value, and that meant that the work of antiquarians was treated with respect.[50]

The ancient-constitution theory was at odds with popular accounts, but, until the 1670s, was given regular reiteration as much because of its essential untenability as because it met many serious challenges from men of power and influence. However, Sir Henry Spelman, in the first part of his *Glossarium* issued in 1626, used Domesday Book as evidence that feudal tenures had been introduced by the Normans; and in the later section, not published until 1664, propounded the view that Parliament was not an immemorial institution but had grown out of the King's Council after the Conquest.[51] Sir Robert Filmer attacked the antiquity of the Commons from a royalist viewpoint; the storm caused by his *Freeholder's Grand Inquest*, issued in 1648 and republished in 1679, reverberated for almost half a century. In his *Baronage* of 1675, Dugdale echoed Filmer's thesis; and from 1676, William Petyt, a rising Whig, began to collect materials for a refutation of Filmer's views on the origins of Parliament.[52]

In the early 1680s, these constitutional arguments were of considerable immediate importance. The heir to the throne, the future James II, was disliked by the Whigs for his pro-Catholic sympathies, and attempts were made in Parliament to exclude him from the succession. In 1680, Petyt published his *Antient Right of the Commons*, a tract aimed against royal absolutism, which restated the thesis that Parliament and the laws were immemorial and predated the monarchy. It further suggested that freeholders had enjoyed the same rights before and after the Conquest and that

William I conquered England, not in the sense of enslaving it, but in the sense of acquiring it:

all of which is most plain and justified infallibly by Domesday Book, made in that king's reign, and subsequent records, where the title and claim of many common persons to their own and ancestors' possessions, both in his time and the time of the Saxon kings, are clearly allowed.[53]

Petyt went on to discuss tenurial arrangements in Domesday Book, a subject on which, despite the fact that he had probably looked at the original,[54] his enthusiasm greatly exceeded his knowledge. In particular, he misunderstood the meaning of the initials T.R.E., which appear frequently in Domesday's text and which stand for *tempore regis Edwardi* (in the time of King Edward).

It is recorded in Domesday Book, that King William had certain rights in demesne, viz., the lands which were in the hands of King Edward, and entitled *Terrae Edwardi Regis*, and other lands, which were forfeited to him by those who took part with Harold, entitled *Terrae Regis*.[55]

The distortion of the evidence consequent on this misreading undermined his whole thesis. Moreover, he used other erroneous information to demonstrate William's generosity to the conquered Saxons; and a similar line was adopted by William Atwood in a tract issued in the same year.[56]

The Tories, supporters of absolute monarchy and the royal prerogative, now gained a polemical champion in Dr Robert Brady, Master of Gonville and Caius College, Cambridge, physician to the king, and a member for Cambridge University in the 1681 and 1685 Parliaments. His earlier medical career had brought him eminence, but had provided no obvious inspiration or training for the historical research which he was to undertake in middle age, and in which he was to gain lasting distinction.[57] His *Full and Clear Answer to a Book by William Petit Esq.*, published in 1681, was a powerful refutation of the views of Petyt and Atwood on the Norman Conquest and on the origins of Parliament. Its style and arrangement were those of other political and historical treatises of the day: its substance set it far apart from them, for it was based on thorough and careful research in original sources, including Domesday Book. Petyt's assertions about *Terrae Regis Edwardi* were lambasted by Brady as

a great mistake, for there is no such title in that book as *Terrae Regis Edwardi*. Of *Terra Regis* there is, first in every county in the top of the leaves, which were in the hands of the Conqueror; for the truth of this I appeal to the book.[58]

47. *Early eighteenth-century portrait of Dr Robert Brady, master of Gonville and Caius College, Cambridge.*

Brady gave many accurate examples to show that William dispossessed the Anglo-Saxons and granted their lands to the Normans. Domesday Book, he considered, demonstrates that the Normans came not to remove Harold, an illegal usurper, from the throne, but to take England by conquest. 'Sure I am, if this gentleman be so well acquainted with Domesday Book, as he pretends to be, he cannot believe, nor any one that ever perused it but one half an hour.'[59]

Dr Brady's book proved highly unpopular with the Whigs and received unfavourable criticism in the House of Commons;[60] the Oxford antiquary Anthony Wood believed that, if the session had lasted two more days, the work might have been burned.[61] Nor did Brady's opponents waste any time before launching their attack. William Atwood, whose scholarship rested on foundations even less substantial than those of Petyt's, declared that

The Domesday Book, to which [Brady] appeals, manifestly destroys the foundations of his pernicious principles. . . . He has the confidence to refer to Domesday Book in every county, for this fiction, that William the Conqueror divided all the land in England amongst his great followers. Now, what if I show out of himself, and this great book of judgments concerning lands and services, that he divided very little of the lands in England to his followers, to be sure that he was far from distributing it all?[62]

Both Atwood and Edward Cooke, a lawyer who in 1682 published a pamphlet to prove that the Conqueror made no absolute conquest of England by the sword,[63] cited many details purporting to come from Domesday in support of the Whig argument. So misunderstood and garbled were their references, that Brady in a further reply railed against that 'ignorant, confident, self-conceited man's [i.e., Cooke's] wretched abusing, partial citing, and false applying of records and history'.[64]

To concentrate too heavily on the polemical side of Brady's work is to do him a disservice; although in part a product of the politics of their day, his works have a more lasting significance as the fruits of detailed and meticulous record scholarship and, for its time, far-sighted historical analysis. Thus, his collection of earlier pamphlets, issued in 1684, contained a glossary and a discussion of serjeanty tenures using material from many records, including Domesday Book, and a valuable catalogue of Domesday tenants-in-chief.[65] In it, and in the first volume of his *Complete History of England*, which appeared in 1685,[66] he set out his historically precocious opinions of the Norman Conquest. He understood that the reign of William I brought about a fundamental break with the past, a change in the legal, governmental and tenurial system; and much of his evidence was drawn from Domesday Book.

In the 1680s, Brady, with government backing, had a special and privileged place at the Tower Record Office, where much of his research and the transcription of documents was carried out by clerks on his behalf.[67] His knowledge of Domesday Book, however, was probably derived almost entirely from first-hand work. Peter le Neve, deputy chamberlain from 1684 to 1712, wrote in 1708 that in the 1680s Brady had 'sat all morning long many mornings one after the other' at the table in Tally Court, searching the records.[68] Much of Brady's research for his last published historical work, a treatise about cities and boroughs, issued in 1690, was carried out almost a decade earlier. At that time, le Neve's senior colleague as deputy chamberlain, John Lowe, was making notes about Domesday boroughs which he collected carefully into a book, writing them in Domesday script.[69] Brady, in his preface, remarked that Domesday formed the basis of his study, and the extensive references and quotations he cited from the Conqueror's survey suggest a lengthy period of research under Lowe's tutelage.[70]

In 1689, after the revolution of the previous year, Petyt was appointed as keeper of the Tower Record Office and Brady was excluded from his sources there. Whiggish detestation of his pro-absolutist theories ran so strongly that his judicious historical interpretation was totally unacknowledged; and Brady was unable to reply to tirades against him. One of those, John Tyrell's *History of England*, which appeared in 1700, the year of Brady's death, is overburdened with an immense preface and introduction devoted almost entirely to listing the 'ignorances' and omissions in Brady's work.[71] In 1724, John Oldmixton looked back on Brady as a man 'who read the records, as witches say their prayers, backwards, [so] that he [made] them speak quite contrary to what was intended'.[72] Although his reputation improved again later in the eighteenth century, it was not until the twentieth that Brady's importance as a historian and scholar was fully appreciated. If the occasionally distasteful polemical and propagandist elements in his writings are disregarded, his achievements in historical interpretation may be better evaluated. Certainly, in his understanding of Domesday Book and its context, he broke new ground, and it is unfortunate that his solid scholarship was at first swept aside in the company of his more ephemeral and didactic pronouncements.

The seventy years which followed the Restoration saw a flowering of medieval scholarship. The Anglo-Saxon language was studied, chronicles were edited, and great collections of ecclesiastical, administrative and diplomatic documents were made. The accessibility of the records was a vital prerequisite to allow such work to proceed, and at the Tally Court before 1712 the deputy chamberlains gave assistance and encouragement to record scholars, often beyond that required for their standard fee. For most of that time, the more senior deputy chamberlain was John Lowe.

Lowe, who helped Brady with his researches, had a strong interest in Domesday. A number of copies he made for antiquarian purposes have survived,[73] as also have

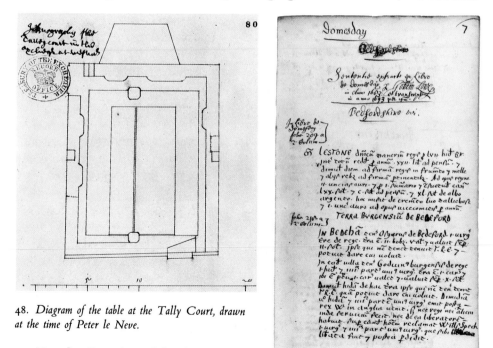

48. *Diagram of the table at the Tally Court, drawn at the time of Peter le Neve.*

49. *Notes from Domesday Book by John Lowe.*

books containing his notes and extracts from Domesday, parts of which are in Domesday script. One is mainly a list of holdings in Domesday;[74] another, a list of towns;[75] the third, an abstract of tenurial information with an index.[76] The last two, completed in 1693, have inscriptions in the front stating that Lowe had bequeathed them to his son and family and showing his pride in his work.

I, John Lowe, desire my son John Lowe that this book may be kept in his name and family by him, by his sons and their sons and grandchildren from age to age and generation to generation, and if there be any of them educated towards the law to be kept by them . . . and so transmitted from hand to hand, always preferring the elder brother's issue. . . . I charge all persons that they do not to initiate any suit or suits for this book, for if any do, then the gift . . . shall be void, but if this book be devised to be delivered to any person who thinks he hath just right to it, I charge him to lose it rather than sue for it, but let him endeavour by fair means and good words only, to get it if he can.[77]

Lowe's colleague at the Treasury of Receipt was Peter le Neve.[78] Born in 1661, he early developed his lasting interests in Norfolk antiquities and in heraldry. In 1689, he was appointed to the College of Arms and in 1704 attained the office of Norroy King of Arms. Justly famed and respected for his knowledge of records and antiquities, in 1708 he became the first president of the revived Society of Antiquaries of London.[79] In 1684, he bought the office of deputy chamberlain of the Exchequer, which he held until ejected from it in 1712. Considerable personal hostility arose

50. *Portrait of Peter le Neve in heraldic garb.*

between him and his senior colleague John Lowe, who in 1690 complained bitterly of le Neve's failure to arrive at the Tally Court before eleven or twelve o'clock and of his negligence in striking tallies. Le Neve riposted by showing that he had spent much of his own time, as well as the hours in his office, in digesting and listing various records: his numerous surviving indexes fully bear out his assertions.[80] He emphasized that those volumes were intended to be left behind in Tally Court 'contrary to the precedent of Mr Lowe who [for] some years since has made some tables and abbreviations of some records but keeps them all at home for private information (except for that called Domesday)'.[81] Lowe's complaint was dismissed in 1691, on the grounds that le Neve had performed valuable work in cataloguing the records and that his clerk was regularly in attendance before nine o'clock.[82]

Domesday Book was another area of tension between the two men. Le Neve kept a register of the searches he had made in the records, which reveals that Domesday was frequently looked at, both for antiquarian searches and to determine ancient demesne.[83] In 1685, le Neve used it to try to ascertain whether 'Gravelthorpe' and 'Gripthorpe' in Yorkshire were the same place; in 1699, to prove that Houghton Regis in Bedfordshire was ancient demesne;[84] however, in the early 1690s, he noted that 'Mr Lowe found several things [from Domesday] which he would not communicate'.[85] Undeterred by Lowe's uncooperativeness, le Neve continued to work on Domesday, and later in the 1690s he recorded that he had 'made a copy of the whole county [i.e., Hertfordshire] out of Domesday for Sir Henry Chauncy Knight and received of him therefor £15 viz. £7 10s. down and £7 [sic] when done'.[86] This, le Neve's best-known transcript from Domesday, was made for Chauncy's history of Hertfordshire,[87] published in 1700. So pleased was Chauncy with his purchase that in 1714 he was still expressing appreciation in his correspondence with le Neve.[88]

Like Agarde, and like their medieval predecessors, le Neve made free annotations on the records in his custody, and Great Domesday bears his hand in three places. He made notes about parks for wild beasts, and other minor jottings, including the correct observation that the section listing the fees of Robert de Bruis postdated the rest.[89] He was less accurate in his annotations of the Domesday *Abbreviatio*. On a page preceding the illuminated depictions of the miracles of the Confessor, he wrote that he, Peter le Neve, one of Queen Anne's deputy chamberlains, believed the pictures to date from the reign of King Henry VII.[90]

Le Neve left no great historical works to posterity; his strength was his unrivalled knowledge of the records in his care, which he was unfailingly glad to share with others. As the result of unsuccessful machinations, he lost the post of deputy chamberlain in 1712, but continued with his treasured collection of notes for a history of Norfolk until his death in 1729.[91] They were used by the antiquary Francis

Blomefield for a county history first published in parts from 1739. In his preface, he calls them 'the greatest fund of antiquities for this county that was ever collected for any single county in this kingdom'.[92] Le Neve's collection, consisting of extracts from, and notes about, a wide range of sources, including Domesday Book, and written in other hands as well as his own, was conveniently arranged under manors; and Blomefield incorporated many of those references into his work.[93]

John Lowe died in 1708 and Peter le Neve left office in 1712, and their disappearance ushered in a less favourable régime for would-be record scholars at Tally Court. John Lawton, a successor of Lowe's, made extracts from Domesday Book,[94] but spent much of his time in the office in striking tallies and was less willing than le Neve or Lowe to work more than his normal hours. As in earlier years, the fabric of the Chapter House, which had become the principal storage-place for the Treasury of Receipt records, was a constant source of worry; and new demands were made by a House of Lords Committee inquiring into the state of the records, which wanted more sorting and listing of documents to be done. In 1719, Lawton and Dudley Downes complained about their lack of assistance in such work and the Committee took the matter in hand.[95] Lawton was given the new post of keeper of the records at the Chapter House in 1724 and by 1732 he had managed to make some headway with the mounds of 'undigested' records in his care.[96] Such problems allowed him far less time than his predecessors had found for helping and advising scholars, and it is significant that the possibilities of publishing an edition of Domesday Book began seriously to be canvassed during his time. Robert Harley, earl of Oxford, made frequent mention of a scheme for engraving it by means of copper plates, and his fellow antiquarian, Thomas Hearne, while disagreeing with the proposed method, thought it would be of the greatest use to publish 'this most venerable monument of antiquity'.[97] Moreover, with the printing of major collections of records, such as the diplomatic and administrative documents in Rymer's *Foedera* and the ecclesiastical material in Wilkins's *Concilia*, the idea of treating Domesday Book in a similar fashion was not an impractical one.[98] Yet an edition of the whole text was not to be produced until 1783.

Meanwhile, historians and antiquarians interested in Domesday Book had to rely on existing work in print and on borrowing or purchasing transcripts from one another. Investigations by the Society of Antiquaries in the 1750s into Domesday extracts produced a limited list of transcripts in print, almost all of which had been made before 1712 and many of which were felt to be inaccurate. The extracts in manuscript were far more numerous,[99] but many were clearly as dubious in authenticity as was a copy belonging to a Mr Erdeswick, which had received a highly unfavourable mention in a letter from Richard Wilkes to Dr Lyttleton, dean of

Exeter, in 1753.[100] Not only might such a transcript be full of inaccuracies, but further errors could result each time it was recopied. Yet that was the only way in which texts could be disseminated among the antiquarians: thus in 1758, William Cole notified the secretary of the Society of Antiquaries that he possessed a Domesday transcript for Cambridgeshire, which he had taken from another copy ten years before.[101]

Eighteenth-century authors of local histories, like those a hundred years earlier, continued to show an interest in Domesday, extracts from which appeared in a number of topographical works, including Morton's history of Northamptonshire (1712), and Gale's work on Richmond, Yorkshire (1722). However, there were many such writers, perhaps more than in the seventeenth century, who found it unnecessary or impossible to allude to the Conqueror's survey; one was Ralph Thoresby, whose history of Leeds was published in 1715. Only the more serious antiquarians were willing or able to grapple with this difficult source, and among those the Reverend Philip Morant deserves pride of place.

Morant cited Domesday extensively in his history of Colchester, first published in 1748, and in his substantial work on Essex, which appeared in parts during the 1760s. For his *magnum opus*, Morant used a Domesday transcript of Essex, which he had acquired in 1750 or 1751 as part of the topographical collections of Thomas Jekyll. These manuscripts, first gathered together in the age of Agarde, were subsequently handed down and augmented by numerous antiquarians.[102] Morant was thus able to quote Domesday verbatim in the footnotes to the parish histories of which his book is composed. In his introduction, he devoted two closely printed pages to a translation of the text, an explanation of some of the terms, and a reproduction of the passage about the Domesday inquest from the *Inquisitio Eliensis*. The first page is headed by an engraving of the Domesday extract for Barking, well executed by John Bayley.[103] Morant's work on Colchester, reprinted as the first volume of his Essex history, similarly contains a transcript of its Domesday entry,[104] as well as numerous extracts from other records. Indeed, Morant's detailed and meticulous, not to say pedantic, approach to his subject was vigorously lampooned by John Clubbe in a satirical account of the mythical village of Wheatfield.[105] Such satire is indicative of the lack of respect accorded to antiquarians in the age of reason, similarly symptomatic of which is the well-known verse penned by Alexander Pope on the death in 1735 of Thomas Hearne, that obsessive editor of original sources:

> But who is he, in closet close y-pent,
> Of sober face, with learned dust besprent ...,
> To future ages may thy dullness last,
> As thou preservdst the dullness of the past.[106]

As the eighteenth century progressed, Whig writers gradually divided into two different camps. On the one hand were men such as William Blackstone[107] and Edmund Burke, who continued to subscribe to the idea of the ancient constitution. From that notion was derived Burke's doctrine of traditionalism, which was based on the tenet that a nation's institutions were the fruit of its experience and took shape only slowly.[108] Burke's abridgment of English history portrays the Conqueror as a man of 'moderation and greatness of mind', who was driven to oppress the English only in reaction to their opposition and hatred; he treated them cruelly and harshly, but Lanfranc, archbishop of Canterbury, preserved some small degree of liberty for them. Domesday Book, Burke considered, was, as the product of a general survey, 'a grand monument of the wisdom of the Conqueror'.[109] A similar, if less sophisticated, line was followed in some of the more popular histories of the period, which showed William I as a benign ruler who voluntarily subjected himself to the laws of England, and Domesday as the proof of his generosity to the conquered Anglo-Saxons. To Thomas Carte, William's intention in ordering the Domesday survey was

to get a true account of the value, as well of his own demesnes, as of his lands held by his commissioners in capite. [Domesday] seems to have been designed by the Conqueror, not so much for his own service, as for the benefit of his successors.[110]

There was, on the other hand, a new strand in Whig ideology which grew in strength from the 1730s and which was, ironically, far closer to the ideas of Brady than to those of his opponents. Popular with the court Whigs, it saw 1689 as the true turning-point and as the time from which the English people began first to enjoy their rightful liberties.[111] It dismissed the Anglo-Saxons as crude and barbaric and saw the Conquest as having introduced feudalism. But it also removed the historical dimension from Whig arguments and made the events of the Conquest an irrelevancy to current developments. By the 1760s, this view had become government orthodoxy, whereas the opposition Whigs stressed the idea of the ancient constitution.[112]

In the first half of the eighteenth century, the most popular history of England was by Rapin de Thoyras, translated from the French and augmented by Tindal. This work uneasily combines ideas drawn from proponents of the ancient constitution with longstanding notions of Norman oppression of the English. William, Rapin suggested, was initially generous to the English and preserved their liberties, but their hostility towards him brought out his cruelty and avarice. Domesday Book, known also as the great 'terrar' (i.e., terrier or list of tenants) and the 'land-book of England', was a manifestation of his greed.[113] In the 1750s, Rapin's history was replaced by David Hume's as the most widely read and influential account of England's development. Hume, who strove for impartiality, found himself at odds with much of traditional Whig thought, and in particular with the theory of the ancient constitution. He considered that the Anglo-Saxons had once been free, but by the eleventh century had become degenerate. The Conquest had unfavourable initial effects, in that it led to the cruel oppression of the English and to the introduction of feudalism, although it was to bring many longer-term benefits. Domesday Book stood out from the other achievements of the harsh and ambitious king as 'an undertaking which proves [his] extensive genius and does honour to his memory.... [It is] the most valuable piece of antiquity possessed by any nation.'[114]

From the 1770s, there was a revival of interest in the Norman Conquest among radical pamphleteers on both sides of the Atlantic. George III and his ministers were seen by the colonists in America as a reincarnation of William the Conqueror and his barons, so that 'whatever is of Saxon establishment is truly constitutional, but whatever is Norman . . . partakes of a tyrannical spirit'.[115] Yet this interest in history did not extend to documentary details, and, unlike the pamphleteers of the 1680s, they paid virtually no heed to Domesday Book or to other records.

The advent of Abraham Farley at Tally Court was to usher in a new era of Domesday scholarship. He was appointed one of the deputy chamberlains in 1736, and was to be granted the office of keeper of the Chapter House records, jointly with George Rose, in 1773. By the time of his death in 1791 he had gained material prosperity and a secure reputation as a record scholar.[116] His immediate superior on appointment was John Lawton, who was keeper of the records until 1740. Lawton and his successor, Richard Morley, faced considerable problems with the deterioration of the fabric of the Chapter House. So bad did matters become that the

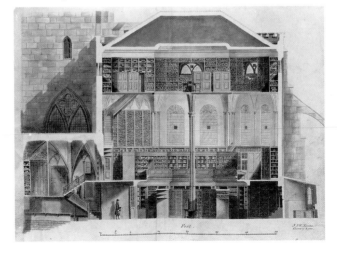

51. *The Chapter House at Westminster, as reconstructed in the mid-eighteenth century to hold the records.*

vault collapsed in 1751 and the building was then reconstructed to hold more records.[117] Nevertheless, Domesday Book, which was still kept in Tally Court in 1739, was at some time in the 1740s moved to the Chapter House, where by 1807 it was kept in a 'closet on the stairs'.[118]

Farley began to work on Domesday Book in or before 1741. Like Peter le Neve before him, he made copies and answered queries; and he also showed Domesday to visiting antiquaries. There is a letter in his correspondence, dating probably from the 1760s, in which the herald Isaac Heard

presents his best compliments to Mr Farley, [and] takes the liberty of recommending some American gentlemen, his friends, curious in matters of antiquity, to Mr Farley's politeness. They are particularly desirous of seeing Domesday Book.[119]

Farley revived le Neve's practice of keeping a register of searches, which he entered in le Neve's own book, not added to since 1703. That volume shows, for example, that in 1742 Farley searched Domesday for mentions of the river Trent and made a copy for a Mr Collins; he found the entry for Montacute, Somerset; and he looked unsuccessfully for Winkfield in Berkshire for Mr Manilove, an attorney from Fetherston Buildings.[120] In 1755, he made several copies of extracts relating to the lands of St Benet of Hulme Abbey for the bishop of Norwich.[121] In 1757, when he was keeping only a draft register, which he was never to copy into le Neve's book, he made Domesday extracts totalling thirty-eight lines for the earl of Uxbridge, who failed to pay or to take delivery of his order until 1761.[122] A Mr Parry was equally dilatory, ordering copies about Cannock Forest and being billed for £22 4s. 2d. in 1757, but similarly not settling his account until 1761.[123] In the early 1760s, Farley carried out a research project for the earl of Egmont with the Reverend Dr John Strachey, the work for which included making several Domesday extracts. Egmont paid their fees, but gave 'nothing for their trouble and attendance in searching and copying at the several offices'.[124]

Unlike their predecessors, Farley, his colleagues and clerks no longer imitated Domesday Book in the extracts they made. Otherwise their copies followed the same general format as earlier, with an explanatory clause at the beginning and an attestation at the end. The example in Plate 52 was made by Farley in 1754 and gives entries for royal lands in Oxfordshire.[125] Farley also made or helped with transcripts of larger sections of Domesday Book. He copied the Kent folios for inclusion in Hasted's history of that county, and charged him a mere third of the normal rate.[126] In the 1770s, he advised Owen Manning on the initial stages of the facsimile engravings which Manning was preparing for his history of Surrey. However, as Farley's own work on a parliamentary edition of Domesday became more time-

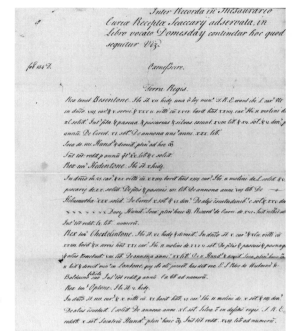

52. *Certified copy from the Oxfordshire section of Domesday Book, made by Abraham Farley in 1754.*

consuming, he was increasingly less helpful to scholars. Manning had problems with his engravers, who demanded extortionate rates for poor work, and he found Farley's uncooperative attitude a further irritation. In 1775, he wrote to Richard Gough that 'Mr Farley's indolence and backwardness in [checking the proofs] had quite tried me', and that he intended to use George Rose rather than Farley to do the verification. Similarly, it was Rose rather than Farley who in the same year checked the plates for Tredway Nash's history of Worcestershire.[127] Some capital letters in red were written at about this time at the end of Great Domesday. They read 'WERECE'SCIRE', 'WEREC'IRE' and 'WER', and they may be connected with the preparation of Nash's volume.[128]

In 1753, Farley began to make copies of documents in the Chapter House for Philip Carteret Webb. Webb combined the roles of antiquarian, lawyer and politician, using one interest to further the others. He was a fellow of the Society of Antiquaries, member of Parliament for Haslemere from 1754 until 1768 and joint solicitor to the Treasury from 1758 to 1768, a position which gave him notoriety in his prosecution of John Wilkes.[129] It was his interest in Haslemere which brought him to the Chapter House, where in 1753 he had Farley make a copy of an assize-roll entry for 1279 relating to that manor. At the same time, Farley produced a copy of the Domesday entry for Haslemere for him and waived his fees, charging only for the

stamped paper.[130] Webb may have thereby become aware both of the value of
Domesday Book and of the problems at the Chapter House. When in December
1755 he read a paper to the Society of Antiquaries, explaining what Domesday Book
was and suggesting that it should be published, he made much of the dangers which
threatened it.[131] The minute book records that

this inestimable remain of antiquity, Mr Webb observes, runs every hour the risk of being
irretrievably lost, should a fire happen in the neighbourhood of the Chapter House, as
formerly happened to the Cottonian Library [in 1731]; to which accident, the Chapter
House, by its situation, is much more liable.[132]

Webb's paper, written perhaps with the advice of Farley, gave a valuable and
balanced account of the contents and significance of Domesday Book. The
Antiquaries took up the cause with enthusiasm and endorsed Webb's call for
Domesday's publication. Several more papers about it were read at subsequent
meetings; and early in 1758 a circular was distributed to fellows asking them for
particulars of any Domesday transcripts in their possession, to be used as the basis
of a published version. The response revealed that there were more than twenty
transcripts of various county sections known to the fellows, in addition to those listed
in Webb's pamphlet; but many, as already noted, appear to have been of doubtful
authenticity or value.[133] Despite the Society's efforts, its funds proved insufficient for
printing Domesday and the project had to be shelved.[134]

One fellow, however, the irascible and pedantic under-librarian at the British
Museum, Dr Charles Morton, had a particular interest in Domesday Book and
appears to have resented Webb's leading role in the discussions at the Antiquaries.
Events leading up to the decision of Parliament to print Domesday Book are obscure,
but there is a possibility that Morton may have persuaded some influential contacts to
add the Conqueror's survey to the substantial number of parliamentary records
which were accepted for publication at that time. Certainly, it was Morton who was
put in charge of the printing of Domesday when the project was finally approved in
Parliament in March 1767.[135]

Although he had the backing of Parliament, Morton was to encounter
considerable opposition to his scheme. His intention was to use a specially cast
facsimile type, which he hoped would reproduce the precise appearance of the
Domesday hands, but he and his transcribers were considerably hampered in their
attempts to look at the record itself by Richard Morley, the keeper at the Chapter
House, and his staff. Indeed, Farley demonstrated his dislike of Morton's scheme by
submitting a memorial to the lords of the Treasury in June 1768. He told them that he
had had custody of the record for the last thirty years or so and had gained a detailed

understanding of its text. He had made many transcripts from it and, because he had to attend his office each morning, would be suitably placed to oversee its publication. He enclosed a specimen of a facsimile page which had been engraved under his supervision, the tracing for which is reproduced in Plate 53.[136] The Treasury considered his memorial, but took no immediate action.[137]

53. *Tracing of a page from* Great Domesday *by Abraham Farley.*

ELAS SSSA· · · Teppe Regiy· hundpet de bepdeytapla·
Benplet tenuit hapold tepope pegiy Edduapdi ppo uno mane
pio 7 p viii· hidiy M cuytodit hoc manepiu Ranulf yp ilgepi in
manu pegiy· Tc· xu· uillant· m·xxi· Sep· vi· boy· Tc· iii· yepuiym· iii·
Tc· iii· cappuce in dnio· m· ii· Tc· xi· cappuce hominu· m· v· 7 xxx·
acpe yilue· laytupa · cxxx· ouib; Dimidiu molendini· Tc apptiatu
e· viii· lib· M peddit· xii· y; tam non e apptiatu n· viii· lib· In hoc
manepio epat tc tepopiy quida lib homo de dimidia hid· qui m effet e
un de uillaniy· 7 e i yupiopi copoto· De hoc manepio data fuit cuida
eccle de alio manepio· dimidia hida teppe· pegiy· E· Poytqua aut hoc
manepiu uenit in dnio pegiy ablata fuit de eccla· 7 iace itepu i manepio·
In toto hoc hundpet ht pex· xviii· liboy hoey tenentey· dimidiam
hida· 7 xlviii· acpay· 7 paytupa· xx ouib; Apptiatu e· x· yol·
In dnio yupdicti manepiu e· i· puncin· 7 i· apin· 7 xxx· popci· lxx·auey·

54. *Specimen of a Domesday extract, printed in Charles Morton's facsimile type.*

There was by that time official recognition of Morton's difficulties. His experiments had, within little more than a year, cost almost £3,000.[138] Surviving specimens of his work, although pleasing, show little to justify so inflated a figure.[139] The Treasury asked the Antiquaries for their opinions about Morton's scheme and its progress, and was informed that, in the Society's view, the use of facsimile type would fail to reproduce the diversity of hands and would lead to great error. If the task was to be tackled properly by such means, it would take more than five hundred years to complete. Instead, on Webb's suggestion, the Antiquaries proposed (like Farley) that copperplate engravings should be used. In 1769, they put forward a detailed scheme for that method which, they believed, would take only five years. But it would cost £13,000 at the very least.[140]

The lords of the Treasury felt that the Antiquaries' scheme, although an improvement on Morton's, was still too expensive. However, in 1770 Morton produced an entirely new proposal for printing Domesday Book, in which the original text was to be transcribed with the words rendered in full rather than in abbreviated form and then set up in common type. His estimates were far more acceptable than those for an engraved version: £4,525 for 1,250 copies. The Treasury agreed to that plan and gave Morton an advance of £1,000 and authorization to proceed. But Farley was at the same time appointed as co-editor of the work. Tension between him and Morton was soon to become considerable; Farley found Morton to be an impediment to any progress, and, according to John Nichols, the printer of Domesday Book, refused to take any further advice from him after 1774.[141]

It was in that year that a final scheme for the printing of Domesday was approved: the use of record type to reproduce the abbreviated form of the original text. In 1773, John Nichols had developed such a type for a transcript of the Dorset section, to be included in John Hutchins's *History and Antiquities of Dorset*. The officials at the Chapter House, including Farley, had helped to check the transcript and were evidently much impressed with the results, as were the members of Parliament and judges to whom Nichols showed the type. When, in December 1774, Farley and Nichols proposed a similar format for the official Domesday transcript, the Treasury once more accepted the change of plan.[142]

From 1775, Farley made transcripts of Great and Little Domesday. The former was completed by 1779, and the work as a whole went through four revisions while it was in the press. By March 1783, Domesday Book had been printed in two volumes and it was distributed to government officials, universities and learned bodies, including the Society of Antiquaries, in the course of that year. As a work produced for Parliament and paid for from Treasury funds, it was not published in the modern sense or put on sale to the public, but was merely issued to interested parties, together with *Rotuli Parliamentorum* and the *Lords' Journals*, at the discretion of the secretary of state. Indeed, such was the haste in which *Domesday Book* was sent out that it lacked even a table of contents and title-page.[143]

Farley received a total of £2,500 for his work, the last £1,000 of which was consequent on its completion. In March 1783, he reported to the Treasury that the edition was finished and the Treasury once more called upon the Society of Antiquaries for its advice. A committee of the Society compared the transcript with the original and replied favourably: 'The copy is faithfully and accurately printed, and ... great care and attention have been paid by Mr Farley in transcribing the record and in correcting the press.'[144] Farley was asked to draft a title-page and table of contents and, having done so, was paid the balance in November 1783. These preliminaries were not, however, printed – an omission which met with much contemporary criticism.[145]

Plates 55 and 56 show a Great Domesday entry and the printed version of Farley's transcription of it. The lands described are those of Westminster Abbey, which include the manors of Westminster, Hampstead and Staines.[142] Farley, in his edition, followed the pagination and layout of the original, so that the words, lines and pages of Great Domesday Book corresponded exactly with the printed version. For Little Domesday he adopted a similar approach, except that he put the texts of the recto and verso of each folio on to one side of the printed sheet, and gave page, rather than folio, numbers in the volume. Nichols's record type, a common type to which were added special supplementary characters to represent the suspension, contraction and other marks, was not a true facsimile, but allowed the original to be reproduced with the minimum of editorial intervention. It was a method of printing records which continued to be used into the present century.

Farley's edition has, ever since it was published, met with approval and admiration

55. The lands of Westminster Abbey, Middlesex, from Great Domesday.

56. Abraham Farley's edition of the same passage as in Plate 55.

from scholars. Such is its quality that subsequent attempts to reproduce the text of Domesday Book in print have, rather than attempting a new edition, either used a photographic process (as with the photozincographic version of the 1860s and with the new facsimile) or have incorporated the Farley version with a new translation (as with the Phillimore volumes).[147] The 1783 edition made a definitive version of the survey available to scholars and politicians for the first time. The interpretation and analysis of the text could take place without recourse to the original, and the benefits soon became apparent in new publications. However, the lack of a table of contents, a glossary and indexes made Farley's edition difficult to use, and, although private enterprise did something to fill the gap almost immediately,[148] it was to be more than two decades before any official effort was made.[149] Indeed, the full potential of Farley's work was not to be realized until well into the nineteenth century, when it was used by several eminent historians to reach a new understanding of the purpose and significance of Domesday Book.

CHAPTER VI

Domesday Book since 1800

In 1816, Thomas Evans, the leader of a group of radical London artisans, produced a pamphlet which, like many others of its day and kind, called for the total and forcible abolition of the current system of landownership. Its unusual feature was Evans's singling-out of Domesday Book as the symbol of the tyrannical Norman yoke:

Our divine institutions, our real constitution, established by our Saxon ancestors, was destroyed by the tyranny of the Norman Conquest. . . . If conquest gives right, and right is the best title to possession of land, as our laws allow, and our lawyers contend, and the Domesday Book, made by William the Norman, is the most ancient and efficient record to which our courts refer, now is the time to cancel this record, to call upon those proprietors and possessors by conquest for a restoration.[1]

This passage is an extreme example of the way in which some early nineteenth-century radicals, like the Levellers before them, believed that the ancient constitution had been perverted by the tyranny of Norman rule.[2] Such theories later became widely accepted in a less revolutionary form by the conventional middle classes. The years between 1820 and 1880 witnessed the 'Gothic revival', the cult of the medieval as expressed in architecture, art, literature and political writing. Popular novels, such as Sir Walter Scott's *Ivanhoe* and Charles Kingsley's *Hereward the Wake*, and poems, such as Alfred Lord Tennyson's *Harold*, are prominent examples of a multitude of literary works which, like many popular histories since the middle ages, depicted the Saxons as cruelly oppressed by their Norman conquerors.[3]

Such views were also increasingly held by more serious historians. Augustin Thierry, whose work on the Norman Conquest first appeared in his native France in 1825, emphasized the destructiveness of the Conquest, but also suggested that the Saxons were not completely subjugated: throughout the middle ages, the native English and their Norman rulers struggled for preeminence, and did not reach a fusion until the sixteenth century. He regarded Domesday Book as an interesting source, but not as a work of political genius, as many others had believed; it merely stemmed from William's need to impose order. Throughout history, other conquerors had made similar inquests.[4] Henry Hallam, a solid, unromantic writer of the Whig school, who made judicious use of sources, likewise saw the Conquest as marking a break. In his comparative study of European institutions, written to combat the all-pervasive influence of Hume, he followed many traditional Whig ideas, but also admitted that others, such as a denial of the significance of the Conquest, were untenable. Thus, the Anglo-Saxon nobles, he believed, had been dispossessed and the people brought under the yoke, but 'we owe no trifling part of our self-esteem to the Norman element in our population and our policy'.[5] He admired Domesday Book as an 'incomparable record', of singular value both as a source for Anglo-Saxon and Anglo-Norman history and as a record of post-Conquest changes in landholding.[6] Sharon Turner, whose study of Anglo-Saxon England was highly influential, wrote a general history of England published between 1814 and 1823. Like Hallam, he saw the Conquest as a cataclysm which disrupted English society and established a new aristocracy, but which left the essential Germanic institutions unchanged. By 1066, the Anglo-Saxons had, he believed, become degenerate, submissive and unwarlike, and William I had therefore served a useful purpose in conquering and invigorating them. As for Domesday Book, it marked the most important financial operation of the reign and was intended to establish the legal rights of the Crown.[7]

Those writers reached a broad audience, because a new interest in history spread throughout English society during the 1820s and was to persist thereafter. The publication of major historical works was greeted with enthusiasm in all walks of society. People valued history for providing moral, improving lessons and for explaining the present,[8] but they also required it to entertain, and the borders between history and fiction were often ill-defined. The historical novels of the 1830s and 1840s, written in imitation of Sir Walter Scott, were frequently overburdened with irrelevant and undigested antiquarian detail, and had flimsy, romantic and implausible plots; whereas, as a reaction, the next generation of such works was founded on detailed and meticulous historical research. Some historians adopted a narrative approach and current literary conventions to reach a similar market.[9] Sir Francis Palgrave, for example, wrote in the 1830s a flowery and bombastic history of England and Normandy, which, like several of his other works, did much to feed the voracious popular appetite for the middle ages. His comments on Domesday Book are typical. He described the Conqueror's commissioners as a 'worshipful company', and Domesday itself as 'fresh and perfect as when scribe put pen to parchment, the oldest cadastre, or survey of a kingdom, in the world'.[10]

Palgrave was, however, a versatile man, and it is interesting to compare such flowery effusions about Domesday Book with his more sober judgments. From 1834, he was keeper at the Chapter House and, from 1838, the first deputy keeper of the records, thus remaining Domesday's custodian. In one of his official reports, he described Domesday as 'a survey of a kingdom unparalleled for its singularity and its

57. Sir Francis Palgrave, 1823.

curiosity, which stands at the head of [Her] Majesty's records'.[11] He also gave it serious discussion in its historical context:

It is not unusual to describe Domesday as a badge of Norman tyranny. That the survey was prompted by stern and rigid principles of government adopted by the Conqueror cannot be denied; but instead of being calculated to enlarge his authority, it was in truth an admission of the restriction of his power.[12]

This somewhat controversial view, stemming from Palgrave's qualified belief in the ancient constitution, has been recently revived.[13] Palgrave discussed his sources in what was, for his day, a critical and non-anachronistic manner which foreshadows the historical work of the last years of Queen Victoria's reign. His account of the genesis of Domesday owed much to the recently published *Introduction* by Sir Henry Ellis,[14] but also illustrates something of his own approach. He was highly suspicious of the forged Crowland chronicle as evidence for Alfred's mythical Domesday, and he made perceptive use of the Anglo-Saxon Chronicle, the *Inquisitio Eliensis* and Exon Domesday.[15] His experience in record work undoubtedly helped him as a historian. Between 1822 and 1834, with the assistance of several clerks, he edited, among other records, a massive collection of parliamentary writs for the Record Commission. It has recently been suggested that he and his subordinates at the Record Office developed new standards of historical professionalism which were to prove an important formative influence on the new 'scientific' history of the later nineteenth century.[16] This new approach was increasingly to render the study and practice of history the preserve only of a specialized élite.[17]

In the 1840s, the idea that the Anglo-Saxons had governed themselves as a loose collection of independent confederations became increasingly popular. Local self-government was seen as a feature of Teutonic societies and was considered one of the most important features of the ancient constitution. Strengthened by a growing admiration for Germanic institutions in general, the notion proved politically influential.[18] Joshua Toulmin Smith, an earnest and indefatigable political crusader,[19] exercised a considerable ascendancy over middle-class thought through his pamphlets directed towards the devolution of power to local communities. Helped by the failure of the central government effectively to organize the Crimean campaign, his views attained the status of orthodoxy during the 1850s and 1860s. The Metropolitan Board of Works, created in 1855, was one of their principal monuments.[20]

In arguing his case for local self-government, Toulmin Smith deployed his considerable antiquarian knowledge and drew upon a wide range of medieval sources. Domesday Book, which he saw as providing incontrovertible proof of his views, was perhaps his favourite.

The case is simple. History proves that three, five, eight, ten and more centuries ago, local self-government did exist in England, and was of force to keep in check the most ambitious of monarchs. ... Our fathers stand out before us, in their 'very habit as they lived', in Domesday Book (so grossly misrepresented by the ill-informed), in hundred rolls, in *inquisitiones nonarum*, and in a thousand other unimpeachable records. We find that, whether it were in the crowded city or the rural parish, the men of England, including the 'villeins', were in the habit of handling their own business, and knew how to handle it.[21]

In another tract, Toulmin Smith explained contemporary misapprehensions about Domesday Book.

Domesday Book, so often misrepresented by those who have never studied it, is, in fact, nothing more nor less than the record of the action of the institutions of local self-government of a free people, in almost every county of England. It brings up a vivid picture, full of life and interest, of how men in England did their own business for themselves eight hundred years ago.[22]

Medieval history in the mid-Victorian era was dominated by the triumvirate of William Stubbs, Edward Augustus Freeman and John Richard Green. Green showed little interest in Domesday, but both Stubbs and Freeman had much to say on it in print and a little in their correspondence with one another.[23] There were great differences between their approaches to history, but they remained on amicable terms throughout their careers. Stubbs was a country parson who became regius professor of modern history at Oxford in 1866, bishop of Chester in 1884 and bishop of Oxford in 1888. He was a conservative and a high churchman, who was convinced of the moral purposes of history, but was at the same time considered humorous and affable. His greatest strength was, perhaps, his ability as an editor, displayed in his many editions of manuscripts published in the Rolls Series and elsewhere. His principal work of historical interpretation was his *Constitutional History*, which has remained influential for generations,[24] some would suggest with malign results.[25] Like his contemporaries, Stubbs felt that 'the roots of the present lie deep in the past, and nothing in the past is dead to the man who would learn how the present comes to be what it is'.[26] Although he recognized the importance of Saxon liberties, he believed that the stability of England under the Confessor was threatened by the power of the great earldoms. 1066 was to him a crucial turning-point which took England into Europe and brought the beginnings of modern government. 'The Norman Conquest was a Good Thing, as from this time onwards England stopped being conquered and was able to become top nation': the parody of *1066 and All That* is not far removed from Stubbs's real views.[27]

In one of his lectures, Stubbs spoke admiringly of Domesday Book. It was, he said,

as perfect as when it was written, and constituting for Englishmen, perhaps, the most interesting record in existence; on religious grounds less interesting than the gospels given by St Gregory to Augustine, or some of the early collections of laws and chronicles, but in its completeness and uniqueness beyond all comparison with any record of this or any other nation of Europe. It is indeed to English history what the books of Numbers and Joshua are to the Bible.[28]

In his *Constitutional History*, Stubbs used Domesday evidence to show that, after the Conquest, not only was the Saxon nobility dispossessed by Normans, but the king dominated his barons in a new and unprecedented fashion. Domesday itself was to Stubbs a register of land, a record of royal revenue, but also a rate book, 'the first step in a continuous process by which the nation arrived ultimately at the power of taxing itself'.[29] He was, however, well aware of the difficulties of Domesday evidence: when a protégé said that he would like to 'get into Domesday', Stubbs replied that 'it was much more important to get out of it'.[30]

Freeman was a gentleman scholar who succeeded Stubbs as regius professor of modern history at Oxford in 1884, when he was already over sixty. A passionate liberal who espoused the cause of Hungarian liberties in the 1870s, he propounded the importance of free Anglo-Saxon communities with great vigour. Unlike Stubbs, he had an aversion to manuscripts and worked only from printed sources, which, however, he followed rigorously in his voluminous narrative histories.[31] By modern standards, his works are prolix, rambling, full of pedantic attention to irrelevant detail, and deeply imbued with the beliefs that historical developments led inevitably to the present and that history provided useful moral guidance: in short, the very opposite to canons of modern historical scholarship.[32] John Horace Round,[33] who was to promulgate the idea of history as the analytical study of original sources, criticized Freeman long and bitterly for his narrative style, his liberal and his anachronistic interpretation of events, his pedantry and his 'gross errors'. But Freeman, for all his shortcomings, was a magisterial writer of historical narrative, and the recent enhancement of his reputation is long overdue.[34]

Freeman's greatest work was a five-volume history of the Norman Conquest, published between 1867 and 1879. Not until the third volume did he reach 1066: the first and second were devoted to an examination of the Anglo-Saxon 'background' and stressed the vital importance of the local communities of free Englishmen. Here his views bordered on a 'socialist' version of the ancient-constitution theory.[35] The Conquest, Freeman thought, extinguished those ancient liberties, but they were to revive in the twelfth century and to go from strength to strength. Freeman's optimism led him to attribute even to the Conqueror some of the qualities of a far-seeing statesman: the king was neither purely benevolent nor purely scientific, 'but we may believe that William could see, in some measure, what experience allows a modern government to see more clearly', namely, that authority can be excercised effectively only if those in power have a knowledge of the land they govern.[36] Therefore William commissioned the Domesday survey, which was intended to reveal to him the full extent of his resources.[37] Although Freeman's analysis of the making of Domesday lacks conviction, he was emphatic about its worth.

The great record, the work of our foreign king, stands as a national possession side-by-side with [the Anglo-Saxon Chronicle]. Each is unique in its own kind. No other nation has such material to draw on in its history.[38]

The final volume of the history contains a number of critical appendixes discussing various aspects of the Domesday evidence. His work on those led Freeman to call for a new edition of the record which was 'in truth, a picture of the nation, and nothing else'.[39]

The scholars of the nineteenth century who wrote about Domesday Book could do so with far greater familiarity and accuracy than their predecessors, because of Farley's excellent edition. In 1800, that still lacked any critical apparatus and even any preliminary pages, but within two decades it had been augmented with much valuable material through the efforts of the Record Commission. The origins of this body lay in a wide-ranging inquiry held in 1799, which found that the national archive was scattered through some sixty repositories in the capital: 'in many offices unarranged, undescribed and unascertained ..., many of them ... exposed to erasure, alienation and embezzlement and ... lodged in buildings incommodious and insecure'.[40] The first Record Commission, appointed in 1800, and its five successors, collectively known as the Record Commission, therefore organized programmes for the sorting, listing and repairing of documents; arranged for a substantial number of record publications; and advised on suitable archival accommodation. In all three areas, it showed only dubious competence and, by the 1830s, criticism of its activities had become acrimonious and widespread. Despite its shortcomings, however, it performed some useful functions, not least in promulgating the idea of a national collection of records.[41]

Abraham Farley's edition of Domesday Book was much admired by the Commission. At its first session in July 1800, it ordered that a title-page and list of contents should be prepared on the lines suggested by the Society of Antiquaries in 1783, and that work on indexes of persons and places should commence forthwith. By 1805, a list of contents and a title-page, dated 1783, were ready, but were added only to the commissioners' personal copies of the Farley volumes. The indexes took much longer. They were compiled by two Chapter House clerks, John Clarke and John Thompson, under the supervision of the keeper, George Rose, and with the assistance of Alfred Tomlins. The subject index was compiled by Henry Ellis of the British Museum.[42] Clarke's index of places, compiled county by county, at first made good progress, but in 1804, when it was already in the press, was found to be highly inaccurate and had to be revised by Tomlins. Thompson's general index of places, also made in conjunction with Tomlins, was compiled more slowly, hampered by the loss of part of the manuscript copy, but all the indexes were issued for the first time in 1811.[43] In the same year, the Commission took over from Parliament the responsibility for 250 sets of the Farley edition, the bulk of the remaining stock. In 1817, they circulated many of them in the normal way with their own title-pages inserted – an addition which has caused much subsequent bibliographical confusion. They included two further volumes with each set: a revised reprint of the indexes, which had been completed by 1814, and an edition of four 'satellite' surveys. These were Exon Domesday, the *Inquisitio Eliensis*, the Winchester Domesday and the Boldon Book, a later twelfth-century survey of the estates of the bishopric of Durham (scholars today would place only the first two in the 'satellite' category).[44] Printed in 1816, the 'satellites' volume was the work of Henry Ellis, a somewhat unworldly scholar who was keeper of printed books and later principal librarian at the British Museum.[45] From 1814, he was also secretary to the Society of Antiquaries, which had the Winchester Domesday in its custody and had given active support for publishing the 'satellites'. The four-volume sets at last provided a comprehensive means of reference to the Farley volumes and background texts for the critical study of Domesday.[46]

Meanwhile, Ellis had also been working on a general introduction to Domesday Book. The commissioners reviewed it in 1814 and found it defective, and Ellis had to make substantial alterations before it could be published in full in 1816. It was issued both as part of the index volume and separately; and, in 1833, an expanded version was published by the Commission in a smaller size.[47] Despite Ellis's initial difficulties, his work was innovatory in his day and was to provide a vitally important guide to Domesday for subsequent generations up to the present one. Ellis discussed the way in which the survey might have been made; he analysed its contents; and he provided abstracts of population and compiled indexes of tenants-in-chief, under-tenants and landholders in 1066. His efforts did not meet with unqualified approval at the time. The Record Commission was allowed to expire in 1837 amidst widespread accusations of inefficiency, incompetence and extrava-gance. The publications programme was singled out by many critics, and a Committee of the House of Commons, investigating the Commission's activities in 1836, expressed unease about the large sums paid to Ellis, among others, for editorial work.[48] Sir Henry Cole, polymath extraordinary, who for many years worked for the Record Commission and the Public Record Office,[49] considered that Ellis totally misunderstood Domesday Book: 'his commentary was like a splash of mud upon it'.[50] Ellis himself was unhappy with the typographical policy of the Commission. Impressed by the record type used in the Farley Domesday volumes, the commissioners had had it developed by Vincent Figgins, who had been an apprentice to Farley's typecutter. They used it as the standard type in most of their publications, including the Domesday 'satellites'.[51] In 1840, Ellis looked back on its employment with regret. The so-called Domesday type, he said, introduced confusion and ambiguity and was a deterrent to scholarship.[52]

In 1838, the records of existing and defunct courts of law were at last brought together under the custody of the master of the rolls and the day-to-day supervision of the deputy keeper of the public records.[53] Sir Francis Palgrave, the first deputy keeper,[54] set up his headquarters at the Rolls Estate in Chancery Lane, from where he controlled the other branch offices, principally the Chapter House, the old riding-school at Carlton House and the Tower of London. Arrangements were made in 1852 for the transfer of older records of government departments to his custody and in 1854 the State Paper Office came under Public Record Office control. Heated controversies about a suitable site and style for a new repository had delayed until

THE ROLLS HOUSE AND CHAPEL.

58. Rolls House and the Rolls Chapel shortly before their demolition in the 1890s.

1851 the laying of a foundation stone for the Public Record Office on the Rolls Estate. The first stage, designed by James Pennethorne and completed in 1858, was a secure and fireproof structure and a fine example of Victorian functional design, but at the same time had Gothic ornamentation befitting its role as the treasure-house of the national records. To Sir Henry Cole, it was 'an architectural design full of truth, originality and ... purpose'.[55]

59. Watercolour by Sir James Pennethorne, depicting the first block of the Public Record Office to be built, c. 1851.

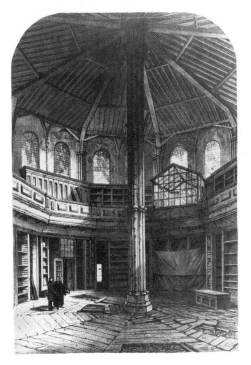

60. *The Chapter House after being emptied of the records, c.1859. It was subsequently restored by Sir George Gilbert Scott.*
61. *The 'Tudor' binding of Great Domesday, showing damage from woodworm.*

Domesday Book was not to be moved to the new Record Office until 1859. Until then, it remained at the Chapter House in Westminster, in conditions far less safe and secure than in earlier centuries. At first kept in its cupboard on the stairs, by 1846 it had been moved to a room known as the Library, which was situated above the Chapter House porch.[56] As a result of the publication of the 1783 edition, the original manuscript was probably used far less than before. In 1819, John Caley, keeper of the records at the Chapter House, reported some alarming facts about Domesday to the record commissioners:

In this repository the condition of the venerable record of Domesday naturally demanded the earliest attention, and it having been ascertained by minute inspection that worms had already pervaded the coverings of these volumes and had begun to feed on the vellum of the leaves..., measures were instantly taken for the rebinding of the volumes by a skilful person in the Office, and it may be reported that both the volumes are very handsomely and substantially bound in Russia leather.[57]

The damage from the worms may still be seen in the discarded boards of the 'Tudor' binding. The Record Commission binding saved Domesday from further harm, but was deplored by many critics, including Palgrave, for its tightness[58] and

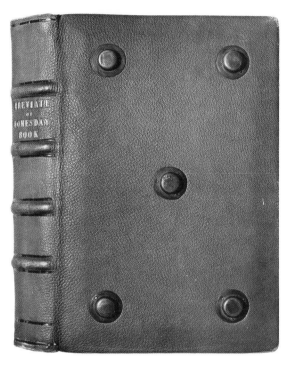

62. *Record Commission cover of the Domesday Breviate, as rebound in 1819. Domesday Book was bound in a similar style, but those covers are now lost.*

was to be replaced within fifty years.[59] Its covers have not survived, but were probably similar in style to those of the Breviate, which was repaired and rebound at the same time.[60]

Worms did not pose the only threat to Domesday Book. In his quarterly reports to the Treasury, Caley had made frequent mention of the potential dangers from fire at the Chapter House. In 1821, he complained of the proximity to it of outbuildings belonging to the dean and chapter, and he feared that fires which were often lit there might get out of control.[61] Five years later, he regretted that no effective steps had been taken to combat the threat.[62] The dangers were all too vividly demonstrated when, in October 1834, most of the palace of Westminster was consumed by a conflagration which began with the burning of an excessive number of tallies in a stove beneath the House of Lords. On that night, Palgrave, then keeper at the Chapter House, stood with the dean of Westminster on its roof, watching the flames. When a gust of wind seemed to be blowing them in that direction, he begged the dean to allow him to carry Domesday Book and other valuable records into the abbey for safe keeping. With a remarkable lack of common sense, the dean refused to agree without first obtaining a warrant from Lord Melbourne, the prime minister,[63] and it was fortunate for the records that the fire went no further.

As deputy keeper of the records, Palgrave continued to worry about the fire hazards, in particular from the wash-house, which was very near to the Library windows.[64] However, he regarded the offices at Carlton Ride and the Rolls Estate as being at even greater risk than the Chapter House,[65] where he was much concerned with remedying Caley's failure to ensure the security of the records by locking them safely away. Even Domesday Book, he reported, had been left unsecured under the previous régime.[66] In 1847, he was able to assure his superiors that the Library was never warmed and was thus eminently suitable for preserving Domesday in its excellent condition,[67] but he still had strong private reservations about its safety. In 1846, he had considered moving Domesday and other documents to the Stone Tower used for the Augmentations Office records, and had asked Henry Cole, the assistant keeper in charge, to prepare presses for them. Nothing came of the idea,[68] although Cole would certainly not have opposed it: in 1849, he remarked that the brewhouse and wash-house still remained in the neighbourhood of the Chapter House, 'jeopardizing Domesday Book, the most priceless record in Europe'.[69] In 1854, Frederick Devon, the assistant keeper at the Chapter House, again proposed moving Domesday and its companions out of the porch.[70] Perhaps in response, the possibility of taking Domesday to the Rolls Chapel was raised in 1855. It was not a new idea; many years earlier it had been considered and a press had been constructed and placed under the oriel window there. However, the installation of heating pipes beneath the chapel floor had at that time rendered the temperature far too high. Palgrave now felt that, despite the heating, the chapel would still be the best place for Domesday – but again nothing further was done about it.[71] When Domesday Book eventually left Westminster in 1859, under the careful custody of Joseph Burtt, the assistant keeper upon whom had devolved the charge of the Chapter House after Devon's death in 1858,[72] it was to be placed, not in the Rolls Chapel, but in a far safer room at the new Record Office.[73] It had survived one of the least secure periods in its entire history relatively unscathed.

Although it was called upon with a decreased frequency, Domesday remained available for searches and copying while it was at the Chapter House. Until 1840, the fee for Domesday searches was 6s. 8d., and for other Chapter House records, 8s. 4d. For each line of Domesday copied, fourpence was charged, and one shilling for every seventy-two words of other documents.[74] The Public Record Office Act brought about a considerable reduction in fees: one shilling for a general search in the catalogues, one shilling for an inspection of any individual record for up to a working week, and 1s. 6d. for any copy of three folios of ninety words each, with sixpence for every extra folio. Domesday was no longer singled out for a special rate. In the early 1850s, charges were remitted altogether for 'literary' searches but were retained for legal inquiries, including Domesday searches for the purposes of litigation.[75]

Domesday's practical uses were, however, very much eclipsed by its growing importance as a museum piece. Thus in 1854, Frederick Devon commented that Domesday was

seldom or never asked for as a book of record, or reference, or evidence, but only looked on as a curiosity or relic . . ., and, as a relic, I would religiously preserve it, even as they preserve the thirteen (original) heads of John the Baptist . . . on the Continent; for it would be equally efficacious in working miracles and can boast of greater antiquity than most of them.[76]

In the 1840s and 1850s, Domesday Book was, as earlier, shown to dignitaries, as when in 1845 the French ambassador went to the Chapter House,[77] and to other visitors, as when in 1857 an American visitor, a Mr Hazard of Rhode Island, was given permission to inspect it.[78] But there was increasing pressure from within the Record Office to put it on show to a wider public. The chief proponent of the idea was Henry Cole, who remained an assistant keeper until 1850 and who had many interests and a growing influence outside the Office. His early innovative schemes in art and design were carried out while he presided at the Carlton Ride repository, and his work in organizing the Great Exhibition of 1851 led to his elevation to a secretaryship at the newly constituted Department of Science and Art.[79] Not only was he the inventor of the Christmas card, but also, as 'Felix Summerly', won design awards for tea sets which went into commercial production, and wrote a number of popular books. In one, a guide book to Westminster Abbey published in 1842, he described the Chapter House and its contents in enthusiastic terms.

This – a most interesting part of the abbey – is not a recognized public sight; and permission to examine its many great curiosities, both architectural, decorative and historical, can only be obtained from the authorities at the Public Record Office at the Rolls House in Chancery Lane. . . . The greatest treasure of the place is William the Conqueror's Domesday Book. You must not touch the text or writing – a rule which has been kept from time immemorial and to which the excellent condition of the record may be partly ascribed.[80]

The year before, Cole had attempted to persuade Lord Langdale, the master of the rolls, to put Domesday Book and other choice records on show to the public at the Chapter House. He gained the support of Devon, who suggested threepence as a suitable fee. Lord Langdale expressed a guarded interest, but the idea was quashed by Palgrave, ostensibly on the grounds of the unsuitability of the buildings.[81] Palgrave's hostile reaction in 1855 to another proposal that Domesday might be displayed at the Rolls Chapel suggests that, in fact, he had a deep-rooted objection to exposing the record to the public gaze: 'It would be very inexpedient to render the record repository a museum or showcase, but such a unique document as Domesday ought to have a species of respect rendered to it.'[82] However, Palgrave's successor from 1861, Thomas Duffus Hardy, sympathized with Cole's views on the matter and in the late 1860s Domesday was to emerge as an important national relic.

The gradual popularization of Domesday Book began in the early 1860s, when a pioneering photographic process gave a far wider section of the public access to its text. Sir Henry James, the idiosyncratic and self-willed director of the Ordnance Survey Department, had developed a new process called photozincography. The original document was photographed in the open air on to a wet collodion glass negative, which was developed and used to produce a gum bichromate paper print. This in turn was inked and pressed on to a zinc plate, which was then etched for printing. Despite some opposition within his department, James determined to prove its worth by reproducing medieval manuscripts.[83] Early in 1861, he secured the agreement of the master of the rolls, Lord Romilly, of Palgrave and of Treasury officials for Domesday to be disbound and the Cornwall folios to be transported to Southampton and to be photozincographed as an initial, modest experiment.[84] Gladstone, as chancellor of the Exchequer, took a personal interest in the project. The Record Office binder, Hood, took Great Domesday apart, and on 4th February the appropriate sheets were taken to Southampton by train by Joseph Burtt. By 14th February, they were back at the Office, the experiment completed.[85] The resulting volumes were offered for six shillings leatherbound and 4s. 6d. clothbound, and by

63. *Satirical drawing of Sir Henry Cole in middle age.*

June 1862, 138 copies had been sold and thirty-two presented. Their recipients included Queen Victoria, Prince Albert and the Prince of Wales.[86] Burtt displayed the results at the Archaeological Institute, where he was triumphantly received.[87]

The Treasury considered the venture a success and, in October 1861, having the reassurance of substantial advance subscriptions from several further counties, authorized four more sections, Hampshire, Middlesex, Surrey and Cheshire, to be photozincographed. It was proposed to transfer the equipment to the Record Office, but James insisted that such a procedure would be scarcely feasible and highly expensive, adding that, since the process had to be done out of doors, the better climate in Southampton would prove of considerable advantage. Thus, in November, Burtt returned to Southampton with the whole of Great Domesday.[88] James had every intention of photozincographing the whole of the volume as soon as possible, and appeared to be exceeding his instructions in cavalier fashion, which irritated the Treasury. There was also strong opposition from the Reverend Lambert Larking, an antiquarian who had received one of the circulars advertising for advance subscriptions. He wrote to the Treasury to complain that the scheme would destroy the financial viability of his own engraved version of the Kent folios, which was rapidly nearing completion. When, in December 1861, James was somewhat reluctantly given permission to photozincograph the rest of Great Domesday, he was expressly forbidden to print the Kent section; and the other counties could be printed only when adequate subscriptions had been raised.[89]

64. *Early process camera, probably the photozincographic machine, in operation at Southampton, c. 1860s.*

Early in January 1862, Burtt was summoned back to London by Hardy, who had succeeded Palgrave as deputy keeper, on the grounds that no one else could find or retrieve records from the classes on which Burtt was working. He was replaced by William Basevi Sanders, who took Little Domesday with him to Southampton and was to remain there for many years, supervising the Domesday and several subsequent photozincographic projects.[90] During 1862, James made stalwart efforts to raise subscriptions for all the Great Domesday counties. He was helped by that eccentric and influential pamphleteer Joshua Toulmin Smith, who devoted much space in his parliamentary journals to describing the project and to castigating local worthies who would not contribute towards it.[91] By April 1863, all the counties save Kent had been printed. Larking had meanwhile become so incapacitated through illness that he was unable to finish his engravings (which were not to appear until 1869) and he gave his permission for James to proceed with the Kent folios.[92] Little Domesday was also photozincographed and the results printed between April and December 1863, a remarkably short space of time. In his final report on the facsimile, Sanders expressed his admiration for James and for his chief photographer, Sergeant James McDonald, and stressed the excellence of their work.[93] Great and Little Domesday were then issued as complete bound volumes, and reprints were soon in train for several county sections. The continuing popularity of the work is shown by the attempts of an enterprising printer to issue a pirated version in 1876.[94] The whole project had cost the Treasury £2,128 2s. 10d., an expense which was recouped only in part and over many decades.[95]

By modern standards, the photozincograph of Domesday Book has certain defects. The process could not differentiate between light and heavy strokes of the pen, and the results give the script only in silhouette. The image was defective in places and had to be retouched, a process which introduced certain inaccuracies and which left the Farley edition as the generally more reliable version of Domesday's text. Marks and erasures on the parchment of the original cannot be distinguished in the photozincograph, and some of the later annotations in the text, and the preliminary notes and jottings by antiquarians, were not included. But given the newness of the process and the unsophisticated lenses and other equipment available, the photozincograph is a remarkable achievement. Further, the rubrication was overprinted very successfully and gives the facsimile an attractive appearance. Indeed, it has proved so useful as a working copy in conjunction with Farley's version that, since it was made, few scholars have felt the need to consult the original. It has also been far more accessible to a wider public than Farley's work.

In 1862, Vacher and Sons proposed to supply an official accompanying edition with extended words in modern type and with an English translation. The Treasury, however, did not agree; nor did it favour new indexes, as suggested by the

65. *The photozincographic version of the Great Domesday entry for the lands of Westminster Abbey.*

archdeacon of London. Despite Lord Romilly's support for both, Gladstone insisted that the photozincograph alone should go on sale.[96] It was left to private enterprise to produce such apparatus, and in the next few years, extended texts for nine counties, some with translations, were published. Sanders gave his editorial assistance to several of them.[97] Subsequently, new translations were issued in the Victoria County History series and by Phillimore county by county, but it was not until the 1980s that new indexes and a revised translation for Domesday as a whole were to be produced with official backing to accompany a facsimile of the complete manuscript.[98]

In March 1864, both volumes of Domesday Book were back at the Record Office. The photozincograph had made the survey better known, but its custodians were now to try almost to apotheosize it, to show it to be a historical relic of which all patriotic Englishmen could be proud. Thus, Lord Romilly wrote to George Hamilton at the Treasury that, now Domesday was 'detached from [its] objectionable and unsuitable bindings', it could be rebound in a fashion 'worthy of the record and of the nation to which it belongs'.[99] A number of different proposals for a new cover were considered, but wrangles about its materials and design, compounded with bureaucratic bungling, delayed the rebinding for six years. The Treasury, on first sanctioning the scheme, suggested that Domesday should be bound in a style appropriate to its period, but placed in a decorated casket to be designed by the Department of Science and Art at South Kensington. Lord Romilly objected to that idea, on the grounds that a casket might allow mildew to grow on the documents. Instead, he suggested that both volumes should be encased in silver gilt, with a design symbolizing Domesday's era and contents.[100] Henry Cole, as joint-secretary of the Department of Science and Art, was asked to commission drawings for the cover and in February 1865 handed over a highly ornamented design to Romilly and Hardy for comment. In a letter to Cole, Hardy made a number of suggestions for improvements. He considered that the proposed jewelled metal bosses should be replaced with enamel medallions, and that

first there ought to be some legend around the Conqueror, giving his compellations, such as *Willelmus D G Rex Anglorum et Dux Normannorum*, also the date, 1066, immediately over the battle of Hastings; and the date, 1085 [*sic*], immediately under the taking of Domesday. With respect to the reverse, the Queen to be in the centre, with her titles around her with a similar legend to that of William the Conqueror; in the same place as the battle of Hastings on the other side, the opening of the Great Exhibition of 1851 as being symbolical of the difference between war and peace, the obverse representing war, the reverse peace with all nations; at the bottom where the taking of Domesday is, on the other side, a representation symbolical of the results of the penny postage; the Conqueror's pointing to the imposition of the tax, the Queen's to a relief from a tax.[101]

Cole, as one of the originators of the penny post, might well have felt flattered. However, by September he had come round to the view that Domesday Book should be covered with plain oak boards, but that it could then be enclosed in an ornate casket. 'If bound in an ancient style, it is an affectation, if in a modern one, it is something of an anachronism.' Hardy agreed to send a copy of the photozincograph for experimentation.[102] but the unfortunate death of the intended binder, Sykes, in 1866 meant that nothing was achieved in that year. In February 1867, Cole recommended one Cayley, 'a most learned artist working in metal', to produce a design for a suitable casket. Cayley set to work and proposed a monstrous 'shrine' in the Byzantine style, made from copper, platinum and gold, which would have cost more than £2,000 to make.[103]

Hardy rapidly rejected Cayley's suggestions and asked Cole to send him the sample bindings, of plain design, which Cole had meanwhile commissioned from another craftsman, Robert Rivière. Cole was unable to do so until the end of the year, because they were on show at the Paris exhibition. When eventually they arrived back, Hardy and Romilly examined them and Romilly considered the metalwork

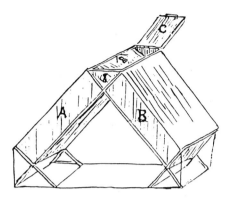

66. *Cayley's design for a Byzantine 'shrine' for Domesday Book, 1867.*

67. *Sample binding for Great Domesday by Rivière, 1866–67.*

on them far too heavy and the design insufficiently linked with English history. He suggested, therefore, that a competition should be held to find the best binder.[104] Cole reacted with disappointment. He agreed that the metalwork was too cumbersome, but foresaw a repetition of earlier experiments; before any further progress could be made, it was necessary to decide whether or not an ornamented cover was required. For his own part, he favoured simplicity and excellence.[105] Hardy hastily tried to soothe Cole's feelings and reminded him of the reservations that they both had had about earlier, elaborate schemes; nevertheless, a competition might be a useful way of settling matters. Cole replied that, to him, competitions were 'one of the humbugs of the age'. He refused to have any part in one and, at the same time, recommended three possible binders, suggesting that Hardy make an immediate choice. Hardy did so, selecting Poynter, a decorative designer and metalworker, and he asked Cole to expedite the production of a decorated cover.[106] However, within two days Lord Romilly reversed that decision, insisting that Domesday should be rebound in a plain style. Cole was pleased with that and once again recommended Rivière, but his triumph was short-lived. Romilly, wearied by the delays, took over the project himself and placed it under the control of the Stationery Office.[107]

The new régime did little to speed the progress of the rebinding. With bureaucratic correctness, W.R. Greg of the Stationery Office resolved to hold a competition. Three well-known binders were selected and were received at the Record Office by Hardy, who showed them Domesday Book. That was in May

1868; in November, Hardy expressed concern that no decision had as yet been reached, and it was not until 12 January 1869 that the specimens were ready for inspection.[108] Ironically, Rivière emerged as the victor. He set up his workshop at the Record Office, and at last, in November 1869, he handed over both Domesday volumes handsomely bound and ornamented with silver. Hardy and Romilly expressed unqualified approval of their appearance.[109] Rivière billed the Treasury for £138 5s. for his work, which included the repairs, rebinding and covers. The total was higher than he had originally estimated, largely because he had had to have some of the damaged centrefolds of the sheets made good, but it was still far from excessive.[110] Like others who had worked on Domesday before him, the repairer, Kew, left his mark on it, in this case in the form of his signature on two of the pages of Little Domesday. Unlike the contributions of Agarde and le Neve, it was hidden beyond the sewing holes.[111]

The removal of the Record Commission's tight binding was undoubtedly beneficial to Domesday Book; a judgment on the style of the new covers is more a matter of taste. Only to men who had considered ornamenting Domesday with enamels depicting the battle of Hastings and the penny post would the design have seemed simple. It incorporates silver bosses decorated with Tudor roses, heavy strips of silver used as edgings for the boards, and elaborately tooled leather with the title 'DOMESDAY BOOK' embossed upon it. By modern standards, it is ornate and impractical, but it gives a vivid illustration of official Victorian views of Domesday Book.

68. *Domesday Book in its final Rivière bindings.*

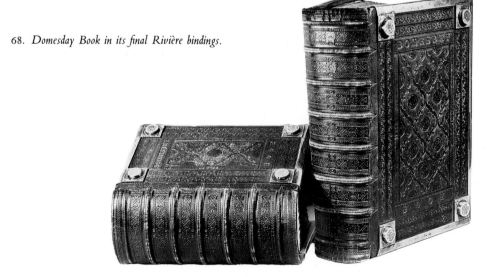

As a celebration of the rebinding, Romilly hoped to have Ellis's *Introduction* revised and reissued, but nothing came of the plan.[112] The rebound volumes needed a suitable setting to show off their new attire, and, after stringent negotiations between Romilly, Hardy, the Office of Works and the Treasury, two glass cases were ordered for their display.[113] Once completed, they were placed in the Domesday or Norman tower in the newly finished east wing of the Record Office. There Domesday was to remain until 1896, when a further part of the Office, designed by John Taylor and facing Chancery Lane, was ready for occupation. A room on the first floor, immediately over the gateway, was reserved as a museum for records of special interest and importance. Among them, Domesday Book had pride of place.[114]

The years after the issuing of the Domesday facsimile saw a gradual growth in Domesday scholarship. In 1876, the *Inquisitio Comitatus Cantabrigiensis*, noticed by Webb in 1756 but subsequently ignored, was published in full.[115] It was soon recognized as the key to Domesday's genesis, perhaps even to the neglect of other analogous records.[116] The Reverend R.W. Eyton, however, primarily used Exon Domesday in his detailed and meticulous work on Domesday Somerset and Dorset, which, with his studies of Staffordshire, led him to important speculations on the nature of Domesday society.[117]

Further stimulation to Domesday studies was provided by the octocentennial celebrations of 1886, which marked the first active commemoration of a Domesday anniversary. They were mooted by Walter de Gray Birch in a letter to *The Athenaeum*

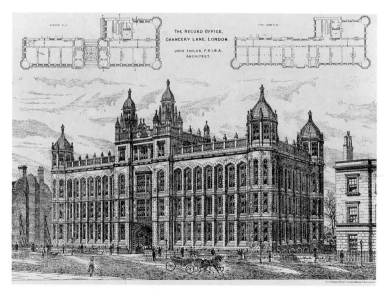

69. *Design for the Chancery Lane façade of the Public Record Office. This part of the building was completed in 1896.*

in April 1885, in which he lamented that Domesday and its related manuscripts were kept in so many different places that it would prove impossible ever to bring them together. However, he proposed that a Domesday Society should be founded along the lines of the many other record societies of the day. Its principal aim should be to issue a new edition of Domesday Book with a translation in octavo volumes, produced by editors well-qualified for the task. Copyright laws permitting, the works of Ellis and Eyton might also be republished.[118] There was then an acrimonious exchange of correspondence with Stuart Moore, a barrister, over errors which he had noticed in Birch's letter,[119] but no further action was taken until December 1885, when, at a council meeting of the Royal Historical Society, 'Mr Hyde Clarke gave notice that at the next council meeting he would call the consideration of the council to the measures desirable to be taken for the 800th commemoration of the Domesday record the following year'.[120] His motion was deferred, but at the session of 18 February 1886, it was eventually agreed that a committee was to 'consider the means of commemorating the 800th year from the completion of the Domesday survey in connection with historical studies'. A committee was duly elected[121] and began to make preparations. It co-opted extra members and also admitted delegates from numerous record societies and analogous bodies, a sign of the serious, if tardy, interest taken in the commemoration by historians of the day. Among its number were F.W. Maitland, Sir Frederick Pollock, J.H. Round, W. de Gray Birch and Sir Henry Maxwell-Lyte, deputy keeper of the records. In August 1886, it issued a circular to the members of all the societies, proposing to organize exhibitions, to have a bibliography compiled, to run a programme of lectures and, eventually, to publish a book of Domesday studies. Recipients were asked to pay a guinea to cover admission charges and the cost of the volume. Varied and wide-ranging topics were suggested as possible subjects for lectures, but there remained little more than two months for their compilation.[122]

The celebrations took place between 25 and 29 October 1886. The programme opened with an exhibition of documents at the Public Record Office. It included Domesday Book, the Breviate and *Abbreviatio*, the Black Book of the Exchequer, pipe rolls, tallies and ancient deeds. At 3.30 p.m. on 25 October, the 338 visitors heard a paper from Hubert Hall, an assistant keeper, on the official custody of Domesday Book. After a vote of thanks from Lord Aberdare, the president of the Royal Historical Society, the proceedings ended at 5.00 p.m. In the evening, there was a lecture by Canon Isaac Taylor in the great hall at the Society of Arts, which was well attended, although *The Athenaeum* commented that many of his arguments were open to question.[123] The following day, the British Museum exhibited manuscripts, including the *Inquisitio Eliensis*, the *Inquisitio Comitatus Cantabrigiensis* and the Margam abbreviation, and printed books, including the works of Webb,

70. *Drawings from the* Illustrated London News, *depicting the 1886 Domesday celebrations.*

Farley, Sanders and Eyton, and the photozincograph. A bibliography – un⁄
fortunately incomplete – was later compiled by Henry Wheatley.[124] That evening
and on the next three days, ten further lectures were given by Moore, Birch, Taylor,
Round and others. The *Illustrated London News* gave a brief but enthusiastic account
of the celebrations, whereas *The Athenaeum* reported the proceedings in more detail
and less flatteringly. Its correspondent was exasperated by the length and obscurity of
some of the contributions, and commented unfavourably on the 'marked deficiency
of papers on the more important branches of biography and history',[125] an opinion
confirmed by a perusal of *Domesday Studies*, in which the papers were subsequently
published. Despite widespread interest among leading historians in the celebrations,
the lectures were mainly amateurish contributions by amateurs; but there were two of
value, both by Round. One was, typically, devoted in part to destroying a
misconception of Freeman's, the other was a brilliant exposition of Round's
fundamental belief that Domesday was a geld book.[126]

The personality of J.H. Round dominated medieval historical studies in the late
nineteenth and early twentieth centuries. He was a pupil of Stubbs, for whose work
he retained a lifelong admiration, but there were few other medieval historians

who escaped his powerful, venomous criticisms. His output was immense but fragmented, and he never wrote a complete history of the Norman Conquest, partly because of his persistent ill-health, partly because he feared to expose himself to the criticism of those with whom he had dealt so fiercely.[127] It was Round's staunch Toryism which initially led him into bitter conflict with Freeman, whose liberal, Germanist views about the origins of Parliament stood for all that Round despised. Round enjoyed attacking the works of others from a historical standpoint, but his campaign of vilification against Freeman became a political crusade as well as a scholarly duty.[128] Among the multitude of Freeman's supposed errors and misconceptions which Round criticized to an unfair extreme were his views on Domesday Book. Round mocked his ignorance of the *Inquisitio Comitatus Cantabrigiensis*, his failure to look at manuscripts, his confusion between Domesday and the geld rolls: 'In spite of [his] unquestionable enthusiasm, there is reason to doubt if Mr Freeman always understood his Domesday, and he did not, it may safely be said, advance our knowledge on the subject.'[129]

One of Round's great strengths was his proficiency as a genealogist, and he investigated numerous peerage and pedigree claims for the government.[130] He traced pedigrees with great skill and accuracy for the *Complete Peerage*, and vilified the many who made bogus claims to descent from the Domesday aristocracy. The editors of the rival *Burke's Peerage* and *Burke's Landed Gentry* were regularly the victims of his ire. He castigated them for the way in which, when compiling a fake pedigree for the Sneyd family, they had relied on the appearance of the names of Godwine and Wulfric in Domesday Book as sufficient proof of ancestry, although these were the English names most commonly found there. As for a chimerical pedigree of the Fitzgeralds, Round observed that it contained 'a gross blunder on the date of Domesday'.[131]

Round's exposition of what he believed were the origins of Domesday Book held sway almost universally for half a century. He developed the geld hypothesis of his 1886 paper at greater length in his *Feudal England*, published in 1895.[132] He saw the *Inquisitio Comitatus Cantabrigiensis* not only as providing the key to the formation of Domesday Book, but also as a record showing that the 'original returns' which were sent to Winchester were in the shape of great hundred rolls, now lost. They were arranged by hundreds and then villages, and were intended to provide the information for the new geld assessments. It was for that reason that the whole survey was produced, but such was the bulk of the rolls that they were then summarized into their Domesday forms, almost as an afterthought. This interpretation not only concentrates too narrowly on geld, but it also ignores much of the evidence of the *Inquisitio Eliensis* and of Exon Domesday. Nevertheless, such was Round's power of exposition that it was not until 1942 that it came under serious attack.[133]

Round's magisterial work as author and editor for many of the Domesday sections in the *Victoria County History* has stood the test of time far better than his explanation of Domesday's origins. The *VCH* was founded in 1899 and owed much of its early success to Round's support.[134] Although centrally planned and directed, it was divided into a series of volumes for each English county. A substantial section in each series was reserved for Domesday, which had 'elaborate and careful treatment … [in an] exposition by an expert'. The text was translated and was given an introduction dealing with points of interest and discussing land tenures; a detailed Domesday map was also included.[135] Round originally intended to write all the Domesday sections himself, but the amount of work required for each one, and his growing ill-health, forced him to abandon that idea. Between 1900 and 1908, however, he produced thirteen Domesday introductions, one in collaboration with L.F. Salzman, and edited all the accompanying translations, in some cases translating the text himself. He also edited a further eleven sections prepared by others. His unrivalled knowledge of topography and genealogy, his meticulously researched maps, his familiarity with the Domesday text, all gave his labours for the *VCH* a great and lasting value. With him worked some able editors, particu-larly James Tait and Frank Stenton, who themselves were to make important contributions to Domesday studies.[136]

1897 saw the publication of F.W. Maitland's *Domesday Book and Beyond*. Its author, a man of charming, liberal disposition, was a barrister by training. He had turned to legal history in the 1880s under the influence of P. Vinogradoff, a Russian who was an expert on English medieval villeinage and manorial society. Maitland became Downing professor of the laws of England at Cambridge in 1888 and then collaborated with Sir Frederick Pollock to write a masterly history of English law, which is still widely used. During its preparation, he worked on Domesday in some depth, but his findings were not included, and he then held back their publication until after the appearance of Round's *Feudal England*. Maitland was a Germanist by inclination: his sympathies and interests lay largely with the Anglo-Saxons, where Round's were with the Normans. But both men believed that Domesday was primarily a geld book, and in *Domesday Book and Beyond*, Maitland developed that idea with clarity, cogency and elegance.[137] The book consists of three essays on the plan and content of Domesday Book, on England before the Conquest, and on the hide. They represent a Germanist answer to the contentions of F. Seebohm that the English manor and English villeinage owe their origins to the Roman villa,[138] and, like Seebohm, Maitland worked backwards from thirteenth-century manorial records, through Domesday Book, to Anglo-Saxon laws and land-books. However, his work transcends the confines of narrow historical debate. It is at once a masterly analysis of the legal conceptions of Anglo-Saxon England, an explanation of how they operated in practical terms, and a guide to broad social developments.

Above all, Maitland brought a philosophical approach to his subject, which enabled him to determine the fundamental questions to ask of his evidence. It is that quality which has given *Domesday Book and Beyond* its place among the great works of historical scholarship.[139]

Soon after the book's publication, Maitland's belief that the manor was a unit of geld assessment and his emphasis on the military origins of the borough were challenged by Tait in a searching critique in the *English Historical Review*. Maitland took the unusual step of writing to thank him for the lucidity of his criticism, but after that he moved away from Domesday, confessing to R.L. Poole in 1900 that *Domesday Book and Beyond* was 'of all that I have written, that [which] makes me most uncomfortable. I try to cheer myself that I have given others a lot to contra-dict.'[140] He died in 1906 without ever returning to his exploration of Domesday.

Round's and Maitland's ideas have subsequently been questioned, developed and complemented by numerous historians, and the feudal and legal, as well as the fiscal, dimensions of Domesday Book have been explored.[141] New areas of Domesday studies have opened up, as, for example, in Professor H.C. Darby's *Domesday Geography of England*, which uses the survey as a source for historical geography.[142] Analysis of the Domesday text by computer[143] will complement Darby's work and will also suggest further new lines of research. One of the most disputed matters, however, remains the origins of Domesday Book. Round's thesis about the 'original returns' was accepted with some reservations until 1942, when a crucially important article by V.H. Galbraith, 'The making of Domesday Book', appeared in the *English Historical Review*. Further developed in his book of the same title, published in 1961, its central thesis was that Great Domesday represents the intended final stage of the survey, and Little Domesday, Exon and the 'satellites' its earlier stages. Galbraith, who was regius professor of modern history at Oxford from 1948 to 1957, had been an assistant keeper at the Public Record Office in the 1920s, but his interest in Domesday was a later development, stemming from his discovery of the manuscript of the Herefordshire Domesday in 1930. From there he went on not only to question Round's 'original returns' thesis, but also to attempt to place the survey in its administrative context.[144] His work left many areas unexplored and many paradoxes unexplained, but its implications are still being worked out.[145]

The existence of the Farley text and the photozincograph of Domesday Book enabled almost all of these studies to be carried out without recourse to the original. The manuscripts themselves meanwhile remained on display at the Public Record Office. From 1902, they were kept in the fine purpose-built museum constructed on the site of the Rolls Chapel, which had collapsed (perhaps, in view of its decrepit and highly flammable structure, with some assistance) during the building of what was

71. *The Public
Record Office
museum in the
early twentieth
century.*

to be the final block of the Record Office.[146] The glass and monuments were saved
and incorporated in the museum, which had Domesday Book, as its principal
exhibit, placed on the table in its centre.[147]

The year after the First World War began, the museum was closed, and early in
1918, there was considerable concern about the threat to its contents from bombing.
Sir Henry Maxwell-Lyte, the deputy keeper, therefore decided to have the most
valuable records taken to a place of safety. At first it was hoped that Domesday Book
could be lodged in the Post Office underground railway near Newgate Street, but
because accommodation there was not immediately available, it was decided instead
to send it to Bodmin Prison, already reserved as an emergency record store. Maxwell-
Lyte wrote that 'the sentimental value attached to Domesday Book is so great that we
are anxious to have it removed to a place of safety without further delay'.[148] The other
documents chosen for evacuation went to Cornwall by train and furniture van,
whereas Domesday was taken by C.G. Crump, an assistant keeper, in person.[149]
His colleague in charge of the records at the prison, A. Story Maskelyne,
telegrammed the Public Record Office on 20 February 1918, 'BOOK SAFE'.[150]
Conditions in the prison were acceptable during the summer months, but in the
winter the prison became very damp and, once the war had finished, existing plans to
return the records to London had to be expedited.[151] Domesday was among the last
to leave in February 1919, and, having been returned to the Record Office with the
requisite care, was soon on display in the museum once more.[152] The solemnity of its

ENTERTAINMENTS AT WHICH WE HAVE NEVER ASSISTED.
A READING FROM DOMESDAY BOOK AT THE RECORD OFFICE.

72. A satirical look at Domesday's custodians, from Punch, *1926.*

custodians and of their treatment of it is well satirized in a *Punch* cartoon of 1926.[153]

As Britain moved towards war in the 1930s, the security of the records again became a matter of concern. A new fireproof steel case was ordered for Domesday Book in 1937, into which it was carefully installed, but it did not remain there for long. In the summer of 1939, the museum was once more shut down and the documents from it were evacuated to the women's wing of Shepton Mallet Prison, Somerset, one of the Record Office's emergency storeplaces. A large-scale operation to move other documents was already under way and was not without its problems. Conditions on arrival were unsatisfactory, because the heating boilers at the prison did not at first operate adequately, and there were many leaking pipes in the building. Nor did the lorries used prove either watertight or mechanically reliable, and it was therefore decided to move Domesday Book and the other museum documents as a full military operation. They were packed in a container marked 'G' and, on 29

73. The women's wing of Shepton Mallet Prison, Somerset, during the Second World War.

Opposite:

74. Two Record Office officials, H.C. Johnson and R. Collie, with Domesday Book at Shepton Mallet Prison.

75. The Public Record Office in the Blitz, 1941.

August 1939, were transported under armed guard. The plan succeeded so well that the vehicle arrived early at Shepton Mallet and the guard and driver parked the lorry near the Market Cross and went off to a café, leaving Domesday Book unattended for half an hour. Later that day, however, L.C. Hector, the assistant keeper in charge, reported that the museum documents had arrived safely and had been duly unpacked.[154] In September 1939, Hector was replaced by H.C. Johnson, who, with the assistance of a repairer, looked after the record store until its final clearance in January 1946.[155] Although some bombs fell in the vicinity of the prison, the Treasury considered the site among the safest available,[156] and Domesday was certainly better protected there than at the Record Office, which in September 1940 lost its south-eastern turret in the Blitz.[157]

The museum documents, including Domesday Book, were returned to the Public Record Office on 26 July 1945, as soon as was safely possible. Domesday was on occasions brought out of store, to be shown to parties of Americans serving in the forces and to other visitors, until in September 1946 the museum reopened once again.[158] In 1952, however, the government made major cuts in civil service manpower and the deputy keeper, Sir Hilary Jenkinson, decided to close the museum rather than to impair the Record Office's statutory functions. His action was widely reported in the press and, as intended, created strong opposition. The *Sunday Graphic*, for example, complained that 'the museum you never knew about, a museum that tells the story of Britain's greatness, will remain unknown, unless you move fast. ... What have you missed seeing? The Domesday Book. ...'[159] In his *Report* for 1952, Jenkinson melodramatically stressed that the museum documents were suffering from poor ventilation and lack of cleaning due to the closure; he had been compelled to employ one man to wipe mildew from them each day.[160] In his

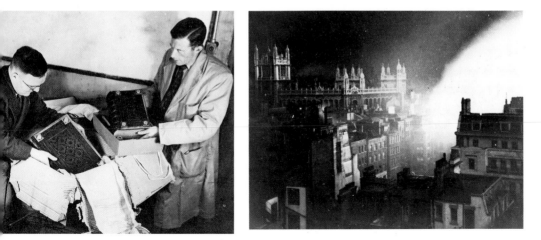

1953 *Report*, however, he had better news: staff numbers had been restored earlier in the year and there were plans to refurbish and reopen the museum.[161]

Meanwhile in August 1952, Jenkinson, who was nearing the end of his distinguished career, decided to have Domesday Book rebound once more. The volumes were gradually dismembered during August and September. The Record Office staff were interested in the anatomy of Domesday Book, its quires and their organization, the bindings and the writing; and careful, detailed research was done on both volumes in their unbound state, principally by Dr D.H. Gifford, as officer-in-charge of the museum, and by R.E. Ellis, as head of the conservation department. Leading Domesday scholars, including Galbraith and Stenton, were invited to view the manuscripts, an experience which they found highly rewarding, and the script was also carefully analysed by A. Fairbank.[162] In 1953, Domesday was rebound by T.E. Hassall between plain oak boards. There was some contemporary criticism of the thickness of the parchment guards and of the tightness of the sewing, but the results were generally well received.[163] The rebound volumes were then put on show to the public, Great Domesday with a selection of coronation documents in June 1953, Little Domesday in November. The museum was meanwhile being completely refurbished. New teak cases, lined with asbestos, were made for a redesigned display, among them a case specially constructed for Domesday which could be wound down to safety at night.[164] The museum was reopened in June 1956 and the display, with Domesday in its place against one wall, was to remain substantially unaltered until 1984.[165]

In August 1953, Jenkinson finished writing *Domesday Rebound*, a booklet which had been researched by several of the assistant keepers. In drawing their work together, he lost a number of valuable opportunities. Important preparatory work on Domesday's history had been carried out, but most of it was presented in a highly summarized form without adequate footnotes.[166] Nor was Jenkinson, who commented to a critic that he had written as an archivist rather than as a historian, prepared to commit himself on how the survey was made, even though he found room for self-conscious comments about Domesday in relation to modern bureaucratic practices.[167] However, the bulk of the booklet, analysing the make-up of the volumes, the material, the gatherings, rulings and earlier repair work, remains a vital tool for Domesday scholars.[168]

Since 1900, Domesday has on occasions been shown to those pursuing serious research, and rules about its custody and handling remain as strict in the twentieth century as they were in the sixteenth. However, the great majority of queries addressed to the Public Record Office about Domesday Book have been of a non-specialist nature, such as requests for information about people or places, or orders for

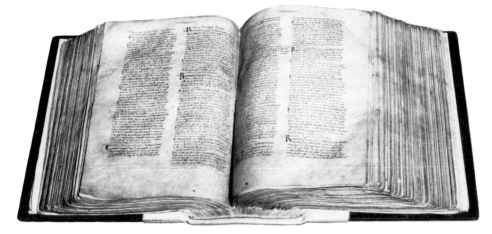

76. *Great Domesday as rebound in 1953.*

77. *Domesday Book in its case, 1956.*

reproductions of short sections. Others show emphatically that the Domesday myth has continued to flourish. One such inquiry, made in 1932 and reported by Jenkinson, is a good example: 'How much would it cost to have Domesday opened up? . . . I want to see it about a royal birth. . . . Oh, it took place about 1885. . . . But surely you keep it up to date?'[169]

As in earlier centuries, Domesday is still frequently quoted in error to lend spurious antiquity to objects or buildings. In 1919, for example, an oak tree at Great Yeldham, Essex, which was decaying and in urgent need of preservation, was said by *The Times* to have been mentioned in Domesday.[170] The name of Domesday is, moreover, still sometimes attached to other records. Thus in 1910, the Valuation Office was set up to levy duty on the appreciation of land values; the country was divided into valuation districts, for each of which income-tax schedules were collected as the basis of a survey and bound into volumes known as 'Domesday Books'.[171] Other general 'Domesday' surveys of various kinds have been proposed since then, as for example in 1931, 1958 and 1972.[172] The BBC's 'Domesday survey' of 1986 has created 'a people's database, [an] electronic Domesday Book to learn about Britain in the 1980s just as we today refer to the original Domesday Book in order to understand life in the years following the Norman Conquest'.[173]

In 1969, plans were laid for a new facsimile of Domesday Book and of the satellites with an introduction by Galbraith. Nothing came of the facsimile scheme, but Galbraith's introduction was published in 1974 as his second book on Domesday.[174] Subsequently, Domesday's text has become widely available in English through an edition launched by Phillimore in 1975. It contains the Farley edition and a new, simplified translation in parallel, each county being covered by one or two volumes. Some of the work on place-names and some of the notes and appendixes are of considerable value.[175] The 1986 anniversary is being celebrated with, *inter alia*, a de luxe Domesday published by Alecto Historical Editions. It includes a revised translation, based closely on the *Victoria County History* Domesday sections; new indexes of persons, places and subjects, generated by computer at the University of California at Santa Barbara; profuse and detailed maps; and scholarly introductions to the survey as a whole and to each county section. The *pièce de résistance* is a new facsimile using the latest photographic techniques, which will prove an invaluable aid to Domesday scholarship. To make that possible, the keeper of public records,[176] Dr G.H. Martin, decided in 1983 to have Domesday Book disbound once more. Research on the manuscripts was carried out under the direction of Dr H. Forde,[177] and the books were repaired and rebound in five parts by Mr F. Haynes, Mr D. Gubbins and Mr J. Abbott for display in 1986.

Although, in the nineteenth and twentieth centuries, Domesday Book has been notable chiefly as a museum piece of national importance and as a focus of scholarly research, its legal uses have not been extinguished. It still remains admissible evidence in a court of law,[178] and during the last two centuries has been cited for a great variety of purposes. Many are familiar from earlier periods. When, in 1773, the rector of Halton in Lancashire made a claim in the Exchequer for tithes from the estates of Halton Hall, one of the principal exhibits was 'a copy of part of the book called Domesday, kept in the Chapter House at Westminster'.[179] An extract from Domesday was also produced in a dispute over the tithes of Bradford on Avon, Wiltshire, heard in the Exchequer in 1792,[180] and in 1832, another was made for a case turning upon whether or not a lessee of the corporation of Northampton had the right to levy tolls on traffic passing through the town.[181] Although Domesday's

78. Three Domesday bindings: the Rivière trial binding, the 1953 binding and the 'Tudor' covers.

79. Model for the 1985 rebinding.

evidence was of little practical relevance in many such cases, the book remains the starting-point for any inquiry into ancient rights.

In 1832, Domesday was used in a case which was transferred from the summer assizes at Nottingham to the court of King's Bench, involving the allegedly felonious demolition of Nottingham Castle. Domesday proved unfavourable to the plaintiff, because it showed Nottingham as a borough outside the hundredal organization, but enough later evidence was found to show that it had subsequently come under the jurisdiction of Broxtowe hundred, and so to enable him to win substantial damages.[182] Domesday has also been cited in cases about the ownership of foreshore and river beds. For example, in a suit heard in Chancery in 1849–50, its evidence was taken to prove that, because it does not mention weirs on the seashore, they are therefore of right in private ownership.[183] In 1904, it was used to demonstrate that the ancestors of the duke of Beaufort had owned a fishery in the river Wye a little above Chepstow, although the duke had to produce other, later, evidence to show that he also owned the river bed. He thereby prevented the defendants from transporting stone from wharves they had built there.[184] Another ancient right, that of holding a market, was verified by Domesday evidence in 1958 in a rating case involving Taunton market and its method of valuation.[185]

Domesday Book was cited in a celebrated case in the House of Lords in 1902, to determine which peer should hold the title of lord great chamberlain.[186] The problem arose when, on the accession of King Edward VII, the earl of Ancaster, the marquess of Cholmondeley, and Lord Carrington all laid claim to the title, which brought with it the right to exercise various honorific functions at a coronation. A large amount of evidence was produced, amongst it an extract from Domesday listing the lands of Aubrey de Vere. It was certified by G.R. Handcock, an assistant keeper, who was required to attend the House of Lords on 28 January 1902 to attest its authenticity.[187] Although the extract was the earliest evidence of the family's English possessions to be presented, it was the grant of the office of the great chamberlain to a later Aubrey de Vere in 1133 which proved of greater interest. The House of Lords heard all the evidence, but was unable to decide which of the three families, all descended from co-heiresses of the Vere house, had the best claim, and the three lords were ordered to appoint a deputy or, if they could not reach agreement on that, to refer the matter to the king.[188]

After the abolition of fines and recoveries in 1833, the ancient-demesne courts lost their *raison d'être* and faded away, but memories of the tenure and its privileges have lingered. In 1860, representatives of the people of Aylesford, Kent, were brought to King's Bench for failing to pay their rates. They argued in defence that their lands were ancient demesne and as such were quit of tallages and taxes granted by Parliament unless specifically mentioned in fiscal legislation; the recent land-tax laws had made no mention of ancient demesne. The case went against them, on the grounds that the county rate was not an imprest granted by Parliament, but a local tax.[189] An attempt to revive a defunct ancient-demesne due was made in 1901. The lord of the manor of Rothley in Leicestershire claimed a customary payment for the transfer of a piece of land in an outlying part of the manor. He cited Domesday Book to prove that it was part of the manor and ancient demesne, but he was unsuccessful in his claim, on the grounds that villein custom had long since been extinguished at Rothley.[190] The Law of Property Act 1922 ruled that copyholds and customary tenures, including by implication those in ancient demesne, should be enfranchised and held as freeholds. But ancient-desmesne rights, together with those of the foreshore, were involved in a case heard in Queen's Bench Division in 1960. The matter at issue was whether the defendants could repair boats at a quay at Bosham. It was proved that Bosham was ancient demesne, and that its lord, the plaintiff, owned the right of foreshore. The defendants claimed their rights to freedom from tolls and other dues as privileged tenants of ancient demesne, and the tenure was discussed at some length and with some mystification, with Coke, Pollock and Maitland, and Vinogradoff among the authorities cited in court. Eventually, judgment went in favour of the lord of the manor, because the tenants, notwithstanding their privileges, were deemed to have no right to use the quay as their place of business.[191]

Despite the final disappearance of the ancient-demesne courts after 1833, the existence and purpose of two were still specifically mentioned in *Halsbury's Laws of England* in 1909. One was the Kingston upon Thames court, said to have been defunct since the early seventeenth century, the other 'is a court of ancient demesne for the levying of fines and recoveries of ancient demesne within the manor of Basingstoke'.[192] The second and third editions of the work changed the reference to Basingstoke to the past tense,[193] but when in the early 1970s proposals were made to abolish ancient feudal courts, it was among those investigated by the Law Commission. A number of the manorial and other courts were still flourishing, mainly for ceremonial purposes and for the management of various commons, for which they were allowed to retain their existence by the Administration of Justice Act 1977 (although their remaining jurisdictional functions were removed). The manorial court at Laxton in Northamptonshire was, indeed, preserved intact. By contrast, many other courts, including the Basingstoke court of ancient demesne, were found to have no remaining use,[194] and these were abolished in the 1977 Act. Ancient demesne has now become a matter only of minimal legal importance, but lawsuits involving ancient rights must still have reference to Domesday. In a case heard in Liverpool Crown Court in 1965, turning on whether or not a motor-car registration book is a public document, the judge discussed the interpretation which should be put on the expressions 'public document' and 'official document'.

Following *Halsbury's Laws*, he discussed surveys, assessments, inquiries and reports in that context. Tellingly he added that Halsbury 'refers to "records relating to Crown property and directly affecting the revenues of the Crown" as being within that category. This would include, for example, Domesday Book.'[195]

Such citations demonstrate that, even after nine centuries, Domesday Book may still be used for one of its original purposes: to investigate landholding and rights. Although much of its detailed information had already been superseded as early as the 1170s, and although the precise meaning of much of its terminology was no longer understood by the 1330s, it has never lost its place as the starting-point for certain legal inquiries. That status was sustained by the immutability of legal procedures, by Domesday's importance as proof of ancient-demesne tenure, and by Domesday's reputation, which spread far beyond the lawyers and administrators who alone, for many centuries, had access to the material which it contained.

There has, indeed, frequently been a considerable descrepancy between the reputation of Domesday Book and its reality. Its name has always been far better known than its contents. Thus, to some medieval landlords, it was the embodiment of their manorial rights, and yet, to some tenants, the symbol of future escape from burdensome services. Its investigation as a historical source began in the Elizabethan period and has continued ever since, but until recently, that understanding has not been disseminated beyond a very few, even within the educated élite. In consequence, Domesday has continued to be popularly endowed with the mythical quality of containing information universal in its scope. Another aspect of its reputation arose largely from its rebinding by the Victorians in a lavish style designed to emphasize its place as England's first and greatest public record. That opened the way for Domesday subsequently to be exhibited and admired by all as a relic of the past. Through its nine centuries, Domesday Book has therefore been seen in a multiplicity of guises: as a museum piece, as the focus of a myth, as a historical source, and as a working record. It is this very diversity of perspectives which continues to make it one of the most interesting and remarkable of all written records.

Notes

CHAPTER I, pages 11–31

1 *DB*, ii, f. 450; *EHD*, ii, 878.
2 D. Bates, *Normandy before 1066* (1982), pp. 73–85; D.C. Douglas, *William the Conqueror* (1964), pp. 31–80.
3 *ASC*, pp. 163–64.
4 E.M. Hallam, 'The king and the princes in eleventh-century France', *Bulletin of the Institute of Historical Research*, liii (1980), pp. 143–56, esp. pp. 152–53, 155–56.
5 Bates, *Normandy before 1066*, pp. 130–31; E.M. Hallam, 'Monasteries as "war memorials": Battle Abbey and La Victoire', *Studies in Church History*, xx (1983), pp. 47–57.
6 *ASC*, p. 163.
7 Hallam, 'Monasteries as "war memorials"', pp. 52–54.
8 Loyn, *Governance of Anglo-Saxon England*, pp. 118–22; Campbell, 'Observations'; Harvey, 'DB and its predecessors'; Clanchy, *Memory to Written Record*, pp. 11–17.
9 Warren, 'Norman efficiency'.
10 *ASC*, pp. 161–62.
11 Clanchy, *Memory to Written Record*, p. 18; below, pp. 32–34.
12 F.M. Stenton, *Anglo-Saxon England*, 2nd edn (Oxford, 1967), pp. 608–9; Douglas, *William the Conqueror*, pp. 346–47; R.A. Brown, *The Normans and the Norman Conquest* (1969), pp. 200–1.
13 Harvey, 'DB and Anglo-Norman governance', pp. 182–83.
14 *ASC*, p. 161.
15 M.T. Clanchy, *England and its Rulers, 1066–1272* (Douglas, 1983), pp. 63–64; R.H.C. Davis, 'The Norman Conquest', *History*, li (1966), pp. 279–86.
16 Harvey, 'DB and Anglo-Norman governance', pp. 183–84.
17 Douglas, *William the Conqueror*, pp. 355–56.
18 Galbraith, *Making of DB*, p. 77.
19 W.J. Corbett in *Cambridge Medieval History*, v (Cambridge, 1926), chapter XV, esp. pp. 507–15; Clanchy, *England and its Rulers*, pp. 63–64.
20 *ASC*, p. 161.
21 Galbraith, *Making of DB*, pp. 180–88.
22 Loyn, *Governance of Anglo-Saxon England*, pp. 94–130, 187–95; Campbell, 'Observations', pp. 39–41; C. Hart, *The Hidation of Northamptonshire* (Leicester, 1970); Galbraith, *Making of DB*, pp. 87–107.
23 R.S. Hoyt, 'A pre-Domesday Kentish assessment list' in P.M. Barnes and C.F. Slade, ed., *A Medieval Miscellany for D.M. Stenton*, Pipe Roll Soc., new ser., xxxvi (1962), pp. 189–202; Harvey, 'DB and its predecessors', pp. 755–56, 761–73; *DB*, i, ff. 379–82.
24 Harvey, 'DB and its predecessors', pp. 770–71; 'DB and Anglo-Norman governance', pp. 178–79.
25 Translated from Stevenson, p. 74.

26 Galbraith, 'Making of DB', pp. 66–67; R.W. Finn, *The Domesday Inquest . . .* (1961), pp. 81–
    88; H.R. Loyn, 'Domesday Book', *Procs. of the Battle Conf.*, i (Ipswich, 1979), pp. 121–30
    esp. pp. 126–27.

27 Darby, *Domesday England*, p. 7.

28 Loyn, *Governance of Anglo-Saxon England*, pp. 137–38; D. Roffe, 'The Lincolnshire Hundred',
    Landscape History, iii (1983), pp. 27–36; J. McDonald and G.D. Snooks, 'Were the tax
    assessments of Domesday Book artificial? The case of Essex', *Econ. Hist. Review*, 2nd ser.,
    xxxviii (1985), pp. 352–72. I am grateful to Professor Loyn for discussion of these matters.

29 Galbraith, *Making of DB*, pp. 123–36.

30 Ibid., pp. 136–42.

31 *EHD*, ii, 882. A number of other documents apparently related to these earlier stages of the
    Domesday survey have also survived in later copies and have generated much academic
    dispute: Harvey, 'DB and its predecessors'; 'DB and Anglo-Norman governance', pp. 175–
    80; Galbraith, *DB, Its Place . . .*, pp. 73–99; P.H. Sawyer, 'The Original returns and DB',
    EHR, lxx (1955), pp. 177–97; see also F. and C. Thorn, ed., *Domesday Book, Worcestershire*
    (Chichester, 1982), apps. iv–v.

32 Galbraith, *Making of DB*, pp. 140–42.

33 Douglas, *Feudal Documents*, introduction; Harvey, 'DB and its predecessors', p. 761, but cf.
    Galbraith, *DB, Its Place . . .*, pp. 76–78.

34 Fowler, 'Early Cambridgeshire feodary', pp. 442–43.

35 Finn, *Domesday Inquest*, pp. 92–111.

36 H. Clover and M. Gibson, ed., *The Letters of Lanfranc . . .* (Oxford, 1976), pp. 170–71; F.
    Barlow, 'Domesday Book: a letter of Lanfranc', *EHR*, lxxviii (1963), pp. 284–89.

37 P.H. Sawyer, review of *Making of DB . . .*, in *EHR*, lxxix (1964), pp. 101–5; F. and C. Thorn,
    ed., *Domesday Book, Devon*, i–ii (Chichester, 1985), notes on Exon Domesday. I would like
    to thank Mrs Thorn for valuable discussion of Exon Domesday. For the 'penultimate draft'
    view of the manuscript, see Galbraith, *Making of DB*, pp. 102–22; R.W. Finn, *Domesday
    Studies: The Liber Exoniensis* (1964), pp. 26–54, 157–58; *Domesday Inquest*, pp. 150–70.

38 N.R. Ker, *Medieval Manuscripts in British Libraries*, ii (Oxford, 1977), p. 807; Exeter Cathedral
    MS. 3500, f. 534v; Finn, *Liber Exoniensis*, p. 1.

39 Galbraith, *DB, Its Place . . .*, pp. 56–64; Finn, *Domesday Inquest*, pp. 173–78.

40 Harvey, 'DB and its predecessors', p. 770. I am grateful to Mr M. Gullick for information on the
    scribes.

41 Galbraith, *Making of DB*, esp. pp. 180–88; *DB, Its Place . . .*, pp. 47–56; *Domesday Rebound*, esp.
    pp. 35–38; Finn, *Domesday Inquest*, pp. 179–88. For a useful introduction, see Nicol,
    Domesday Book.

42 *Dialogus*, p. 31; I am grateful to Dr A. Williams for this reference.

43 R. Reed, 'Report on Domesday volumes', produced for Conservation Dept, PRO, in August
    1984; my thanks to Dr H. Forde for making the report available to me.

44 Galbraith, *Making of DB*, pp. 200–1; *Domesday Rebound*, pp. 22–24.

45 *Domesday Rebound*, pp. 24–29 and app. II.

46 Galbraith, *Making of DB*, pp. 8, 203–4.

47 Galbraith, *Making of DB*, pp. 29, 31; *Domesday Rebound*, pp. 29–31.

48 Ex inf. Dr H. Forde; below, p. 35.

49 E 403/193, m. 10.

50 E 31/3; *Domesday Rebound*, pp. 38–40 and plate VIII.

51 Below, p. 150 for its subsequent fate.

52 Below, pp. 150–51, 157–60, 170, 172.

53 W.G. Sinnigen and A.E. Boak, *A History of Rome to AD 565*, 6th edn (New York, 1967), pp. 73, 170, 271, 299, 445; St Luke, II, 1–3; G. Ostrogorsky, *History of the Byzantine State*, trans. J. Hussey (Oxford, 1968), pp. 40, 137, 188.

54 Campbell, 'Observations', p. 48; F. Ganshof, *The Carolingians and the Frankish Monarchy*, trans. J. Sondheimer (1971), pp. 130–32; E. Lesne, *Histoire de la propriété ecclésiastique en France*, iii (Lille, 1936), pp. 1–30.

55 Campbell, 'Observations', pp. 48–49; C.E. Perrin, *Recherches sur la seigneurie rurale en Lorraine* (n.p., 1935), pp. 3–90, 607, 614.

56 Campbell, 'Observations'.

57 G. Sivéry, 'La description du royaume de France par les conseillers de Philippe Auguste et par leurs successeurs', *Le Moyen Age*, xc (1984), pp. 65–84.

58 C.W. Hollister and J.W. Baldwin, 'The rise of administrative kingship: Henry I and Philip Augustus', *American Historical Review*, lxxxiii (1978), pp. 867–905.

59 F. Lot, 'L'état des paroisses et des feux de 1328', *Bibliothèque de l'École des Chartes*, xc (1929), pp. 51–107; E.M. Hallam, *Capetian France* (1980), pp. 286–88.

60 Bates, *Normandy before 1066*, p. 154; C.H. Haskins, *Norman Institutions* (Cambr., Mass., 1918), pp. 42–44.

61 D. Clementi, 'Notes on Norman Sicilian surveys', in Galbraith, *Making of DB*, pp. 55–58; A. Ahmed, *A History of Islamic Sicily* (Edinburgh, 1975), p. 66.

62 D.C. Douglas, *The Norman Achievement, 1050–1100* (1969), pp. 186–87; J. Riley-Smith, *The Feudal Nobility and the Kingdom of Jerusalem, 1174–1277* (1973), pp. 40–41, 58–59.

63 Translated from B. Guérard, ed., *Le Polyptique de l'abbé Irminon*, i (Paris, 1844), p. 25.

64 T. Hearne, *A Collection of the Curious Discourses written by eminent Antiquaries . . .*, i (1771), pp. lxii–lxiii.

CHAPTER II, pages 32–51

1 *Dialogus*, pp. 62–64.

2 Ibid., pp. xiv–xxii.

3 E 31/2, f. o.

4 E 36/266, f. 33.

5 E.g., IND 17176, ff. 91–93.

6 J. Stow, *Annales . . .*, continued by E. Howes (1631), p. 118; J.H. Round, 'The early custody of Domesday Book', *The Antiquary*, xv (1887), pp. 246–49; G.R.C. Davis, *Medieval Cartularies of Great Britain . . .* (1958), no. 45. My thanks to Professor C.N.L. Brooke for information about this cartulary.

7 R. Baker, *A Chronicle of the Kings of England*, 3rd edn (1660), p. 28.

8 R.A. Brown, 'The "treasury" of the later twelfth century', in J. Conway Davies, ed., *Studies presented to Sir Hilary Jenkinson* (Oxford, 1957), pp. 35–49; C.N.L. Brooke and G. Keir, *London, 800–1216: The Shaping of a City* (1975), p. 232.

9 Below, p. 56.

10 W.L. Warren, *King John* (1961), pp. 253–54.

11 *DB*, ii, f. 450; *Herefordshire Domesday*, p. xxv; T. Madox, ed., *Formulare Angicanum* (1702), p. 238.

12 *Herefordshire Domesday*, pp. xxv–vi.

13 Ibid., p. xxvi; *Reg R*, ii, no. 1000; *DB*, i, f. 332v (addition of *c*.1120–29); E. Searle, ed., *The Chronicle of Battle Abbey* (Oxford, 1980), pp. 48–49, 60–61.

14 *Reg R*, ii, nos. 1111, 1488, 1500, 1515; R.R. Darlington, ed., *The Cartulary of Worcester Cathedral Priory*, Pipe Roll Soc., new ser., xxxviii (1968), pp. 26–27; Hemming, i, 298.

15 E.g., G.F. Warner, ed., *Giraldi Cambrensis Opera*, RS, viii (1891), p. 316; *Plac. Abb.*, p. 22; *Rot. Cur. Reg.*, ii, 6; Round, *Feudal England*, p. 175.

16 *Ann. Mon.*, ii, 34.

17 *CRR*, x, 68; the name appears in the title of an early Abingdon survey but was almost certainly added by a later copyist: D.C. Douglas, 'Some early surveys from the abbey of Abingdon', *EHR*, xliv (1929), pp. 618–25.

18 Harvey, 'DB and its predecessors', pp. 766–67.

19 Hemming, i, 288, 298; F. and C. Thorn, ed., *Domesday Book, Worcestershire* (Chichester, 1982), app. V.

20 Douglas, 'Early surveys', p. 623; Harvey, 'DB and its predecessors', pp. 766–67.

21 Harvey, 'DB and its predecessors', p. 767.

22 Ibid., pp. 766–67.

23 Gransden, ii, 400, 490–91.

24 Harvey, 'DB and Anglo-Norman governance', pp. 176–77; W. de Gray Birch, ed., *Chronicles of Crowland Abbey* (Wisbech, 1883), pp. 140–41.

25 Below, pp. 42–47.

26 Above, pp. 16, 20.

27 Stevenson, p. 77.

28 *EHD*, ii, 130–31; M. Brett, 'John of Worcester and his contemporaries', in R.H.C. Davis and J.M. Wallace-Hadrill, ed., *The Writing of History in the Middle Ages ..., Essays ... to R.W. Southern* (Oxford, 1981), pp. 101–26.

29 Translated from B. Thorpe, ed., *Florentii Wigorniensis Monachi Chronicon ex Chronicis*, ii (1848), p. 18.

30 *ASC*, p. 161, note 6; above, p. 16.

31 F. Liebermann, *Ungedruckte anglo-normannische Geschichtsquellen* (1879), p. 21; *EHD*, ii, 853.

32 Translated from T. Arnold, ed., *The History of the English by Henry, Archdeacon of Huntingdon*, RS (1879), p. 207.

33 R. Howlett, ed., *Chronicles of the Reigns of Stephen, Henry II and Richard I*, RS, iv (1899), p. 44; Gransden, i, 199–200.

34 H.R. Luard, ed., *Matthaei Parisiensis Chronica Maiora*, RS, ii (1874), p. 18; Gransden, i, 356–79.

35 Translated from F. Madden, ed., *Matthei Parisiensis Historia Anglorum ...*, RS, i (1886), p. 27.

36 Ibid., iii (1869), p. 172.

37 Gransden, i, 367–72; R. Vaughan, *Matthew Paris* (Cambridge, 1958), pp. 139–60.

38 Below, pp. 122–23.

39 Below, chapters III–IV.

40 Galbraith, *DB, Its Place ...*, p. 100.

41 Harvey, 'DB and Anglo-Norman governance', p. 193.

42 Warren, 'Norman efficiency', p. 128.

43 Richardson and Sayles, pp. 28–29.

44 Clanchy, *Memory to Written Record*, pp. 18–21.

45 Below, pp. 172–76.

46 J. Green, 'William Rufus, Henry I and the royal demesne', *History*, lxiv (1976), pp. 337–52, esp. p. 339; C.F. Slade, ed., *The Leicestershire Survey, c. AD 1130* (Leicester, 1956); Round, *Feudal England*, pp. 149–59, 175–81, 196–214.

47 *DB*, i, ff. 332v–333; G.F. Jensen, 'The Domesday Book account of the Bruce fief', *The English Place-Name Society Journal*, ii (1968–69), pp. 8–17.

48 M. Biddle, ed., *Winchester in the Early Middle Ages . . . The Winton Domesday* (Oxford, 1976), pp. 9–10.

49 F.R.H. du Boulay, *The Lordship of Canterbury* (1966), pp. 42–43; D.C. Douglas, *Time and the Hour* (1977), p. 230.

50 Fowler, 'Early Cambridge feodary'; BL Sloane MS. 986, f. 67.

51 E.g., lists from Peterborough and Shaftesbury Abbeys: Douglas, *Feudal Documents*, p. lxxxi; Round, *Feudal England*, pp. 175–81; BL Harl. MS. 61, ff. 37–76v.

52 Douglas, *Feudal Documents*; Galbraith, *DB, Its Place . . .*, pp 76–78; Harvey, 'DB and its predecessors', p. 761.

53 D.C. Douglas, ed., *The Domesday Monachorum of Christ Church Canterbury* (1944), pp. 1–33, 81–98; cf. Galbraith, *DB, Its Place . . .*, pp. 79–84; cf. Harvey, 'DB and its predecessors', pp. 756–59.

54 A. Ballard, ed., *An Eleventh Century Inquisition of St Augustine's Canterbury*, British Academy, Records of Soc. and Econ. Hist., iv (1920), pt II.

55 Douglas, 'Early surveys'; Round, *Feudal England*, pp. 142–46; Harvey, 'DB and its predecessors', pp. 759–60.

56 W. Hunt, ed., *Two Chartularies of the Priory of St Peter at Bath*, Som. Rec. Soc. Publs., vii (1893), pp. 67–68; R.V. Lennard, 'A neglected Domesday satellite', *EHR*, lviii (1943), p. 32; Galbraith, *DB, Its Place . . .*, pp. 88–91; Harvey, 'DB and its predecessors', pp. 760–61.

57 P.H. Sawyer, ed., 'Evesham "A", a Domesday text', *Worcestershire Hist. Soc., Miscellany*, i (1960), pp. 3–36; Galbraith, *DB, Its Place . . .*, pp. 84–88; Round, *Feudal England*, pp. 169–80.

58 F. Barlow, *William Rufus* (1983), pp. 233–34; Galbraith, *Making of DB*, pp. 141–42.

59 *Reg R*, i, no. 387; Round, *Feudal England*, pp. 308–14; R.W. Southern, *Medieval Humanism and Other Studies* (Oxford, 1970), pp. 193–94.

60 V.H. Galbraith, 'Notes on the career of Samson, bishop of Worcester (1098–1112)', *EHR*, lxxxii (1967), pp. 86–101, esp. pp. 93–97; Barlow, *William Rufus*, pp. 235–36.

61 Hemming, i, 287–88, 298–316.

62 Galbraith, *DB, Its Place . . .*, pp. 109–11.

63 Cf. also BL Loans MS. 30, f. 10; W. Wrottesley, ed., 'The Burton Cartulary', *William Salt Archeological Soc. Collections . . .*, pt I, v (1884), pp. 7–8.

64 Below, p. 42.

65 *Herefordshire Domesday*, p. xxv; V.H. Galbraith, 'Royal charters to Winchester', *EHR*, xxxv (1920), pp. 382–400, nos. X, XII.

66 *Reg R*, ii, no. 468 (and no. LXXX).

67 Harvey, 'DB and Anglo-Norman governance', pp. 183–84.

68 *Reg R*, ii, no. 1500; *Herefordshire Domesday*, p. xxvii.

69 *Reg R*, ii, nos. 1488, 1515; *Herefordshire Domesday*, p. xxvii.

70 *Reg R*, ii, nos. 976, 1887; *Herefordshire Domesday*, p. xxvii; Hemming, i, 298.

71 R.R. Darlington, ed., *The Cartulary of Worcester Cathedral Priory*, Pipe Roll Soc., new ser., xxxviii (1968), pp. 26–27.

72 *Reg R*, ii, no. 1000; *Herefordshire Domesday*, p. xxvi; J.H. Stevenson, ed., *Chronicon Monasterii de Abingdon*, RS, ii (1858), pp. 115–17; cf. Harvey, 'DB and Anglo-Norman governance', p. 179.

73 *Plac. Abb.*, p. 22; *Rot. Cur. Reg.*, ii, 6.

74 *CRR*, i, 263.

75 Translated in Galbraith, *DB, Its Place . . .*, p. 102, from H. Ellis, ed., *Original Letters Illustrative of English History*, 3rd ser. (1846), pp. 26–27; BL Roy. MS. 6.C.XI, f. 276v.

76 *CRR*, x, 68.

77 *Herefordshire Domesday*, esp. pp. xxi–iv, xxxi–ii.

78 Galbraith, *DB, Its Place . . .*, p. 111.

79 BL Cott. MS. Vitell. C.VIII, ff. 143–56.

80 Collation of the texts of the abbreviations and of the Kentish roll has been carried out by Dr T. Chalmers. I am grateful to him for providing me with this information.

81 E 36/284; *New Paleographical Society Publications*, first ser., ii (1912), plate 240.

82 E 36/284, f. 20.

83 *CChR*, i, 259; *GEC*, x, 800–6.

84 Below, p. 51.

85 R.A. Brown *et al.*, ed., *The History of the King's Works, I, The Middle Ages*, i (1963), pp. 127–47.

86 BL Arundel MS. 153.

87 E 164/1.

88 Galbraith, *Making of DB*, pp. 109–11.

89 F.G. Cowley, *The Monastic Order in South Wales, 1066–1349* (Cardiff, 1977), pp. 196–97.

90 *GEC*, ii, 699–702.

91 Ibid., pp. 702–8.

92 C.A. Seyler, 'The early charters of Swansea and Gower', *Archeologia Cambrensis*, lxxix (1924), pp. 68–78. I am grateful to Dr D. Crouch for discussion of the Breviate.

93 *ASC*, p. 163.

94 Harvey, 'DB and Anglo-Norman governance', pp. 184–85; Southern, *Medieval Humanism*, pp. 186–97; Barlow, *William Rufus*, pp. 237–40; Warren, 'Norman efficiency', p. 131.

95 Harvey, 'DB and Anglo-Norman governance', p. 184; Warren, 'Norman efficiency', p. 131; cf. Barlow, *William Rufus*, pp. 137–40.

96 Harvey, 'DB and Anglo-Norman governance', pp. 184–85; Southern, *Medieval Humanism*, pp. 191–93; *ASC*, p. 176; cf. Barlow, *William Rufus*, pp. 238–39.

97 Barlow, *William Rufus*, pp. 233–34.

98 Green, 'William Rufus, Henry I and the royal demesne', p. 348.

99 W.L. Warren, *Henry II* (1973), pp. 275–81.

100 H. Maxwell-Lyte, ed., *The Book of Fees commonly called the Testa de Neville*, 3 vols. (1920–31).

101 I am grateful to Professor W.L. Warren for suggesting this point.

102 I would like to thank Dr D.Crouch for discussion of these matters.

103 J. Green, 'The last century of Danegeld', *EHR*, xcvi (1981), pp. 241–58; Warren, 'Norman efficiency', pp. 128–31.

104 Green, 'Danegeld' p. 254; A.L. Poole, *From Domesday Book to Magna Carta, 1087–1216*, 2nd edn (1955), p. 418.

105 I am grateful to Professor W.L. Warren for suggesting this point.

106 Below, pp. 74–76.

107 Mitchell, *Taxation*, pp. 321–57.

108 H.M. Cam, *Liberties and Communities in Medieval England* ... (Cambridge, 1944), pp. 174–75; Sutherland, *Quo Warranto*, pp. 6–7.

109 E.g., *CCR, 1242–47*, p. 242; JUST 1/174, mm. 30–39.

110 Cam, *Liberties*, p. 175; Sutherland, *Quo Warranto*, pp. 82–83.

111 E.g., JUST 1/229, m. 19.

112 Cam, *Liberties and Communities*, p. 175.

113 *CLibR*, iv, 282; below, app. IV, no. 1.

114 E 159/41, m. 4. I would like to thank Dr D. Carpenter for this reference.

115 *CChR*, ii, 18, 20; E 368/35, m. 3. I am grateful to Dr D. Carpenter for this reference.

116 DL 25/2266. I am grateful to Professor J.C. Holt for this reference. See also M. Altschul, *A Baronial Family in Medieval England: The Clares, 1217–1314* (Baltimore, 1965), p. 99.

117 Below, pp. 74–76.

118 Translated from JUST 1/1046, m. 23.

119 Below, pp. 100–105.

120 H.G. Richardson and G.O. Sayles, ed., *Select Cases of Procedure without Writ under Henry III*, Selden Soc., lx (1941), pp. 91–92.

CHAPTER III, pages 52–73.

1 Below, pp. 96–97, 100.

2 Below, pp. 105–9

3 Adapted from the translation of BL Cott. MS. Tib.C.IX, f. 195 by I. Taylor, 'On the study of Domesday Book', *DS*, i, 5.

4 BL Egerton MS. 2735, f. 158v; J.D. Martin, ed., *The Cartularies and Registers of Peterborough Abbey*, Northants Rec. Soc. (1978), pp. 13–14.

5 C. Harper-Bill, ed., *Blythburgh Priory Cartulary*, i, Suffolk Rec. Soc. (1980), p. 243.

6 Bodl. MS. Gough Cambs 22, f. 10.

7 BL Add. MS. 43405, f. iib.

8 J.M. Guilding, ed., *Reading Records: Diary of the Corporation*, i (1892), p. 18.

9 BL Egerton MS. 2788, ff. 8–9v.

10 R.R. Sharpe, ed., *Calendar of Letter Books ... of the City of London, Letter Book K* (1911), p. 87.

11 D.H. Willis, ed., *The Estate Book of Henry de Bray* ..., Camden 3rd ser., xxvii (1916); J.S. Davies, ed., *The Tropenell Cartulary*, i (Devizes, 1908), p. 5. My thanks to Dr P.A. Brand for the first reference.

12 H.C. Hamilton, ed., *Chronicon Domini Walteri de Hemingburgh*, i (1848), pp. 17–18; above, p. 36.

13 *Ann. Mon.*, iii, 426; Gransden, ii, 390–91; *DB*, i, f. 30.

14 *Ann. Mon.*, iii, 347.

15 Gransden, ii, 490–91; W.G. Searle, *Ingulf and the Historia Croylandensis*, Cambridge Antiq. Soc. (1894), pp. 7–12.

16 J. Leland, ed., *Joannis Rossi Antiquarii Warwicensis Historia Anglorum* (Oxford, 1745), pp. 107–9; Gransden, ii, 308–27.

17 R. Stewart-Brown, 'The Domesday roll of Chester', *EHR*, xxxvii (1922), pp. 481–500.

18 W.H. Hale, ed., *The Domesday of St Paul's*, Camden Soc., lxix (1858).

19 C.H.E. White, ed., *The Great Domesday Book of Ipswich* ... (Ipswich, 1885).

20 *DB*, i, f. 197; *Cal. IPM*, viii, 75–78.

21 L.O. Pike, ed., *Year Books of ... Edward the Third, Years XIV and XV*, RS (1899), p. 346.

22 Below, pp. 95–99.

23 Palgrave, *Kalendars and Inventories*, ii, 316.

24 Powell, *Repertorie*, pp. 15, 17.

25 C 81/22, no. 2207; J. Topham, ed., *Liber Quotidianus* ..., SAL (1787), p. 69.

26 BL Add. MS. 7966, f. 2v.

27 CP 40/148, m. 164. I am grateful to Dr P.A. Brand for this reference.

28 Translated from W. Stubbs, ed., *Chronicles of the Reigns of Edward I and Edward II*, RS, i (1882), p. 286.

29 E 163/16/83; dated by E 5/30/5; E 5/41/7; (ex inf. Miss M. Condon and Dr R. Ball).

30 AO 1/865/1.

31 Williams, 'Peter le Neve', p. 127.

32 *Rot.Parl.*, ii, 314.

33 E.g., E 36/266, ff. 60, 62, 70–75v.

34 Sainty, *Officers*, pp. 164–77.

35 J.C. Tingey, ed., *The Records of the City of Norwich*, ii (1910), p. 51.

36 E 314/84, no. 26; cf. CROH, GBR, box 1, bundle 13 (the first reference ex inf. Miss M. Condon).

37 E.g., BL Add. MS. 40725 (Blythburgh cartulary), f. i.

38 Below, app. IV, no. 6.

39 IND 17175, opposite f. 1; below, p. 129.

40 Below, p. 64.

41 E. Henderson, *Foundations of English Administrative Law* (Cambr. Mass., 1963), pp. 83–89; S.A. de Smith, 'The prerogative writs', *Cambridge Law Journal*, xi (1953), pp. 40–56.

42 Cf., e.g., below, app. I, no. 5.

43 Below, app. I, no. 211.

44 E 36/266, f. 96v.

45 Below, app. I, no. 70.

46 *DB*, i, f. 65.

47 Below, app. I, no. 9.

48 E.g., CP 40/161, m. 82d (ex inf. Dr P. Brand).

49 Below, app. I, no. 182.

50 Below, app. I, nos. 189–211.

51 Below, app. I, no. 208.

52 Below, pp. 115–17.

53 Printed in Powell, *Repertorie of Records*, p. 132.

54 F. Taylor, ed., 'An early seventeenth-century calendar of records preserved in Westminster palace treasury', *Bulletin of the John Rylands Library*, xxiii (1929), p. 115.

55 E 368/412, m. 33d.

56 Below, p. 134.

57 E 101/337/13.

58 SP 46/139, f. 12; below, p. 152.

59 I am grateful to Mr G. Stanley for his research on the uses of the exemplifications which are listed below in appendix I.

60 CROH, GBR, charters, no. 13; *DB*, i, f. 203v.

61 Below, app. I, nos. 40, 136.

62 H.R. Salter, ed., *Munimenta Civitatis Oxonie* (Devizes, 1920), p. 285.

63 E.g., below, app. I, no. 37.

64 H.C. Maxwell-Lyte, *Historical Notes on the Use of the Great Seal of England* (1926), p. 336.

65 Ibid., p. 283.

66 Although cf. E 101/213/2 and below, app. I, nos. 58, 66–75; E 101/216/12 and below, app. I, no. 165.

67 Listed below in appendix I.

68 Maxwell-Lyte, p. 365.

69 C 66/207, m. 4.

70 C 135/134/4; *Cal. IPM*, x, 262–66.

71 C 44/2/12, nos. 1–7; *DB*, i, f. 299; KB 27/381, rex m. 17; *CCR, 1354–60*, p. 361.

72 E.g., KB 27/309, m. 35d (1337); KB 145/3/10/1, 16 November 1386 (extract enrolled on KB 27/503, m. 62).

73 KB 27/317, m. 78. I am grateful to Dr N.A.M. Rodger for his research on plea roll entries where Domesday Book is cited.

74 KB 27/207, m. 82.

75 Taylor, p. 115.

76 LR: 1 Salk 57.

77 Darby, *Domesday England*, pp. 195–201; *DB*, i, ff. 51–51v.

78 C.R. Young, *The Royal Forests of Medieval England* (Leicester, 1979), pp. 136–41.

79 Below, app. III, no. 1 (ex inf. Miss M. Condon).

80 Ibid., no. 2 and nos. 3–6.

81 BL Add. MS. 7666, f. 2v.

82 *CCR, 1313–18*, pp. 272–74; Young, pp. 143–44.

83 C 47/12/11, mm. 1–2, 4–9.

84 *RH*, i, 840.

85 Below, app. I, no. 19; KB 27/309, m. 35 and 3 schedules; *DB*, i, ff. 154v, 155v, 158.

86 SP 14/94, ff. 182–83; *VCH, Essex*, vii, 11–17, 31–39, 64–72.

87 *VCH, Essex*, vii, 18–19. I would like to thank Dr W.R. Powell for generously providing the material about this incident.

88 Below, app. I, no. 1; *CPR, 1266–72*, p. 100; *DB*, i, f. 280; *VCH, Notts*, ii, 93.

89 CP 40/207, m. 298; *DB*, i, f. 207v.

90 W.C. Bolland, ed., *Year Books of Edward II*, Selden Soc., xviii (1920), pp. 179–91.

91 *Rot. Parl.*, ii, 70–71; *CCR, 1333–37*, pp. 92, 232, 271; E 159/110, m. 124; *VCH, Lincs*, ii, 112; *Feudal Aids Preserved in the Public Record Office* ..., iii (1904), p. 213; below, app. I, no. 30; *DB*, i, 346v.

92 *CCR, 1330–33*, p. 480; *Cal. Inq. Misc., 1307–48*, no. 1313; below, app. I, no. 13; *DB*, i, f. 104.

93 New College, Oxford, MSS. 3277, 3280; *DB*, i, ff. 143v, 149.

94 H. Wood, *A Collection of Decrees by the Court of Exchequer in Tithe Causes* ..., i (1798), pp. 27–30; *DB*, i, f. 89v.

95 Listed below in apps. I and II.

96 Below, app. I, no. 202.

97 *VCH, Worcs*, iii, 114; C 66/1264, mm. 30–31.

98 SP 46/186/88; *DB*, i, f. 255v. I am grateful to Dr N. Fuidge for the first reference.

99 *Rot. Parl.*, ii, 91.

100 E 159/113, m. 156; G.O. Sayles, ed., *Select Cases in the Court of King's Bench under Edward III*, Selden Soc., v (1958), pp. 97–101; *CCR, 1337–39*, p. 122; *DB*, i, f. 253.

101 Fragment detached probably from E 13/58 (ex inf. Miss M. Condon).

102 *CCR, 1343–46*, pp. 201, 321; *Cal. IPM*, viii, no. 271; *DB*, i, f. 356.

103 *CPR, 1334–38*, pp. 195, 222; *1338–40*, pp. 156–57; *CCR, 1337–39*, p. 322; below, app. I, no. 17; *DB*, i, f. 144v.

104 Above, note 70.

CHAPTER IV, pages 74–113

1 E. Coke, *A Second Part of the Institutes of the Laws of England*, ed. C. Hargrave and H. Butler (1797), p. 542.

2 P. Vinogradoff, *Villeinage in England* (Oxford, 1892), p. 92.

3 Ibid., pp. 94, 105–7; F. Pollock and F.W. Maitland, *The History of English Law . . .*, 2nd edn (Cambridge, 1911), i, 385–86.

4 Vinogradoff, *Villeinage*, pp. 101–5; Pollock and Maitland, i, 388–89.

5 F.W. Maitland, ed., *Select Pleas in Manorial and other Seignorial Courts*, Selden Soc. (1889), pp. 99–129; J. Baigent and J. Millar, ed., *History of Basingstoke* (1889), pp. 221–70; below, pp. 112–13, 175.

6 S.E. Thorne, ed., *Bracton on the Laws and Customs of England*, ii (1968), pp. 37–38.

7 Pocock, *Ancient Constitution*, pp. 33–41; below, p. 123.

8 Below, pp. 165–66.

9 R.S. Hoyt, *The Royal Demesne in English Constitutional History, 1066–1272* (New York, 1950), pp. 171–207.

10 Ibid., p. 192.

11 M.K. McIntosh, 'The privileged villeins of the ancient demesne', *Viator*, vii (1976), pp. 275–328. I am grateful to Professor McIntosh for allowing me to read the typescript of part of her new history of Havering.

12 M.A. Barg, 'The villeins of the ancient demesne', *Studi in Memoria di Federigo Melis*, i (Rome, 1978), pp. 213–37.

13 Hoyt, *Royal Demesne*, pp. 134–70, esp. p. 162.

14 P.R. Hyams, *Kings, Lords and Peasants . . .* (Oxford, 1980), pp. 246–48.

15 Ibid., pp. 63–65, 247–48; McIntosh, 'Privileged villeins'.

16 R.H. Hilton, ed., *The Stoneleigh Leger-Book* (Oxford, 1960), pp. xxiv–xxviii.

17 *RH*, ii, 46; Barg, 'Villeins', p. 219; B. Schumer, *The Evolution of Wychwood to 1400: Pioneers, frontiers and forests* (Leicester, 1984), pp. 46–47; above, chapter III, note 85.

18 McIntosh, 'Privileged villeins', p. 325.

19 Barg, 'Villeins', p. 214; Pollock and Maitland, pp. 393–94, 397; below, pp. 109–10.

20 P. Brand, '"Quo waranto" law in the reign of Edward I . . .', *The Irish Jurist*, new ser., xiv (1979), pp. 124–72, esp. pp. 133–42, 146, 168. I am grateful to Dr Brand for his advice on these matters.

21 Sutherland, *Quo Warranto*, pp. 15–32, 167; H. Cam, *The Hundred and the Hundred Rolls* (1930), p. 28.

22 E.g., Branscombe, Devon: *RH*, i, 68; Barg, 'Villeins', p. 219; *DB*, i, f. 102.

23 E.g., Stonesfield and Combe, Oxon; above, note 17.

24   R.H. Hilton, 'Peasant movements in England before 1381', *Econ. Hist. Review*, 2nd ser., ii
     (1949), pp. 117–36, esp. pp. 122–30.

25   *Plac. Abb.*, p. 185; *DB*, i, f. 43.

26   *Plac. Abb.*, p. 197; *DB*, i, ff. 288–89.

27   *Plac. Abb.*, p. 270; Vinogradoff, *Villeinage*, p. 9; *DB*, i, f. 101.

28   Barg, 'Villeins', p. 223.

29   Below, app. I, no. 7.

30   Z. Razi, 'The struggles between the abbots of Halesowen and their tenants . . .', in T.H. Aston
     et al., ed., *Essays in Honour of R.H. Hilton* (Cambridge, 1983), pp. 151–67.

31   BL Loans MS. 29/55, ff. 1–7v (1272); below, app. I, nos. 3–4 (1275–76).

32   D.G. Watts, 'Peasant discontent on the manors of Titchfield Abbey, 1245–1405', *Proc. Hants
     Field Club and Arch. Soc.*, xxxix (1983), pp. 121–35.

33   Mitchell, *Taxation*, pp. 358–99.

34   T. Madox, *Firma Burgi* (1726), pp. 61–62.

35   E 159/118, mm. 260–61; *DB*, i, f. 162v.

36   G.L. Harriss, *King, Parliament and Public Finance . . .* (Oxford, 1975).

37   J.F. Willard, 'Taxation boroughs and parliamentary boroughs, 1294–1336' in J.G. Edwards
     et al., ed., *Historical Essays in Honour of James Tait* (Manchester, 1933), pp. 417–35, esp. p. 418.

38   R.S. Hoyt, 'Royal demesne, parliamentary taxation and the realm', *Speculum*, xxiii (1948), pp.
     58–69.

39   J.F. Willard, *Parliamentary Taxes on Personal Property, 1290–1334* (Cambr. Mass., 1934), p. 10;
     cf. R.B. Pugh, 'England's earliest gazetteer?', *Bulletin of the Institute of Historical Research*, li
     (1978), pp. 113–23.

40   E 159/14, m. 11.

41   E 368/89, m. 41.

42   Below, app. I, no. 29; *CCR, 1343–46*, p. 289; *RH*, i, 49–50; *DB*, i, f. 273v.

43   E 159/120, mm. 162–64.

44   Ibid., m. 164.

45   C. Oman, *The Great Revolt of 1381*, ed. E. Fryde (Oxford, 1969), pp. 22–31.

46   Below, app. I, nos. 58–80. I am grateful to Professor McIntosh for this suggestion.

47   M. Morgan, *The English Lands of the Abbey of Bec* (Oxford, 1946), pp. 105–6; KB 27/207, m. 82;
     VCH, Wilts, iii, 394–96; xii, 138–60; *DB*, i, ff. 65v, 71 and cf. f. 74.

48   Morgan, pp. 107–9; below, app. I, nos. 22, 134; *VCH, Wilts*, xii, 146, 156.

49   Below, app. I, nos. 37–52.

50   Among the massive literature on the subject, see most recently, R.H. Hilton and T.H. Aston,
     ed., *The English Rising of 1381* (Cambridge, 1984).

51   Faith, 'The "Great Rumour" of 1377', ibid., pp. 43–73. I am grateful to Dr Faith for allowing
     me to see the article in typescript and for discussion of these matters. See also J.H. Tillotson,
     'Peasant unrest in the reign of Richard II', *Historical Studies*, xvi (1974), pp. 1–16.

52   *Rot. Parl.*, iii, 21–22. Translation quoted from R.B. Dobson, *The Peasants' Revolt of 1381*, 2nd
     edn (1981), pp. 76–78.

53   Below, app. I, nos. 58–78 *et passim*. See also E 101/213/2–3 (hanaper accounts); Faith, pp. 71–
     73.

54   Faith, pp. 52–54.

55   Faith, pp. 60–62; B.H. Putnam, ed., *Proceedings before the Justices of the Peace in the Fourteenth and
     Fifteenth Centuries* (1938), pp. 385–86.

56 Tillotson, pp. 5–8; I am grateful to Dr E. Powell for discussion of these matters.

57 *CPR, 1377–81*, p. 20; SC 8/63/3142.

58 *CPR, 1377–81*, pp. 204, 251; SC 8/103/5106.

59 Below, app. I, no. 78.

60 *CPR, 1377–81*, p. 251; Tillotson, p. 7.

61 Tillotson, pp. 7–8.

62 Faith, pp. 54–58.

63 G.R. Owst, *Literature and the Pulpit in Medieval England*, 2nd edn (1961), pp. 294–302.

64 Faith, pp. 63–68; cf. below, app. I, no. 12 (probably obtained by the abbot).

65 Below, app. I, no. 104.

66 I.S. Leadam and J.F. Baldwin, ed., *Select Cases before the King's Council*, Selden Soc. (Cambr., Mass., 1918), pp. ciii–civ, 82–85.

67 Below, app. I, no. 119.

68 N.S.B. Gras, *The Early English Customs System* (Cambr., Mass., 1918), pp. 25–26.

69 CP 40/68, m. 1d (ex inf. Dr P. Brand); KB 27/194, m. 94.

70 I.D. Thornley and T.F.T. Plucknett, ed., *Year Books of Richard II: 11 Richard II* (1937), pp. 175–82; H.J. Hanham, 'A tangle untangled; the lordship and manor of Ashburton', *Devon Assoc. Trans.*, xciv (1962), pp. 440–57; my thanks to Dr D. Bates for the second reference.

71 J.A. Raftis, *A Small Town in Medieval England: Godmanchester, 1278–1400* (Toronto, 1982).

72 CROH, GBR, charters, nos. 1–7. I would like to thank Mr A.D. Hills for discussion of the Godmanchester records.

73 *RH*, i, 198; *PQW*, p. 296.

74 JUST 1/348, m. 10.

75 CROH, GBR, boxes 2, 5–9.

76 E.g., E 179/122/4, 8, 9.

77 *CCR, 1360–64*, pp. 183–84, 338.

78 CROH, GBR, box I, bundle 7, 11 February 1365.

79 Ibid., charters, nos. 8–9.

80 SC 8/176/8761.

81 CROH, GBR, charters, nos. 10–11; *CChR, 1341–1417*, p. 327; C 81/532, no. 7909.

82 Below, app. I, no. 141; CROH, GBR, charters, no. 13, illustrated above, p. 63. The date is confirmed by the attestation of the letters patent by John Frank, who also attested enrolments on the chancery rolls between 1415 and 1435: PRO card index of Chancery clerks.

83 CROH, GBR, charters, no. 15; *CCR, 1422–29*, p. 287.

84 E 368/203, Recorda, Hil, m. 8 (ex inf. Miss M. Condon).

85 CROH, GBR, charters, nos. 16–21.

86 E 134/24/ 5 Charles II/Hil 9 (ex inf. Dr D. Crook).

87 Below, app. I, no. 180; *CPR, 1476–85*, p. 190.

88 A. Everitt, 'The market town', in P. Clark, ed., *The Early Modern Town* (1976), pp. 168–204, esp. pp. 195–98.

89 Below, app. I, nos. 192, 195; *CPR, 1572–75*, p. 76; *CPR, 1575–78*, p. 351.

90 LR: 2 Leo 190; cf. Cro. Eliz. 227.

91 *Records of the Borough of Nottingham, II, 1399–1485* (Nottingham, 1883), pp. 349–59.

92 NRO DDP 7/2 (all references to material about Clipstone, Warsop and Mansfield ex inf. Dr D. Crook).

93 D. Crook, 'Clipstone park and peel', *Trans. Thoroton Soc.*, lxxx (1976), pp. 35–46.

94 *Cal. IPM*, viii, 1, no. 2.

95 Below, note 117.

96 NRO DDP 7/2; below, note 117.

97 W. Blackstone, *Tracts chiefly relating to the Antiquities and Laws of England*, 3rd edn (Oxford, 1771), pp. 199–240.

98 R.J. Robson, *The Oxfordshire Election of 1754* (Oxford, 1949), p. 144.

99 Ibid., pp. 141–45; *LJ*, xxvii, 291–92.

100 D. Crook, 'The community of Mansfield from Domesday Book to the reign of Edward III', *Trans. Thoroton Soc.*, lxxxviii (1984), pp. 14–38; lxxxix (1985), forthcoming; 'The ancient demesne tenants of Mansfield', forthcoming.

101 NRO DPP 17/68.

102 *RH*, ii, 27.

103 KB 27/170, m. 74.

104 NRO DDP 17/1, mm. 6, 7, 9.

105 E 134/ 34 Eliz/Easter 5.

106 D. Crook, 'Lindhurst, No Man's Wood and the manor of Mansfield', *Trans. Thoroton Soc.*, lxxxv (1981), pp. 78–89, esp. p. 81; A.C. Wood, 'A petition relating to the manor of Mansfield, 1602', ibid., xlii (1938), pp. 70–83, esp. p. 72.

107 LR: 2 Burr 1046; Simpson, *Land Law*, pp. 154–56. My thanks to Dr D.L. Thomas for discussion of ejectment.

108 IND 17175, ff. 1, 10.

109 NRO DDBM 14, pp. 430–34.

110 NRO DDBM 15, pp. 382–83 and DDBM 79–80; CP 43/922, mm. 295–97; CP 43/925, m. 356; CP 43/926, mm. 260–61.

111 *DB*, i, f. 39; *VCH, Hants*, iv, 129–33.

112 Baigent and Millard, *Basingstoke*, p. 172.

113 E.g., ibid., pp. 222, 267; HRO 148 M 71/2/1, no. 25 (1429); no. 40 (1440); no. 52 (1447).

114 HRO 148 M 71/2/8, nos. 1–6; below, p. 175.

115 Court Books (1778–1838), manor of Havering, Ansell papers in the custody of Hunt and Hunt, Solicitors, Romford (ex inf. Professor M.K. McIntosh).

116 I am grateful to Professor McIntosh for this information.

117 NRO DDBM 74, pp. 5–11; DDBM 78, pp. 69–76; DRO 239 M/M 10, pp. 170–75.

118 *Commissioners Appointed to Inquire into the Law of England Respecting Real Property, First Report* (1829), pp. 28–29.

119 Idem, *Third Report* (1832), p. 13.

120 LR: 5 Co 84.

121 LR: 2 Burr 1046.

122 3 and 4 Wm IV c 74.

123 Below, p. 175.

CHAPTER V, pages 114–140.

1 H. Spelman, *Archeologus in modum Glosarii ...* (1626), p. 220.

2 H. Owen, ed., 'The description of Pembrokeshire by George Owen ...', *Cymmrodorion Rec. Ser.*, i (1892–97), esp. pp. 370–73; M. McKisack, *Medieval History in the Tudor Age* (Oxford, 1971), pp. 93–94.

3   C. Jenning, *Early Chests in Wood and Iron*, PRO Museum Pamphlets, vii (1974), pp. 6–7; E 31/4.

4   Cf. D.C. Douglas, *English Scholars* (1939), pp. 171–72; Condon and Hallam, pp. 373–74.

5   Above, chapter III, notes 57–58.

6   W. Hamper, ed., *The Life, Diary and Correspondence of Sir William Dugdale* (1827), pp. 170–71.

7   SP 46/139, ff. 81–82; Williams, 'Peter le Neve'; below notes 81–82.

8   Hamper, *Dugdale*, pp. 221–23.

9   P. Leycester, *Historical Antiquities* ... (1673), appendix (1672).

10 Sainty, *Officers*, p. 176.

11 E.g., *Plac. Abb.*

12 Palgrave, *Kalendars and Inventories*, pp. 311–35, esp. p. 316.

13 Powell, *Repertorie*, p. 132.

14 Ibid., p. 133.

15 Bodl. MS. Top. Gen. C 22.

16 T. Gale, *Registrum Honoris de Richmond* (1722), app. I, pp. 8–11; J. Evans, *A History of the Society of Antiquaries* (Oxford, 1956), pp. 12–13.

17 Gale, *Registrum*, app. I, pp. 1–7; McKisack, pp. 86–87.

18 K. Sharpe, *Sir Robert Cotton, 1586–1631* ... (Oxford, 1979), p. 24.

19 Spelman, *Archeologus*, pp. 218–20.

20 Hallam, 'Annotations in Domesday Book'.

21 E 31/2, f. C.

22 E 31/2, f. 272.

23 Below, apps. I, II, IV.

24 Above, p. 33.

25 *DNB*, xiv, 450–53.

26 J.O. Halliwell, ed., *The Autobiography and Correspondence of Sir Simonds D'Ewes*, 2 vols. (1845), ii, 55–56.

27 Ibid., pp. 80–81.

28 Ibid., pp. 78–79; BL Add. MS. 11056, ff. 63–64.

29 Halliwell, *D'Ewes*, i, pp. 81–83.

30 BL Harl. MS. 623; A.G. Watson, *The Library of Sir Simonds D'Ewes* (1966), pp. 257, 303. I would like to thank Dr A. Prescott of the British Library for his advice about manuscripts containing Domesday material.

31 Ibid., f. 1.

32 Ibid., f. 38.

33 Halliwell, *D'Ewes*, i, 31–37; BL Harl. MSS. 362, ff. 42–50v; 597, ff. 104–7; 99, f. 29 (the last three references ex inf. Dr G.H. Martin).

34 Douglas, *English Scholars*, pp. 31–59.

35 W. Dugdale, *The Antiquities of Warwickshire* ... (1654), p. 1.

36 Bodl. MS. Dugdale 2, esp. pp. 1–58.

37 Hamper, *Dugdale*, p. 237.

38 Written against Petyt's *Antient Rights*; below, note 53.

39 Bodl. MS. Dugdale 10, ff. 93v–103.

40 W. Dugdale, *The Baronage of England* ..., i (1675), pp. 20–21.

41 R. Latham and W. Matthews, ed., *The Diary of Samuel Pepys, ii, 1661* (1970), p. 236.

42 E.g., BL Lansd. MS. 330; Hallam, 'Annotations in Domesday Book'.

43 S. Pepys, *Naval Minutes*, ed. J.R. Tanner, Navy Rec. Soc., lx (1926), pp. 96–97, 183–84.

44 I am grateful to Dr N.A.M. Rodger for discussion of Pepys.

45 Q. Skinner, 'History and ideology in the English revolution', *Historical Jnl.*, viii (1965), pp. 151–78, esp. p. 158; J. Hayward, *Lives of the III Normans, Kings of England* (1613), 98–99; above, pp. 34, 36.

46 J. Speed, *The Historie of Great Britaine* (1611), p. 421.

47 W. Howell, *Medulla Historiae Anglicanae* (1679), esp. pp. 109–10.

48 Hill, 'Norman Yoke', pp. 81–87; J. Lilburne, *Regall Tyrannie Discovered* (1647), pp. 90–91.

49 Pocock, *Ancient Constitution*, pp. 30–55.

50 Ibid., pp. 46–48; Skinner, p. 152.

51 Pocock, *Ancient Constitution*, pp. 91–123.

52 Ibid., pp. 148–58, 182–87.

53 W. Petyt, *The Antient Rights of the Commons of England Asserted* (1680), pp. 18–21.

54 Inner Temple MS. 538, vol xvii, f. 481.

55 Petyt, *Antient Rights*, p. 23.

56 W. Atwood, *Jani Anglorum Facies Nova* (1680).

57 Douglas, *English Scholars*, pp. 148–74; J.G.A. Pocock, 'Robert Brady, 1627–1700 ...', *Cambridge Hist. Jnl.*, x (1950–52), pp. 187–204; C.N.L. Brooke, *A History of Gonville and Caius College* (1985), chapter 8; I am grateful to Professor Brooke for showing me the chapter in typescript.

58 Reprinted in R. Brady, *An Introduction to Old English History* (1684), p. 11.

59 Ibid., p. 13.

60 A. Grey, ed., *Debates of the House of Commons*, viii (1763), p. 306.

61 A. Clark, ed., *The Life and Times of Anthony Wood, Antiquary at Oxford, 1632–98* ..., ii (Oxford, 1892), p. 533.

62 [W. Atwood], *Jus Anglorum ab Antiquo* (1681), pp. 73, 77.

63 E. Cooke, *Argumentum Anti-Normanicum* ... (1682); see also J.P. Kenyon, *Revolution Principles; the Politics of Party, 1689–1720* (Cambridge, 1977), pp. 35–37.

64 Brady, *Introduction*, p. 275.

65 Ibid., appendix and glossary.

66 R. Brady, *Complete History of England* (1685), i, esp. pp. 185–216.

67 Pocock, 'Robert Brady', p. 196.

68 SP 46/139, mm. 81–82.

69 IND 17176.

70 R. Brady, *An Historical Treatise of Cities and Boroughs* (1690), pp. ii–iii.

71 J. Tyrrell, *A History of England, ii, 1066–1272* (1700).

72 Quoted by S. Kliger, *The Goths in England* (Cambr., Mass., 1932), pp. 185–86.

73 Below, app. V, nos. 2–10.

74 IND 17177 (1680).

75 IND 17176 (1683–93).

76 BL Add. MS. 28646 (1693).

77 Ibid., f. IV.

78 Williams, 'Peter le Neve'.

79 Douglas, *English Scholars*, p. 132.

80 Williams, 'Peter le Neve', p. 130.

81 SP 46/139, ff. 16–18.

82 Ibid., ff. 24–25.
83 IND 17175, ff. 1–72.
84 Ibid., ff. 31v, 71v.
85 Ibid., f. 14.
86 Ibid., f. 28.
87 H. Chauncy, *The Historical Antiquities of Hertfordshire*, 2 vols. (1700), *passim*.
88 BL Harl. MS. 4712, f. 212.
89 Hallam, 'Annotations in Domesday Book'.
90 E 36/284, facing f. 1; cf. above, pp. 42–44.
91 BL Add. MS. 7524, f. 57.
92 F. Blomefield, *An Essay towards a Topographical History of the County of Norfolk*, 2nd edn, i (1805), p. xv.
93 Ibid., e.g., pp. 1–3, 201, 313, 482; Bodl. MSS. Gough Norfolk 30, 34–39. I am grateful to Mrs M. Clapison of the Bodleian Library for her advice about these manuscripts.
94 E.g., Bodl. MS. Top. Gen. 106, 2 Feb. 1758.
95 *LJ*, xxi, 137–38, 141–42.
96 *Reports of Committees of the House of Commons*, i (1715–35), pp. 508–9.
97 Condon and Hallam, p. 374.
98 Ibid., pp. 349–59; Douglas, *English Scholars*, pp. 278–84.
99 P.C. Webb, *A Short Account ... of Domesday Book ...* (1756), p. 12.
100 BL Stowe MS. 753, f. 248.
101 Bodl. MS. Top. Gen. 106, 15 Jan. 1758.
102 G.H. Martin, introduction to P. Morant, *The History and Antiquities of the County of Essex*, i (repr. Wakefield, 1978), pp. (vii)–(ix).
103 Ibid., pp. xxvii–xxviii.
104 Ibid., book I, apps., pp. 3–4.
105 Ibid., intro., p. (ix).
106 A. Pope, *Dunciad*, ed. J. Sutherland, 3rd edn (1963), pp. 170–72; Douglas, *English Scholars*, pp. 226–48.
107 Above, p. 110.
108 J.G.A. Pocock, *Politics, Language and Time* (New York, 1971), pp. 202–32.
109 W. King, ed., *The Works of the Rt. Hon. Edmund Burke*, rev. edn, vii (Boston, 1866), pp. 338, 343, 353–54, 363–64. I am grateful to Dr. M.J. Jubb for discussion of these matters.
110 T. Carte, *A General History of England*, i (1748), p. 436.
111 H.T. Dickinson, *Liberty and Property; Political Ideology in Eighteenth-Century Britain* (1977), pp. 141–42.
112 J. Brewer, *Party Ideology and Popular Politics at the Accession of George III* (Cambridge, 1976), pp. 259–61.
113 Rapin de Thoyras, *The History of England*, ed. N. Tindal, 2nd edn, i (1732), esp. p. 177.
114 T.S. Hughes, ed., *The History of England by Hume and Smollett*, i (1854), p. 215 (ex inf. Dr M.J. Jubb); D. Forbes, *Hume's Philosophical Politics* (Cambridge, 1975), pp. 267, 301–3.
115 Demophilus, *The Genuine Principles of the Saxon, or English, Constitution* (Philadelphia, 1776), p. 3.
116 Condon and Hallam, p. 377.
117 H.M. Colvin *et al.*, ed., *The History of the King's Works, V, 1660–1782* (1976), p. 415.
118 Condon and Hallam, p. 373, note 335.

119 E 192/92, pt II.

120 IND 17175, f. 74.

121 Ibid., f. 93.

122 BL Add. MS. 21349, f. 42.

123 Ibid., f. 113.

124 Ibid., f. 98.

125 BL Lansd. MS. 329, ff. 4–6.

126 Condon and Hallam, p. 379; BL Stowe MS. 851.

127 Condon and Hallam, p. 379; Bodl. MS. Top. Gen. 43, esp. f. 89.

128 Hallam, 'Annotations in Domesday Book'; E 31/2, f. xxii.

129 Condon and Hallam, p. 362.

130 IND 17175, f. 89.

131 Webb, *Short Account*.

132 SAL Minute Book 7, pp. 229–30.

133 Condon and Hallam, pp. 374–75.

134 SAL Minute Book 10, p. 371.

135 Condon and Hallam, pp. 375–76.

136 E 31/6 (tracing); BL Stowe MS. 851, f. 3 (engraving).

137 T 1/466, ff. 261–62; T 29/39, p. 164.

138 BL Add. MS. 38514, ff. 46–50.

139 Ibid., f. 79.

140 Condon and Hallam, pp. 376–78; SAL Minute Book 10, pp. 532–33.

141 Condon and Hallam, p. 378.

142 T 29/44, p. 112; Condon and Hallam, p. 379.

143 Condon and Hallam, pp. 348–49, 380; below, p. 147.

144 BL Add. MS. 38514, ff. 63–66.

145 Condon and Hallam, pp. 380–81; below, p. 147.

146 E 31/2, f. 128; *DB*, i, f. 128.

147 Below, p. 172.

148 R. Kelham, *Domesday Book Illustrated* (1788).

149 Condon and Hallam, pp. 380–83.

CHAPTER VI, pages 141–176.

1 T.J. Evans, *Christian Policy*, 2nd edn (1816), p. 16; I.J. Prothero, *Artisans and Politics in Early Nineteenth Century London: John Gast and his Times* (1979), p. 88.

2 Hill, 'Norman Yoke', pp. 109–13; A. Briggs, 'Saxons, Normans and Victorians', *1066 Commemoration Lectures* (Sussex, 1966), pp. 89–112.

3 Ibid., pp. 114–15.

4 A. Thierry, *History of the Conquest of England by the Normans*, English transl. (1841), pp. 120–22.

5 H. Hallam, *View of the State of Europe during the Middle Ages*, 10th edn, ii (1853), pp. 307–8.

6 Ibid., pp. 304–7.

7 S. Turner, *The History of England during the Middle Ages*, 2nd edn (1825), pp. 73–74, 132–35, 140.

8 P.B.M. Blaas, *Continuity and Anachronism* ... (The Hague, 1978); T.W. Heyck, *The Transformation of Intellectual Life in Victorian England* (1982); G.O. Trevelyan, ed., *The Life and Letters of Lord Macaulay*, ii (1923), pp. 507–10.

9 J.C. Simmons, *The Novelist as Historian* ... (The Hague, 1973); A. Chandler, *A Dream of Order* ... (1971).

10 R.H. Inglis Palgrave, ed., *The Collected Historical Works of Sir Francis Palgrave*, iii (Cambridge, 1921), pp. 321–22.

11 *DKR*, iv, 35.

12 Palgrave, *Collected Works*, ix (Cambridge, 1922), p. 168.

13 Warren, 'Norman efficiency', pp. 115–23.

14 Below, p. 148.

15 Palgrave, *Collected Works*, ix, 166–70; Blaas, pp. 77–91.

16 P.J.A. Levene, 'The Amateur and the Professional: Antiquarians, Historians and Archeologists in nineteenth-century England, 1838–1886', unpublished D.Phil. thesis, University of Oxford, 1983. I am grateful to Dr Levene for permission to refer to her thesis.

17 Heyck, *Intellectual Life*.

18 M.J.M. Mackenzie, *Theories of Local Government* (1961), pp. 9–12.

19 *DNB*, liii, 95–96.

20 O. Anderson, 'The political uses of history in mid-nineteenth century England', *Past and Present*, xxxvi (1967), pp. 87–105, esp. pp. 103–4.

21 J. Toulmin Smith, *Local Self-Government Unmystified* (1857), p. 32.

22 J. Toulmin Smith, *The Parish*, 2nd edn (1857), p. 486.

23 W.H. Hutton, ed., *The Letters of William Stubbs, Bishop of Oxford, 1825–1901* (1904), pp. 163–64, 173.

24 Maitland in *EHR*, xvi (1901), pp. 417–26; Burrow, *Liberal Descent*, p. 159.

25 Richardson and Sayles, pp. 1–21.

26 W. Stubbs, *The Constitutional History of England*, 5th edn, i (1891), intro.

27 W.C. Sellar and R.J. Yeatman, *1066 and All That*, 8th edn (1930), p. 17; Briggs, 'Saxons, Normans and Victorians', pp. 102–3.

28 W. Stubbs, *Lectures on Modern History*, ed. A. Hassall (1906), p. 186.

29 Stubbs, *Constitutional History*, pp. 282–83, 290, 303, 415–17.

30 F.M. Powicke, *Modern Historians and the Study of History* (1955), p. 175.

31 J. Bryce in *EHR*, vii (1892), pp. 497–509; *DNB*, 1st supp., ii, 247–51.

32 M.E. Bratchel, *Edward Augustus Freeman and Victorian Interpretations of the Norman Conquest* (Ilfracombe, 1969).

33 Below, pp. 163–65.

34 Richardson and Sayles, pp. 48, 92.

35 Burrow, *Liberal Descent*, p. 216.

36 E.A. Freeman, *The History of the Norman Conquest of England* ..., 2nd edn., v (1876), p. 6.

37 Ibid., iv (1876), p. 688.

38 Ibid., pp. 688–91.

39 Ibid., v, 3–4, 734.

40 E.M. Hallam and M. Roper, 'The capital and the records of the nation ...', *London Journal*, iv (1978), pp. 74–94, esp. note 4.

41 P. Walne, 'The Record Commission, 1800–1837', *Jnl. Soc. Archivists*, ii (1960–64), pp. 8–16.

42 Condon and Hallam, pp. 382–83.

43 PRO 36/1, pp. 62, 199; PRO 36/2, pp. 58–59; PRO 36/3, pp. 78, 85; PRO 36/4, pp. 144, 198, 408.

44 Condon and Hallam, p. 383; *DB*, iii–iv; above, pp. 37–39.

45 *DNB*, xvii, 280–82.

46 Condon and Hallam, p. 383.

47 Ibid.; H. Ellis, *A General Introduction to Domesday Book*, 2 vols. (1833).

48 *HC* 1836 (429), xvi, 1.

49 Below, pp. 153–54, 158–59.

50 V and A Library, MS. 55 AA 12, 29 Nov. 1847. I would like to thank Mrs John Bonython for permission to refer to this extract.

51 Condon and Hallam, p. 382. I am grateful to Dr D.H. Gifford for this information.

52 PRO 2/87, pp. 214–15.

53 1 and 2 Victoria c 94.

54 J.D. Cantwell, 'The making of the first deputy keeper of the records', *Archives*, xvii (1985), pp. 22–37. The majority of the references in this chapter to the custody of Domesday Book have been provided by Mr Cantwell and I am most grateful to him for his help.

55 *Fifty Years of Public Work of Sir Henry Cole K.C.B.*, 2 vols. (1884), i, 32.

56 *DKR*, vii, 27.

57 PRO 36/7, pp. 224–25, 229–30, 237; T 1/1882/276.

58 Palgrave, *Kalendars and Inventories*, i, pp. lxiii–lxiv.

59 Below, pp. 157–60.

60 PRO 36/7, p. 241.

61 PRO 36/7, p. 286.

62 T 1/4150, 25 March 1825.

63 E. Walford, *Old and New London*, iii (1875), pp. 453–54.

64 *DKR*, vii, 27.

65 Ibid.

66 PRO 36/49, pp. 19–20.

67 *DKR*, viii, 30.

68 PRO 1/10, 20 Oct. 1846.

69 *The Westminster and Foreign Quarterly Review*, li (1849), p. 168.

70 PRO 4/4, 31 Dec. 1854.

71 PRO 1/19, 24 Oct. 1855.

72 Nicol, *Domesday Book*, plate ix; PRO 2/13, p. 117; *DNB*, viii, 21.

73 *DKR*, xxi, 20 (room C6).

74 *DKR*, i, app., p. 66.

75 *DKR*, ii, app. I, no. 9.

76 PRO 4/4, 31 Dec. 1854.

77 *The Historical Register*, vi (1845), p. 75.

78 PRO 35/6, 8 May 1857; PRO 2/16.

79 E. Bonython, *King Cole* (1983); *DNB*, xi, 268–70.

80 F. Summerly, *A Handbook of Westminster Abbey* (1842), pp. 37, 39.

81 PRO 2/89, pp. 244–48, 255.

82 PRO 1/19, 24 Oct. 1855.

83 H. James, *Photozincography*, 2nd edn (Southampton, 1860); *Blackwood's Edinburgh Magazine*, cxliv (1888), pp. 558–63; W.A. Seymour, *A History of the Ordnance Survey* (1980), pp. 164–65. I am grateful to Dr D.L. Thomas for information about the process.

84 PRO 1/24, 17 Oct. 1860; PRO 1/25, 14 Jan. 1861; *DKR*, xxiii, 7; T 1/6285A/20233 (this and subsequent T 1 references to the photozincograph ex inf. Mr T.R. Padfield).

85 PRO 1/25, 16 Feb. 1861.

86 T 1/6332A/17908.

87 *Gentleman's Magazine*, new ser., x (Jan.–June, 1861), pp. 652–53.

88 PRO 1/25, 21 Oct., 22 Oct., 24 Oct., 29 Nov. 1861.

89 T 1/6332A/17908.

90 PRO 1/26, 24 Jan. 1862; *DKR*, xxiv, pp. ix–x.

91 Above, p. 144; J. Toulmin Smith, *The Parliamentary Remembrancer*, v (1862), pp. 186–88.

92 T 1/6477A/3807.

93 PRO 1/28, 13 Jan. 1864; *DKR*, xxv, pp. ix–xi.

94 PRO 1/41, 29, 30 June 1876.

95 T 1/6591B/18488.

96 T 1/6397A/18385.

97 *Domesday Rebound*, p. 13.

98 Below, p. 172.

99 PRO 1/28, 5 March 1864. My thanks to Dr D.H. Gifford for her unpublished material on the rebinding.

100 PRO 1/28, 9, 12 March 1864.

101 PRO 1/29, 25, 27 Feb., 13, 15 March 1865.

102 Ibid., 13, 28 Sept. 1865.

103 PRO 1/32, 19 Feb. 1867.

104 Ibid., 4 March 1867; PRO 1/33, 11 Jan. 1868.

105 PRO 1/33, 6 March 1868.

106 Ibid., 9, 12, 14, 16 March 1868.

107 Ibid., 19, 22 March 1868.

108 Ibid., 25 April, 11 May, 18 Nov. 1868; PRO 1/68, 12 Jan. 1869.

109 PRO 1/68, 17 Nov., 1 Dec. 1869.

110 *Domesday Rebound*, p. 40.

111 E 31/1, ff. 437, 447 (ex inf. Dr H. Forde).

112 T 1/6869B/7654; PRO 1/34, 20, 24 March, 22, 28 April 1869.

113 T 1/6957A/1173; PRO 1/35, 21, 26 March 1870.

114 *DKR*, lvii, 10 (room B19).

115 N.E.S.A. Hamilton, *Inquisitio Comitatus Cantabrigiensis* ... (1876); P.C. Webb, *A Short Account of Danegeld* ... (1756).

116 Below, note 133.

117 R.W. Eyton, *A Key to Domesday* ..., *Dorset*, 2 vols. (1878); *Domesday Studies* ..., *Somerset*, 2 vols. (1880); *Domesday Studies* ..., *Staffs* (1881); 'Notes on Domesday', *Trans. Shropshire Arch. Soc.*, i (1878), pp. 89–118.

118 *The Athenaeum*, no. 2998, 11 April 1885, p. 472; see also *DS*, ii, 485–515.

119 Ibid., no. 3000, 25 April 1885, pp. 235–36; no. 3001, 2 May 1885, pp. 566–67.

120 R Hist. S Minute Book, 1880–86, p. 232.

121 Ibid., pp. 234–35, 238–39, 240–41.

122 PRO 1/51, 30 Oct. 1886.

123 Ibid; *The Athenaeum*, no. 3079, 30 Oct. 1886, pp. 566–67; *DS*, ii, 623–47.

124 *Royal Hist. Soc. Domesday Commemoration* (1886); PRO 1/51, 30 Oct. 1886; *DS*, ii, 51–95.

125 PRO 1/51, 30 Oct. 1886; *Illustrated London News*, 6 Nov. 1886, pp. 481–82; *The Athenaeum*, no. 3080, 6 Nov. 1886, pp. 602–3.

126 *DS*, i, 77–142; ii, 539–59.
127 *DNB, 1922–30*, pp. 727–31; J. Tait in *EHR*, xliii (1928), pp. 572–77; D. Stephenson, 'The early career of J.H. Round: the shaping of a historian', *Trans. Essex Arch. Soc.*, 3rd ser., xii (1980), pp. 1–10.
128 Stephenson, 'Early career', pp. 4–5.
129 J.H. Round in *Quarterly Review*, clxxv (1892), pp. 1–37, esp. p. 22.
130 E.g., below, note 188.
131 J.H. Round, *Peerage and Pedigree*, ii (1910), pp. 18–21, 46.
132 J.H. Round, *Feudal England* (1895), pp. 3–146.
133 Galbraith, *Making of DB*, pp. 10–27; P.J. Boyden, 'J.H. Round and the beginings of the modern study of Domesday Book', *Trans. Essex Arch. Soc.*, 3rd ser., xii (1980), pp. 11–24.
134 W.R. Powell, 'J. Horace Round, the county historian', ibid., pp. 25–38.
135 H.A. Doubleday and W. Page, *A Guide to the VCH* (n.d., *c.* 1904), p. 5.
136 Powell, 'J.H. Round'; Galbraith, *DB, Its Place . . .*, pp. 149–50, 155–56; for the works of Tait and Stenton, and critical comments, see Bates, *D Bibl.*, general works.
137 C.H.S. Fifoot, *Frederic William Maitland, A Life* (Cambr., Mass., 1971), pp. 146–47 *et passim*; H.F. Bell, *Maitland, A Critical Examination and Assessment* (1965), pp. 1–33.
138 F. Seebohm, *The English Village Community* (1876).
139 F.W. Maitland, *Domesday Book and Beyond*, ed. E. Miller (1960), esp. intro., pp. 16–17.
140 C.H.S. Fifoot, *The Letters of F.W. Maitland*, Selden Soc., suppl. ser., i (1965), p. 271.
141 Galbraith, *DB, Its Place . . .*, pp. 9–17; Bates, *D Bibl.*, general works, for details and comments on these and numerous other areas of research.
142 Darby, *Domesday England*, gives a classic exposition of many of its findings.
143 Work is being carried out at the University of Hull, the University of Santa Barbara, California, USA, Flinders University, Australia and elsewhere.
144 R.W. Southern in *Proceedings of the British Academy*, lxix (1978), pp. 397–425.
145 E.g., above, chapter I, notes 20–41; chapter II, notes 51–64.
146 *DKR*, lvii, 19–47.
147 PRO 8/32; *PRO Museum Catalogue*, 1st edn (1902), p. 23.
148 PRO 1/83, 14 Feb. 1918.
149 PRO 40/17.
150 PRO 1/83, 20 Feb. 1918.
151 Ibid., 7 July 1918; PRO 1/84, 5, 6, 21 Jan. 1919.
152 PRO 1/84, 18 Feb. 1919; *PRO Museum Catalogue*, 9th edn (1922), p. 16.
153 *Punch*, 18 Aug. 1926, p. 185.
154 PRO 18/7; *DKR*, ci, pp. 1–2; further material ex inf. Mr M. Meerendonk.
155 PRO 18/7; *DKR*, cviii, 1.
156 T 162/642.
157 PRO 18/7; *DKR*, ciii, 1.
158 PRO 8/32; *DKR*, cviii, 3; *PRO Museum Catalogue* (1948), p. 11.
159 PRO 1/1322; PRO 1/1324.
160 *DKR*, cxiv, 3–4.
161 *DKR*, cxv, 4–5, 8–9.
162 PRO 8/36; PRO 1/1371.
163 PRO 1/1409; *DKR*, cxiv, 20.
164 PRO 8/41.

165 *DKR*, cviii, 9; *PRO Museum Catalogue* (1956), p. 20; (1966), p. 3; (1974), p. 53.

166 PRO 8/57 (notes presented by Dr D.H. Gifford).

167 PRO 1/1447; *Domesday Rebound*, pp. 36–38.

168 *Domesday Rebound*, pp. 17–46.

169 PRO Miscellanea B, no. 15 (ex inf. Dr J.B. Post).

170 *The Times*, 19 Apr. 1919.

171 PRO leaflet, no. 3: *Valuation Office Records created under the 1910 Finance Act.*

172 *The Times*, 28 Mar. 1931; 27 June, 4 July 1958; 18 May 1972.

173 *BBC Domesday Project, Information Sheet for Women's Institutes* (1984); I would like to thank Mrs B.M. Hallam for this reference.

174 *The Times*, 25 July 1969; Galbraith, *DB, Its Place* ....

175 E.g., ed. F. and C. Thorn, *Domesday Book, Worcestershire* (Chichester, 1982), and *Domesday Book, Devon*, 2 vols. (Chichester, 1985).

176 By the Public Records Act 1958, the deputy keeper of the records was replaced by the keeper of public records; 6 and 7 Eliz II c 51.

177 Above, chapter I, notes 42, 48.

178 I am grateful to Miss C.M. Hallam for her advice on modern legal uses of Domesday Book.

179 H. Wood, ed., *A Collection of Decrees by the Court of Exchequer in Tithe Causes* . . ., iii (1798), pp. 426–34, esp. p. 433.

180 E 127/49, Hil 1792, no. 380; E 126/34, pp. 239–41 (ex inf. Miss M. Condon).

181 C.A. Markham, ed., *The Records of the Borough of Northampton*, i (1898), pp. 8–9; LR: 2 M and Sc 843.

182 LR: 4 Barn and Adol 273; K. Brand, 'The Park Estate, Nottingham . . .', *Trans. Thoroton Soc.*, lxxxviii (1984), pp. 54–75, esp. p. 61.

183 S.A. Moore, *A History of the Foreshore* . . . (1888), p. 478.

184 LR: 20 TLR 602.

185 LR: 4 Ryde Rat Cas 32.

186 H. Maxwell-Lyte, 'Domesday Book', *Pall Mall Magazine*, xxvii (May–Aug., 1902), pp. 209–16; I would like to thank Dr D. Bates for this reference.

187 Below, app. IV, no. 35; PRO 1/67, 27 Jan. 1902.

188 *Peerage Evidence, xxxvii, Lord Great Chamberlain of England* (1901–2).

189 LR: 6 Jur (NS) 297.

190 LR: 1 Ch 842.

191 12 and 13 Geo V c 16, sections 128–37; LR: 2 All ER 668 (1960).

192 Lord Halsbury, ed., *The Laws of England* . . ., ix (1909), pp. 171, 142. I would like to thank Mr A. Rowland for his guidance on the demise of the Basingstoke court.

193 Ibid., 2nd edn., ed. Lord Hailsham, viii (1933), p. 683; ibid., 3rd edn., ed. Lord Simonds, ix (1954), p. 513.

194 Law Commission file on the abolition of ancient courts. I am grateful to the Law Commission for permitting me to see the file and to Mrs E. Smith of the Lord Chancellor's Dept for her help in arranging the visit.

195 LR: 1 All ER 701 (1965).

Appendixes

Appendix I contains Chancery exemplifications as well as writs of *certiorari* and their Domesday returns. The columns used in it convey the following information: date = date of the writ or, if no writ, date of exemplification; nature of request = gist of the writ of *certiorari* or explanation of the request given in the enrolment of the letters patent. (T) at the end of the entry signifies a request by the tenants of the place; (B) likewise by the burgesses. The returns are in the form of extracts from Domesday Book. If nothing was found in Domesday, the writ was endorsed to that effect (above, p. 58). Appendix II lists loose returns for which the writs of *certiorari* do not survive. The summaries and extracts in appendixes III–IV were intended for administrative and legal uses, but the transcripts in appendix V were made for antiquarian purposes. Where the extracts or transcripts do not survive in the original, but are mentioned only in a register of searches (IND 17175), they have been assigned to appendix IV or appendix V according to information given in that register.

Appendix I
Chancery Exemplifications and Extracts from Domesday Book Returned on Writs of Certiorari

Number	Date	Reference	Place	Nature of request
1	1266 May	C 260/1, no. 3	Nottingham (Notts)	Has king right to present to St Mary's church?
2	1266 Oct.	CPR, 1258–66, p. 648	Stoneleigh (Warw)	Who held it in DB?
3	1275 Dec.	C 260/1, no. 9	Meonstoke and Titchfield (Hants)	Ancient demesne?
4	1276 June	C 260/1, no. 27	Titchfield (Hants)	Ancient demesne?
5	1279 Jan.	C 260/2, no. 3	Great Gaddesden (Herts)	Ancient demesne?
6	1279 Oct.	C 260/2, no. 55	Steventon (Berks)	Ancient demesne?
7	1279 Dec.(?)	C 260/2, no. 9	Halesowen (Worcs)	Was manor held by Hailes Abbey (Glos) in DB and Pipe Rolls?
8	1280 Apr.	C 260/2, no. 13	East Markham (Notts)	Ancient demesne?
9	1307 Sept.	C 260/18, no. 1	Weekley (Northants)	Ancient demesne?
10	1311 June	C 260/21, no. 21	Beesby (Lincs)	Ancient demesne?
11	1311 June	C 260/21, no. 22	Ashford (Derb)	Ancient demesne?
12	1331 Sept.	C 260/41, no. 39A	St Albans (Herts)	Ancient demesne?
13	1332 July	C 260/42, no. 37	Otterton and East Budleigh (Devon)	How were they held before they were given to the abbey of Mont St Michel (France)? Consult DB.

Number	Date	Reference	Place	Nature of request
14	1332 Dec.	C 260/42, no. 53	Stareton (Warw)	How was it held? Consult DB and other documents.
15	1333 Apr.	C 260/43, no. 11	Freshwater (IOW, Hants)	Ancient demesne?
16	1333 Sept.	C 260/43, no. 26	Allerthorpe (Yorks ER)	Ancient demesne?
17	1336 May	C 260/47, no. 23	Ilmer (Bucks)	How was it held in DB?
18	1337 May	C 260/48, no. 23	Newington (in Milton, Kent)	Was half of manor held in chief in DB?
19	1337–38	C 260/48, no. 48	Woodstock, Bladon, Hanborough, Combe and Stonesfield (Oxon)	Ancient demesne?
20	1338 Feb.	C 260/49, no. 4	Stafford (Staffs)	Ancient demesne?
21	1338 Nov.	C 260/49, no. 22	Great Leighs (Essex)	How was service of six marks held in DB?
22	1341 June	*CPR, 1340–43*, p. 231	Ogbourne St Andrew and Ogbourne St George (Wilts)	Exemplification of DB text (T).
23	1341 June	*CPR, 1340–43*, p. 253	Harmondsworth (Midd)	Exemplification of DB text.
24	1342 May	C 260/53, no. 41 *CPR, 1340–43*, p. 437	Bampton (Oxon)	Ancient demesne?
25	1342 June	C 260/53, no. 43 *CPR, 1340–43*, p. 475	Meonstoke (Hants)	Ancient demesne? (T)
26	1342 Oct.	C 260/53, no. 56 *CPR, 1340–43*, p. 531	Torksey (Lincs)	Are the burgesses of Torksey free? Consult DB.
27	1343 May	C 260/54, no. 19 *CPR, 1343–45*, p. 30	Meonstoke (Hants)	Ancient demesne?
28	1343 July	*CPR, 1343–45*, p. 53	Rawcliffe (Yorks NR)	Exemplification of DB entry requested by the abbot of Selby (Yorks WR).
29	1344 Feb.	C 260/55, no. 14	Oakham, Langham and Egleston (Rut)	Investigate privileges and ancient demesne status claimed by inhabitants. (T) (petition)
30	1344 July	C 47/7/5, mm. 11–12	Crowland Abbey (Lincs)	List of lands held by abbey in DB requested.
31	1346 Feb.	C 260/57, no. 9 *CPR, 1345–48*, p. 53	South Molton (Devon)	Ancient demesne?

Number	Date	Reference	Place	Nature of request
32	1346 Feb.	C 260/57, no. 10	Hemingbrough (Yorks ER)	Ancient demesne?
33	1347 May	C 260/58, no. 35	Wargrave (Berks)	Ancient demesne?
34	1347 June	C 260/58, no. 46 CPR, 1348–50, p. 7	Powick (Worcs)	Is that part once held by Walter Poucher ancient demesne?
35	1347 Nov.	C 260/58, no. 75	Letcombe Regis (Berks)	Are tenants of ancient demesne status?
36	1348 May	C 260/59, no. 31 CPR, 1348–50, p. 95	Merton (Surrey)	Ancient demesne?
37	1352 Feb.	C 260/6, no. 10 CPR, 1350–54, p. 259 (a)	Wakefield (Yorks WR)	Is service held from king? Consult DB.
38	1353 Nov.	C 260/64, no. 48	Gedney, Holbeach and Whaplode (Lincs)	Ancient demesne?
39	1354 Oct.	C 260/65, no. 31A	Scalby (Yorks NR)	Parcel of Pickering or Falsgrave (Yorks NR)? Consult DB.
40	1355 Mar.	C 47/9/56	Herefordshire	Exemplification of DB extract listing lands of bishop of Hereford in Herefordshire, made at bishop's request.
41	1355 Oct.	C 260/66, no. 43 CPR, 1354–58, pp. 288–89	Moretonhampstead, Colaton Raleigh and Broadhempston (Devon)	Ancient demesne? (T)
42	1359 Feb.	C 260/70, no. 6	Clovelly (Devon)	Ancient demesne?
43	1359 Oct.	C 260/70, no. 35	Savoy (Midd)	Ancient demesne?
44	1360 June	CPR, 1358–61, p. 429	King's Nympton (Devon)	Exemplification of DB extract. (T)
45	1361 Feb.	C 260/72, no. 13 CPR, 1358–61, p. 544	Ottery St Mary and Rawridge (Devon)	Ancient demesne?
46	1363 Nov.	C 260/74, no. 43 CPR, 1364–67, p. 84	Exeter (Devon)	Ancient demesne? (B)
47	1364 July	C 260/75, no. 30	Kings Cliffe (Northants)	Ancient demesne?
48	1365 May	C 260/76, no. 25	Lincoln (Lincs)	Ancient demesne?
49	1365 Oct.	C 260/76, no. 51	Crowle (Lincs)	How held in DB?

(a)   E 101/212/7 (hanaper account): 'Carta Philippe Regine Anglie de exemplificatione liberata per breve de magno sigillo – nichil.'

Number	Date	Reference	Place	Nature of request
50	1366 Apr.	C 260/77, no. 9	Gomshall and Shere (Surrey)	Ancient demesne?
51	1367 Feb.	C 260/78, no. 10	List of DB holdings of Hugh Lasne in Heref, Glos, Salop and Wilts requested.	
52	1367 Oct.	C 260/78, no. 36	Uppingham (Rut)	Ancient demesne?
53	1369 May	C 260/80, no. 21	Montgomery (Mont) castle and manor	How held in DB?
54	1370 June	C 260/81, no. 22	Clothall (Herts)	Is it held in chief? Consult DB and Book of Fees.
55	1372 June	C 260/83, no. 55	Great Faringdon and Great Coxwell (Berks)	Ancient demesne?
56	1376 Oct.	C 260/87, no. 46A	Amberley (Sussex) (b)	Ancient demesne?
57	1376 Nov.	C 260/87, no. 49	Lambeth (Surrey)	Ancient demesne?
58	1377 Mar.	C 260/88, no. 8	Farnham (Surrey)	How were lands held in DB? (T)
59	1377 Mar.	C 260/88, no. 9 CPR, 1374–77, p. 452	Crondall (Hants)	Ancient demesne?
60	1377 Apr.	C 260/88, no. 10	Highclere, Ecchinswell, East Woodhay and Ashmansworth (Hants)	Ancient demesne?
61	1377 Apr.	C 260/88, no. 47	Lincoln (Lincs)	Exemplification of DB entry for Lincoln requested for use in dispute involving abbot of Tupholme (Lincs). (c)
62	1377 Apr.	C 260/88, no. 1	Froyle (Hants)	Ancient demesne? (T)
63	1377 Apr.	C 260/88, no. 14	Thorpe, Egham, Cobham and Chobham (Surrey)	Ancient demesne? (T)
64	1377 May	C 260/88, no. 59	Whitchurch (Hants)	Ancient demesne?
65	1377 June	C 260/88, no. 26	Lands in Ripplesmere hundred (Berks)	Ancient demesne? (T) (Warfield)
66	1377 July	C 260/89, no. 4 CPR, 1377–81, p. 12	All Cannings and Urchfont (Wilts)	Ancient demesne? (T)
67	1377 July	C 260/89, no. 5 CPR, 1377–81, p. 12	Stanton St Bernard and South Newton (Wilts)	Ancient demesne? (T)
68	1377 July	C 260/89, no. 7 CPR, 1377–81, p. 16	Bishops Cannings (Wilts)	Ancient demesne? (T)

(b)   Given erroneously as Essex in writ.   (c)   Writ and return damaged.

Number	Date	Reference	Place	Nature of request
69	1377 Aug.	C 260/89, no. 8 CPR, 1377–81, p. 10	Manningford Abbots and Pewsey (Wilts)	Ancient demesne? (T)
70	1377 Aug.	C 260/89, no. 9 CPR, 1377–81, p. 18	Melksham, Bradford on Avon and Steeple Ashton (Wilts)	Ancient demesne? (T)
71	1377 Aug.	C 260/89, no. 10 CPR, 1377–81, pp. 15, 16	Christian Malford and Sutton Mandeville (Wilts)	Ancient demesne? (T)
72	1377 Aug.	C 260/89, no. 11 CPR, 1377–81, p. 15	Kintbury (Berks)	Ancient demesne? (T)
73	1377 Aug.	C 260/89, no. 12 CPR, 1377–81, p. 15	Wroughton (Wilts)	Ancient demesne? (T)
74	1377 Aug.	C 260/89, no. 13 CPR, 1377–81, p. 23	Badbury, Chiseldon and Liddington (Wilts)	Ancient demesne? (T)
75	1377 Aug.	C 260/89, no. 14 CPR, 1377–81, p. 19	Chilmark and Wylye (Wilts)	Ancient demesne?
76	1377 Dec.	C 260/89, no. 35	Benson (Oxon)	Ancient demesne?
77	1378 Jan.	C 260/89, no. 36 CPR, 1377–81, p. 213	Southease and Donnington (Sussex)	Ancient demesne?
78	1378 Feb.	C 260/89, no. 46	List of DB lands of Chertsey Abbey (Surrey) in one Berks and seven Surrey hundreds requested by abbot of Chertsey.	
79	1378 May	C 260/89, no. 59	Hatfield (Yorks WR)	Is church part of service of manor?
80	1379 May	C 260/90, no. 31	Brigstock and Upton (Northants)	Ancient demesne?
81	1381 Dec.	C 260/93, no. 15	Whiston and Denton (Northants)	Ancient demesne?
82	1383 June	C 260/94, no. 60 CPR, 1381–85, p. 274	Shaftesbury (Dors)	Ancient demesne? (B)
83	1383 Oct.	C 260/95, no. 7	Tintinhull (Som)	Ancient demesne?
84	1383 Nov.	C 260/95, no. 16	Cricket St Thomas, Tintinhull, East and West Chinnock, Closworth, Bishopston and Beercrocombe (Som)	Ancient demesne?

Number	Date	Reference	Place	Nature of request
85	1384 Jan.	CPR, 1381–85, p. 372	Ashburton (Devon)	Exemplification from DB. (T)
86	1384 May	CPR, 1381–85, p. 399	Bromham (Wilts)	Exemplification from DB. (T)
87	1385 May	C 260/96, no. 55	Kingsthorpe (in Northampton, Northants)	Ancient demesne?
88	1385 Oct.	C 260/97, no. 4 CPR, 1383–89, p. 54	Ford (Salop)	Ancient demesne?
89	1386 May	C 260/97, no. 30	Hadleigh (Suff)	Ancient demesne?
90	1386 Oct.	C 260/98, no. 8	Rossall (Salop)	Ancient demesne?
91	1386 Oct.	C 260/98, no. 9	Pentney (Norf)	Ancient demesne?
92	1386 Nov.	C 260/98, no. 14	Pentney (Norf)	Ancient demesne?
93	1387 Nov.	C 260/99, no. 7	Southmere (Norf)	Ancient demesne?
94	1388 Jan.	C 260/99, no. 17	Coston (Salop)	Ancient demesne?
95	1388 Apr.	C 260/99, no. 25	Bosham (Sussex)	Ancient demesne?
96	1388 May	C 260/99, no. 30	Ashreigney, Holcombe Burnell, Halberton and Ashprington (Devon)	Ancient demesne?
97	1388 May	C 260/99, no. 31	Ashburton (Devon)	Ancient demesne?
98	1388 May	C 260/99, no. 32	Long Bennington and Fenton (Lincs)	Ancient demesne?
99	1388 June	C 260/99, no. 33	Finedon (Northants)	Ancient demesne?
100	1391 Nov.	C 260/102, no. 54 CPR, 1388–92, p. 501	Ripplesmere hundred (Berks)	Ancient demesne?
101	1391 Nov.	C 260/103, no. 29 CPR, 1391–96, p. 3	Plympton St Mary (Devon)	Ancient demesne?
102	1392 Feb.	C 260/103, no. 51	Nether Stowey, Spaxton, Perry, Edington, Littleton, Chilton Polden and Ham (Som)	Ancient demesne?
103	1392 Nov.	CPR, 1391–96, p. 195	Plympton St Mary (Devon)	Ancient demesne? (B)
104	1393 Feb.	C 260/104, no. 8 CPR, 1391–96, p. 231	Winkfield (Berks)	Ancient demesne?
105	1394 Jan.	C 260/105, no. 23 CPR, 1391–96, p. 351	Waltham St Lawrence and Wargrave (Berks)	Ancient demesne? (T)
106	1394 Feb.	CPR, 1391–96, p. 530	Barnstaple (Devon)	Exemplification of DB entry. (B)

Number	Date	Reference	Place	Nature of request
107	1395 Jan.	CPR, 1391–96, p. 530	Colaton Raleigh and Whitford (Devon)	Ancient demesne? Exemplification requested. (T)
108	1396 July	C 260/107, no. 49	Spalding (Lincs)	Ancient demesne?
109	1397 May	C 260/108, no. 45	Foulsham, Whitwell and Hingham (Norf)	Ancient demesne?
110	1398 Oct.	C 260/110, no. 15	Wednesbury (Staffs)	Ancient demesne?
111	1399 Oct.	C 260/112, no. 1	Havering atte Bower (Essex)	Ancient demesne?
112	1400 Jan.	C 260/112, no. 11	Odiham (Hants)	Ancient demesne?
113	1400 Jan.	C 260/112, no. 22	Langport (Som)	Ancient demesne?
114	1399–1400	C 260/112, no. 28	Lowestoft (Suff)	Ancient demesne?
115	1400 Nov.	C 260/113, no. 6	Hanley Child and Hanley William (Worcs)	Ancient demesne?
116	1401 June	CPR, 1399–1401, p. 502	Witley (Surrey)	Exemplification of DB entry requested. (T)
117	1402 July	C 260/114, no. 24 CPR, 1401–5, p. 107	Kintbury (Berks)	Ancient demesne? (T)
118	1403 Feb.	C 260/115, no. 23	Baston and Carlby (Lincs)	Ancient demesne?
119	1403 Apr.	C 260/115, no. 27	Thorpe, Egham, Cobham and Chobham (Surrey)	Ancient demesne?
120	1404 Feb.	C 260/116, no. 23	Lists of lands held by Hugh de Port, Hugh Fitz Baldric, the king's thegns and Gilbert de Breteuil in the hundred of Holdshott (Hants) and of the lands of Hugh de Port in the hundred of Thorngate (Hants) from DB requested by Andrew Yonge, clerk.	
121	1404 May	CPR, 1401–5, p. 309	Melksham (Wilts)	Exemplification of DB entry requested. (T)
122	1405 Jan.	CPR, 1401–5, p. 479	Waltham St Lawrence and Wargrave (Berks)	Reissue of exemplification from DB, no. 105 above. (T)
123	1407 Apr.	C 260/119, no. 31	Exemplification, at the request of Thomas, archbishop of Canterbury, of DB extract listing lands of the archbishop in Brixton hundred (Surrey).	
124	1407 June	C 260/119, no. 22	Barnes (Surrey)	How held in DB?
125	1408 Feb.	C 260/120, no. 11A	Leighton Buzzard (Beds)	Ancient demesne?
126	1409 Nov.	C 260/121 no. 8 CPR, 1408–13, p. 44	Houghton Regis (Beds)	Ancient demesne? (T)

Number	Date	Reference	Place	Nature of request
127	1410 Mar.	C 260/122, no. 12	Lewes (Sussex)	Ancient demesne and how held? (B and Thomas, earl of Arundel)
128	1410 Apr.	C 260/122, no. 15	Hintlesham (Suff)	Ancient demesne?
129	1410 June	C 260/122, no. 26	Brandiston, Hunworth and Stody (Norf)	Ancient demesne?
130	1410 June	C 260/122, no. 27A	South Stainley (Yorks WR)	Ancient demesne?
131	1410 July	C 260/122, no. 29	Blythburgh (Suff)	Ancient demesne?
132	1411 June	CPR, 1408–13, p. 296	Clovelly (Devon)	Exemplification of DB extract requested by Thomasia, relict of William Carey.
133	1414 Feb.	C 260/126, no. 14	Willenhall (Staffs)	Ancient demesne?
134	1416 Nov.	CPR, 1416–22, pp. 45–46	Hadleigh (Suff)	Reissue of exemplification from DB, no. 89 above, at the request of John, prior of Christchurch.
135	1417 Oct.	C 260/130, no. 10	Cheddar and Axbridge (Som)	Ancient demesne?
136	1423 Feb.	C 260/132, no. 7	Luton (Beds)	Ancient demesne? (T)
137	1423 July	C 260/132, no. 23	Bilston (Staffs)	Ancient demesne?
138	1423 July	C 260/132, no. 24	Havering atte Bower (Essex)	Ancient demesne?
139	1423 Oct.	C 260/133, no. 2	East Budleigh (Devon)	Ancient demesne?
140	1424 Jan.	C 260/133, no. 8	Kinver (Staffs)	Ancient demesne?
141	1424 May	C 260/133, no. 13 CPR, 1422–29, p. 195	Godmanchester (Hunts)	Ancient demesne? (T)
142	1426 July	C 260/134, no. 20	Great Faringdon, and Great and Little Coxwell (Berks)	Ancient demesne?
143	1426 Nov.	C 260/135, no. 6	Milborne Port (Som)	Ancient demesne?
144	1427 Jan.	C 260/135, no. 10 CPR, 1422–29, p. 389	Godalming (Surrey)	Ancient demesne? (T)
145	1427 Feb.	C 260/135, no. 15A	List of lands held by Hyde Abbey, Winchester (Hants) in DB requested by John, abbot of Hyde.	
146	1427 Apr.	C 260/135, no. 16	Melksham (Wilts)	Ancient demesne?
147	1427 June	C 260/135, no. 21 CPR, 1422–29, p. 413	Thatcham (Berks)	Ancient demesne? (B)
148	1428 Apr.	C 260/136, no. 18	Methwold (Norf)	Ancient demesne?
149	1428 Apr.	C 260/139, no. 19	Kingswinford and Cannock (Staffs)	Ancient demesne?

Number	Date	Reference	Place	Nature of request
150	1430 Jan.	C 260/137, no. 17	Climsom (Corn)	Ancient demesne?
151	1433 June	C 260/140, no. 17B	Bloxham (Oxon)	Ancient demesne?
152	1433 July	C 260/140, no. 21A	Alrewas (Staffs)	Ancient demesne?
153	1433 Nov.	C 260/140, no. 24	Norwich (Norf)	List of land in city of Norwich held by Henry de Norwich from king in DB requested by citizens.
154	1433 Nov.	C 260/140, no. 27	Dunwich (Suff)	Ancient demesne? (d)
155	1434 Feb.	C 260/140, no. 30	Dymock (Glos)	Ancient demesne?
156	1435 Nov.	C 260/141, no. 21	Tideswell (Derb)	Ancient demesne?
157	1435 Nov.	C 260/141, no. 22	Mutford (Suff)	Ancient demesne?
158	1436 May	C 260/141, no. 29	Bromham (Wilts)	Ancient demesne?
159	1440 June	C 260/143, no. 24	Knaresborough (Yorks WR)	Ancient demesne? (T)
160	1441 May	C 260/145, no. 20	Havering atte Bower (Essex)	Ancient demesne?
161	1445 May	C 260/146, no. 20	Condover (Salop)	Ancient demesne?
162	1446 Nov.	CPR, 1446–52, p. 27	Walsall (Staffs)	Exemplification of DB extract requested but nothing found in DB.
163	1447 Feb.	C 260/146, no. 27	Frome (Som)	Ancient demesne?
164	1448 Oct.	C 260/148, no. 1	Exeter (Devon)	Are church and land held by bishop of Exeter in city ancient demesne?
165	1449 Feb.	CPR, 1446–52, p. 223	Britford (Wilts)	Exemplification of DB entry requested by abbess of Shaftesbury. (e)
166	1449 Nov.	C 260/148, no. 17	Odiham (Hants)	Ancient demesne?
167	1455 July	C 260/159, no. 15 CPR, 1452–61, p. 241	Evenlode (Glos)	How held? Check DB and Book of Fees.
168	1455 Oct.	C 260/149, no. 9	Horsford and Horsham St Faith (Norf)	Ancient demesne?
169	1459 May	C 260/149A, no. 7	Kirton in Lindsey (Lincs)	Ancient demesne?
170	1459 July	C 260/149A, no. 8	Wakefield and Sandal Magna (Yorks WR)	Ancient demesne?
171	1461 June	C 260/150, no. 1	Havant (Hants)	Ancient demesne?
172	1461 Nov.	C 260/150, no. 12	Chesterton (Cambs)	Ancient demesne?

(d) Return gives DB text for Ipswich instead.

(e) E 101/216/12 (hanaper account): '*De carta abbatisse Shafton' de manerio de Bretford in comitatu Wiltes' de exemplificatione xvjs iiijd.*'

Number	Date	Reference	Place	Nature of request
173	1461 Nov.	C 260/150, no. 17 CPR, 1461–67, p. 94	Houghton Regis and Sewell (Beds)	Ancient demesne? (T)
174	1463 May	C 260/150, no. 36	Marshfield (Glos)	Ancient demesne?
175	1466 June	C 260/151, no. 5	Easingwold (Yorks NR)	Ancient demesne?
176	1466 June	CPR, 1461–67, p. 512	Great Moulton (Norf)	Exemplification of DB entry requested. (T)
177	1468 Oct.	C 260/151, no. 20	Tardebigge (Worcs)	Ancient demesne?
178	1473 Nov.	C 260/153, no. 21	Wednesbury (Staffs)	Ancient demesne?
179	1477 July	C 260/154, no. 7	Dunton (Norf)	Ancient demesne?
180	1480 May	C 260/154, no. 17	Chesterfield, Whittington, Brimington, Tapton, Boythorpe and Aston (Derb)	Ancient demesne?
181	1484 Nov.	C 260/155, no. 4	Derby (Derb)	Ancient demesne?
182	1488 Jan.	C 260/156, no. 5	Lewisham (Kent)	Ancient demesne?
183	1504 Feb.	C 260/158, no. 46	Plympton St Mary (Devon)	Ancient demesne?
184	1505 Nov.	C 260/159, no. 4	Kinver (Staffs)	Ancient demesne?
185	1511 June	C 260/160, no. 25	Hope (Derb)	Ancient demesne?
186	1514 May	C 260/161, no. 4	Faccombe (Hants)	Ancient demesne?
187	1519 Nov.	C 260/162, no. 1	Coombe Bissett (Wilts)	Ancient demesne?
188	1568 May	C 260/164, no. 15	Little Torrington (Devon)	Ancient demesne?
189	1569 Feb.	C 260/165, no. 12	Calne (Wilts)	Ancient demesne?
190	1570 Jan.	C 260/165, no. 19	Wendover (Bucks)	Ancient demesne?
191	1570 Nov.	C 260/165, no. 24	Bramford (Suff)	Ancient demesne?
192	1573 May	C 260/167, no. 14	Lowestoft (Suff)	Ancient demesne?
193	1574 Nov.	C 260/168, no. 27	Brampton (Hunts)	Ancient demesne?
194	1575 June	C 260/168, no. 42	Kineton and Wellesbourne (Warw)	Ancient demesne?
195	1577 June	C 260/169, no. 21	Bromsgrove (Worcs)	Ancient demesne?
196	1578 Jan.	C 260/169, no. 26B	Tardebigge (Worcs)	Ancient demesne?
197	1582 Oct.	C 260/171, no. 24	Buckenham (Norf)	Ancient demesne?
198	1583 May	C 260/171, no. 35	Buckenham (Norf)	Ancient demesne?
199	1583 June	C 260/171, no. 36	Duddington (Northants)	Ancient demesne?
200	1583 June	C 260/171, no. 37	Winfarthing (Norf)	Ancient demesne?
201	1585 Nov.	C 260/173, no. 2	Sutton Courtenay (Berks)	Ancient demesne?
202	1585 Nov.	C 260/173, no. 3	Feckenham (Worcs)	Ancient demesne?
203	1586 May	C 260/173, no. 8	Kidderminster (Worcs)	Ancient demesne?

Number	Date	Reference	Place	Nature of request
204	1588 June	C 260/173, no. 55	Benson (Oxon)	Ancient demesne?
205	1608 Apr.	C 260/181, no. 5	Easingwold (Yorks NR)	Ancient demesne?
206	1610 Feb.	C 260/179, no. 31	Falsgrave, Pickering, Loft Marishes, etc. (Yorks NR) (f)	Ancient demesne?
207	1627 Apr.	C 260/184, no. 7	Moseley (Warw)	Ancient demesne?
208	1629 May	C 89/17, no. 7	Kirton in Lindsey (Lincs)	Ancient demesne?
209	1630 Apr.	C 260/184, no. 20	Newport (Essex)	Ancient demesne?
210	1630 May	C 260/184, no. 22	Bromsgrove (Worcs)	Ancient demesne?
211	1656 Feb.	C 202/40/2	Swaffham, North and South Pickenham, Foulden, Sculthorpe, Narford, Palgrave and Great Cressingham (Norf)	Ancient demesne?

(f) Writ damaged.

Analysis of Exemplifications and Extracts by Date

1261–70	2	1401–10	16	1541–50	0
1271–80	6	1411–20	4	1551–60	0
1281–90	0	1421–30	15	1561–70	4
1291–1300	0	1431–40	9	1571–80	5
1301–10	1	1441–50	4	1581–90	8
1311–20	2	1451–60	4	1591–1600	0
1321–30	0	1461–70	7	1601–10	2
1331–40	10	1471–80	3	1611–20	0
1341–50	15	1481–90	2	1621–30	4
1351–60	8	1491–1500	0	1631–40	0
1361–70	10	1501–10	2	1641–50	0
1371–80	25	1511–20	3	1651–60	1
1381–90	19	1521–30	0		
1391–1400	16	1531–40	0		

Appendix II

Loose Returns on Writs of Certiorari *Containing Domesday Extracts*

Number	Approx. date	Reference	Place
1	13th century	C 260/186, no. 1e	Chester (Ches)
2	13th century	C 260/208, no. 10	Langar (Notts)
3	13th century	C 260/208, no. 22	Stamford (Lincs)
4	14th century	C 47/9/45	Lands of Gilbert de Gant in Lincs and nine other counties
5	14th century	C 260/208, no. 3	Houghton Regis (Beds)
6	14th century	C 260/208, no. 6	Dorchester, Fordington, Sutton Poyntz, Gillingham and Chilfrome (Dors)
7	14th century	C 260/208, no. 12	Royal lands in Suffolk
8	14th century	C 260/208, no. 13	Merton and Ewell (Surrey)
9	14th century	DL 41/1, no. 1	Lands of Earl Hugh and Ivo Tailbois in Lincs
10	15th century	C 260/208, no. 5	Hope with Edale, Aston, Shatton, Offerton, Tideswell, Stoke and 'Muchedeswell' in Wormhill (Derb)
11	15th century	C 260/208, no. 1	Willenhall and Wolstanton (Staffs)
12	15th century	C 260/208, no. 2	'Westuode' in Llanwarn (Heref)
13	15th century	C 260/208, no. 15	Kineton and Wellesbourne (Warw)
14	Temp. Hen. VII (a)	C 260/208, no. 21	Cannock (Staffs)
15	Later 16th century	C 260/208, no. 16	Middlewich (Worcs)
16	1574–91 (b)	C 260/208, no. 9	Carleton St Peter and Cranworth (Norf)

(a) Cf. script of app. I, no. 182.
(b) Signed by Arthur Agarde and Christopher Fenton as deputy chamberlains of the Exchequer.

Appendix III
Abstracts of Domesday Book, 1299 to 14th Century

Forests

Number	Date	Reference	Place	Subject
1	1299–1300	E 101/136/4	Bucks, Oxon, Hunts, Northants, Hants, Wilts, Dors, Som	List of woodland in royal demesne.
2	Temp. Edw. I	E 32/337	Notts	List of woodland in royal demesne.
3	Temp. Edw. I	E 32/341, mm. 1–2	Som, Devon, Staffs	List of woodland in royal demesne.
4	Temp. Edw. I	E 32/90, m. 4	Northants	List of woodland.
5	Temp. Edw. I	E 32/247, mm. 1–4	Lincs, Berks, Ches, Derb	Evidence about the forests: lists of lands.
6	Temp. Edw. I	C 47/12/11, m. 3	Essex	List of forest lands.

Misc.

Number	Date	Reference	Place	Subject
7	1322	E 403/262 (a)	England	List of towns in royal demesne extracted for tallage purposes.
8	14th century	C 260/208, no. 17	Yorks	List of lands.
9	14th century	E 36/13649	Northants, Som, Dors	List of royal lands.
10	14th century	C 260/208, no. 9; C 47/9/46	Rutland Derb	List of royal lands.

(a) The list itself has not survived, only the records of payment to the clerk.

Appendix IV

Exchequer Exemplifications and Certified Copies from Domesday Book, 1567–1902

Number	Date	Reference	Place	Attestors
1	1567	E 165/12, Hil 9 Eliz	Biddesden (Wilts) (a)	
2	1567	E 165/12, Hil 9 Eliz	A Sussex entry (a)	
3	1568	E 165/12, Trin 10 Eliz	A Devon entry (a)	
4	1570	E 165/12, Trin 12 Eliz	South Molton (Devon) (a)	
5	1572 June	BL Harl. MS. 139, f. 110	Northwich hundred (Ches)	Thomas Burro and Arthur Agarde
6	1572 June	BL Harl. MS. 139, f. 111	Nantwich hundred (Ches)	Thomas Burro and Arthur Agarde
7	1572 June	BL Harl. MS. 139, f. 111v	Ati's Cross hundred (Ches)	Thomas Burro and Arthur Agarde
8	1572 June	BL Harl. MS. 139, f. 112v	Hodnet (Salop)	Thomas Burro and Arthur Agarde
9	1583	E 165/43, Trin 25 Eliz	Lands in Worcs (a)	
10	1612	SP 14/71, no. 37	Colwick (Notts)	Arthur Agarde
11	1628 Jan.	BL Harl. MS. 7573, ff. 4–5v	Lands of William Peverel in Derb	John Bradshaw
12	1636 Mar.	BL Harl. MS. 7573, ff. 6–7	Lands of William Peverel in Notts	Scipio le Squyer
13	1657 Sept.	BL Harl. MS. 7573, ff. 1–3v	Royal lands in Notts	Scipio le Squyer and Edward Fauconberge
14	1666–1708	BL Harl. MS. 7573, ff. 8–9	Lands of William Peverel	John Lowe
15	1685	IND 17175, f. 4	'Cencombe', 'Northon' and 'Warre' (b)	Peter le Neve
16	1685	IND 17175, f. 5	Masham (Yorks) (b)	Peter le Neve
17	1688	IND 17175, f. 7	Ottery St Mary (Devon) (b)	Peter le Neve
18	1689	IND 17175, f. 10	Rising Chase (in Castle Rising, Norf) (b)	Peter le Neve
19	c. 1690	IND 17175, f. 14	Ripple (Worcs) (b)	Peter le Neve
20	c. 1690	IND 17175, f. 18v	Aylesbury (Bucks) (b)	Peter le Neve
21	1690s	IND 17175, f. 34v	Bedale (Yorks) (b)	Peter le Neve
22	1690s	IND 17175, f. 42	Rodmell (Sussex) (b)	Peter le Neve

(a) Referred to in a register of exemplifications.
(b) Referred to in a register of searches.

Number	Date	Reference	Place	Attestors
23	1690s	IND 17175, f. 43	Skirpenbeck (Yorks) (b)	Peter le Neve
24	1690s	IND 17175, f. 48v	Grinton and Bridlington (Yorks) (b)	Peter le Neve
25	1699	IND 17175, f. 70	Clatford (in Preshute, Wilts) (b)	Peter le Neve
26	1741 June	IND 17175, f. 74	Snowshill (Glos) (b)	Abraham Farley
27	1743 May	IND 17175, f. 78	Duffield (Derb) (b)	Abraham Farley
28	1753 Nov.	IND 17175, p. 89	Stansted (Herts) (b)	Abraham Farley
29	1754 Nov.	BL Lansd. MS. 329, ff. 4–6	Royal lands in Oxon	Abraham Farley
30	c. 1760s	BL Add. MS 24724, ff. 159–65	Lands of Westminster Abbey in Worcs	Abraham Farley
31	c. 1760s	BL Add. MS. 24724, ff. 165–8	Lands of Pershore Abbey in Worcs	Abraham Farley
32	c. 1770s	BL Add. MS. 24723, f. 13	Coxwold, Kilburn and Wildon (Yorks NR)	Abraham Farley
33	c. 1770s	BL Add. MS. 24723, f. 14	Boltby (Yorks NR)	Abraham Farley
34	c.1770s	BL Add. MS. 24723, f. 15	'Fridebi' in Felixkirk (Yorks NR)	Abraham Farley
35	1902 Feb.	TS 16/147	Lands of Aubrey de Vere	G.R. Handcock

(b) Referred to in a register of searches.

Appendix V　　*Official Transcripts of Domesday Book, 1650–1783*

Number	Date	Reference	Place	Transcriber or Attestor
1	1650s	BL Harl. MS. 1499, ff. 137–40	Part of DB Yorks folios	Scipio le Squyer
2	c. 1666–70	BL Harl. MS. 6025, ff. 239–85	Surrey	John Lowe
3	1666–72	BL Harl. MS. 1905	Kent	John Lowe
4	c. 1680 or c. 1693	BL Harl. MS. 1903	Glos	John Lowe
5	c. 1680 or c. 1693	BL Harl. MS. 1904	Part of Hants	John Lowe
6	c. 1680 or c. 1693	BL Harl. MS. 1906	Norf	John Lowe
7	c. 1680 or c. 1693	BL Harl. MS. 1907	Sussex	John Lowe
8	c. 1680 or c. 1693	BL Harl. MS. 1908	Worcs	John Lowe
9	c. 1680 or c. 1693	BL Harl. MS. 4953	Yorks	John Lowe
10	c. 1686	BL Lansd. MS. 311	Extracts from DB about boroughs	John Lowe
11	c. 1690–2	IND 17175, ff. 26, 28	Herts (a)	Peter le Neve
12	1690s	IND 17175, f. 37d	Entries where salt pits are mentioned (a)	Peter le Neve
13	1742 Apr.	IND 17175, f. 74	Information about the river Trent (a)	Abraham Farley
14	1752 July	IND 17175, p. 86	Lands of Drogo de Bevrere in Yorks (a)	Abraham Farley
15	1753 Aug.	IND 17175, p. 89	Godalming (Surrey) (a)	Abraham Farley
16	1755 Jan.	IND 17175, p. 93	Lands of St Benet of Hulme Abbey (Norf) (a)	Abraham Farley
17	1755 Mar.	IND 17175, p. 93	Waxham (Norf) (a)	Abraham Farley
18	1755 Nov.	IND 17175, p. 100	Kintbury and Eagle hundreds (Berks) (a)	Abraham Farley
19	1757	BL Add. MS. 21349, f. 42	Royal lands and lands of St Mary's (unspecified) (a)	Abraham Farley
20	1757	BL Add. MS. 21349, f. 113	Entries about Cannock forest (Staffs) (a)	Abraham Farley
21	1760	BL Add. MS. 21349, f. 98	Manors in Somerset (a)	Abraham Farley
22	c. 1767	BL Add. MS. 38514, f. 79	Royal lands in Essex	Printed in facsimile types under Charles Morton
23	c. 1775	BL Stowe MS. 851, ff. 13–119	Kent	Abraham Farley
24	1774–83	MS lost, printed as DB, i–ii	Great and Little Domesday	Abraham Farley

(a) Referred to in a register of searches.

List of Abbreviations

Ann. Mon.: Annales Monastici, ed. H.R. Luard, 5 vols., RS (1864–69).

ASC: The Anglo-Saxon Chronicle, ed. D. Whitelock *et al.* (1961).

Bates, [D.], *D[omesday] Bibl[iography* (1986)].

BL: British Library, London.

Bodl.: Bodleian Library, Oxford.

Cal. Inq. Misc.: Calendar of Inquisitions Miscellaneous, HMSO (1916–69).

Cal. IPM: Calendar of Inquisitions Post Mortem, HMSO (1904–   ).

Campbell, [J.], 'Observations [on English government from the tenth to the twelfth century', *Trans. R Hist. S*, 5th ser., xxv (1975), pp. 39–54].

CCR: Calendar of Close Rolls, HMSO (1900–63).

CChR: Calendar of Charter Rolls, HMSO (1903–27).

Clanchy, [M., *From] Memory to Written Record, [England 1066–1307* (1979)].

CLibR: Calendar of Liberate Rolls, HMSO (1917–64).

Condon, [M.M.] and Hallam [E.M., 'Government printing of the public records in the eighteenth century', *Jnl. Soc. Archivists*, vii (1984), pp. 348–88].

CPR: Calendar of Patent Rolls, HMSO (1903–   ).

CROH: Cambridgeshire Record Office, Huntingdon.

CRR: Curia Regis Rolls, HMSO (1923–   ).

Darby, [H.C.], *Domesday England* [(Cambridge, 1977)].

DB: Domesday Book, seu Liber Censualis . . ., i–ii, ed. A. Farley (1783); iii–iv, ed. H. Ellis, Record Commission (1811, 1816).

Dialogus [de Scaccario and Constitutio Domus Regis, ed. C. Johnson (Oxford, 1983)].

DKR: Reports of the Deputy Keeper of the Records (1840–1958).

DNB: Dictionary of National Biography, 65 vols. and supplements (1885–   ).

Domesday Rebound, [Notes on the Physical Features and History of the Record, PRO Handbooks, no. 2, HMSO (1954)].

Douglas, [D.C., ed.], *Feudal Documents [from the abbey of Bury St Edmunds*, British Academy, Records of Social and Economic History, viii (1932)].

DRO: Derbyshire Record Office, Derby.

DS: Domesday Studies . . ., ed. P.E. Dove, 2 vols. (1888–91).

EHD: D.C. Douglas and G.E. Greenaway, ed., *English Historical Documents*, ii, *1042–1189* (1953).

EHR: English Historical Review (1886–   ).

Fowler, [G.H.], '[An] early Cambridge feodary', [*EHR*, xlvi (1931), pp. 442–43].

Galbraith, [V.H.], *D[omesday] B[ook], Its Place [in Administrative History* (Oxford, 1974)].

Galbraith, [V.H., 'The] Making of D[omesday] B[ook', *EHR*, lvii (1942), pp. 161–77].

Galbraith, [V.H.], *The Making of D[omesday] B[ook* (Oxford, 1961)].

GBR: Godmanchester Borough Records.

GEC: The Complete Peerage by G.E.C., ed. V. Gibbs *et al.*, 13 vols. (1910–40).

Gransden, [A, *Historical Writing in England,*] i, [c. *550–c. 1307* (1974);] ii, [c. *1307 to the Early Sixteenth Century* (1983)].

Hallam, [E.M.], 'Annotations in Domesday Book [since 1100', in A. Williams, ed., *Domesday Middlesex* (1986)].

Harvey, [S.P.J.], 'D[omesday] B[ook] and Anglo-Norman governance', [*Trans. R Hist. S*, 5th ser., xxv (1975), pp. 175–93].

Harvey, [S.P.J.], 'D[omesday] B[ook] and its predecessors', [*EHR*, lxxxvi (1971), pp. 753–73].

HC: Reports of Committees of the House of Commons (1803–).

Hemming: *Hemingi Chartularium Ecclesie Wigorniensis*, ed. T. Hearne, 2 vols. (Oxford, 1720).

Herefordshire Domesday [circa 1160–1170, ed. V.H. Galbraith and J. Tait, Pipe Roll Soc., new ser., xxv (1950)].

Hill, [C., 'The] Norman Yoke', [in idem, *Puritanism and Revolution* (1965), pp. 58–125].

HMSO: Her Majesty's Stationery Office.

HRO: Hampshire Record Office, Winchester.

LJ: Journals of the House of Lords (1777–).

Loyn, [H.R., *The*] *Governance of Anglo-Saxon England* [(1983)].

LR: Law Reports as cited in *Manual of Legal Citations*, i, *The British Isles* (1959).

Mitchell, [S.K.], *Taxation* [*in Medieval England*, ed. S. Painter (New Haven, 1951)].

Nicol, [A.], *Domesday Book*, [PRO Museum Pamphlets, x, HMSO (1981)].

NRO: Nottinghamshire Record Office, Nottingham.

Palgrave, [F., ed., *Antient*] *Kalendars and Inventories* [*of the Treasury of H.M. Exchequer*, 3 vols., Record Commission (1836)].

Plac. Abb.: Placitorum Abbreviatio, ed. G. Rose and W. Illingworth, Record Commission (1811).

Pocock, [J.G.A., *The*] *Ancient Constitution* [*and the Feudal Law* (Cambridge, 1957)].

Powell, [T., *The*] *Repertorie* [*of Records* (1631)].

PQW: Placita de Quo Warranto, ed. W. Illingworth and J. Caley, 2 vols., Record Commission (1818).

PRO: Public Record Office, London.

Reg R: Regesta Regum Anglo-Normannorum, ed. H.W.C. Davis *et al.*, i–ii (1913–56).

RH: Rotuli Hundredorum, ed. W. Illingworth and J. Caley, 2 vols., Record Commission (1812–18).

R Hist. S: Royal Historical Society.

Richardson, [H.G.] and Sayles, [G.O., ed., *The Governance of Medieval England* (Edinburgh, 1963)].

Rot. Cur. Reg.: Rotuli Curiae Regis, ed. F. Palgrave, 2 vols., Record Commission (1835).

Rot. Parl.: Rotuli Parliamentorum, ut et Petitiones et Placita in Parliamento, 6 vols. (1777).

Round, [J.H.], *Feudal England*, [*Historical Studies on the XIth and XIIth Centuries* (1895)].

RS: Rolls Series, alias *Rerum Brittanicum Medii Aevi Scriptores*, 99 titles, HMSO (1858–97).

Sainty, [J.C.], *Officers* [*of the Exchequer*, List and Index Soc., special ser., xviii (1983)].

SAL: Society of Antiquaries of London.

Stevenson, [C., 'A contemporary description of the Domesday survey', *EHR*, xxii (1907), pp. 72–84].

Sutherland, [D.W.], *Quo Warranto* [*Proceedings in the Reign of Edward I, 1278–1294* (Oxford, 1963)].

V and A: Victoria and Albert Museum, London.

VCH: Victoria History of the Counties of England, alias *Victoria County History*, ed. H.A. Doubleday *et al.* (1900–).

Warren, [W.L., 'The myth of] Norman efficiency' [*Trans. R Hist. S*, 5th ser., xxxiv (1984), pp. 113–32].

Williams, [N.J., 'The work of] Peter le Neve [at the Chapter House, Westminster', *Jnl. Soc. Archivists*, i (1955–59), pp. 125–31].

Sources of the Photographs

1. PRO photograph. 2. BL Cotton MS. Dom. A. II, f. 22. 3, 4. Tapisserie de Bayeux, Centre Guillaume le Conquérant. 5. J. Bayley, *History and Antiquities of the Tower of London*, i (1821), facing p. 107. 6. Courtauld Institute of Art. 7. Exeter Cathedral MS. 3500, f. 278. 8. E 31/1, ff. 127v–128 (PRO). 9. E 31/2, f. 299 (PRO). 10. E 31/2, f. 166v (PRO). 11. E 31/3 (PRO). 12. E 36/266, f. 33 (PRO). 13. E 31/2 f. O (PRO). 14. Balliol College, Oxford, MS. 350, f. 4. 15. E 36/284, f. 3 (PRO). 16. E 36/284, f. 1v (PRO). 17. E 36/284, f. 253 (PRO). 18. E 36/284, f. 20 (PRO). 19. BL Arundel MS. 153, f. 82. 20. E 164/1, p. 113 (PRO). 21. E 164/1, p. 56 (PRO). 22. E 164/1, p. 59 (PRO). 23. E. Walford, *Old and New London*, iii (1875), p. 403. 24. E. Walford, *Old and New London*, iii (1875), p. 450. 25. Guildhall Library. 26. BL Harley MS. 139, f. 111. 27. C 202/40/2 (PRO). 28. C 260/89/9 (PRO). 29. C 260/18, no. 1A (PRO). 30. C 260/156, no. 5 (PRO). 31. C 89/17/7 (PRO). 32. Powell, *Repertorie*, p. 132. 33. CROH, GBR, Charters, no. 13. 34. C 66/207, m. 4 (PRO). 35. BL Roy. MS. 14. C. VII, f. 9. 36. *Gentleman's Magazine*, new ser., xliii (1855), p. 37 (BL). 37. BL Roy. MS. 18. E. I, f. 165v. 38. National Monuments Record. 39. MR 8 (PRO). 40. Miss F.R. Bowler, SRN, SCM. 41. E 31/4 (PRO). 42. E 31/2, f. C (PRO). 43. E 31/2, f. 272 (PRO). 44. BL Harley MS. 623, f. 1. 45. BL Harley MS. 623, f. 38. 46. W. Hamper, ed., *The Life . . . of Dugdale*, i (1827), frontispiece. 47. Gonville and Caius College, Cambridge (W. Swaan). 48. SP 46/139, m. 80 (PRO). 49. IND 17176, f. 7 (PRO). 50. College of Arms. 51. MPB 2/99/1 (PRO). 52. BL Lansdowne MS. 329, f. 4. 53. E 31/6 (PRO). 54. BL Add. MS. 38514, f. 79. 55. E 31/2, f. 128 (PRO). 56. *DB*, i, f. 128. 57, 58. PRO photographs. 59. MPD 177 (PRO). 60. PRO photograph. 61. E 31/3 (PRO). 62. E 164/1 (PRO). 63. V and A Museum E. 2178–1932. 64. Ordnance Survey Department, Southampton. 65. Photozincograph of DB, i, f. 128. 66. PRO 1/32, 19 Feb. 1837 (PRO). 67. PRO 8/58 (PRO). 68. E 31/3 (PRO). 69. MPJ 169/10 (PRO). 70. *Illustrated London News*, 6 Nov. 1886, p. 482. 71. PRO photograph. 72. *Punch*, 18 Aug. 1926 (BL). 73, 74. PRO 18/7 (PRO). 75. PRO 8/23 (PRO). 76, 77, 78, 79. PRO photographs.

Acknowledgments
I would like to thank the British Library Board for permission to reproduce plates 2, 19, 26, 35, 36, 37, 44, 45, 52, 54 and 72; the Town of Bayeux for 3 and 4; the Courtauld Institute of Art for 6; the Dean and Chapter of Exeter Cathedral for 7; the Master and Fellows of Balliol College, Oxford, for 14; the Guildhall Library, City of London, for 25; Cambridge County Council for 33; the National Monuments Record for 38; Miss F.R. Bowler, SRN, SCM for 40; the Master and Fellows of Gonville and Caius College, Cambridge, for 47; the College of Arms for 50; the Trustees and Director of the Victoria and Albert Museum for 63; and the Ordnance Survey Department, Southampton, for 64. All other photographs are from the Public Record Office.

Select Glossary

Ancient desmesne	land held by the king in 1066 or 1086. Proof of the tenure was normally in Domesday Book.
Assart	woodland cleared for agricultural purposes.
Borough	town with customs and privileges and with its own court.
Burgess	inhabitant of a borough who had special burghal privileges.
Cartulary	record-book of deeds and charters.
Carucate	measurement of land varying between 60 and 120 acres, used in former Danish areas, and denoting land ploughable by eight oxen. Cf. Hide.
Certiorari	prerogative writ ordering information from or text of a legal record to be copied and certified to another court.
Copyhold	land held by the title of a deed enrolled on the manorial court roll.
Cottar	cottager; an unfree peasant holding a small piece of land.
Danegeld	*see* Geld.
Demesne	manors held directly by the lord, as opposed to those held by his men; that part of a manor exploited on a lord's behalf rather than that part held by his tenants.
Escheat	land reverting to the lord of a fee if the tenant died without heirs or broke his feudal contract.
Escheator	official who enforced the royal right to escheats.
Farm	a fixed sum or rent in cash or kind, usually due annually.
Fee, Fief	landed estate held from a lord by feudal tenure.
Fee farm	rent payable from the holder of a fee to his lord.
Fee tail	entail; specific and limited arrangement for the inheritance of land.
Geld, Danegeld	tax levied by the Crown on the hide to pay for the defence of England.
Hanaper	office levying payments for sealing letters with the great seal.
Hide	measurement of land equivalent to a carucate. Both were used as the basis of tax assessment.
Honor	group of estates held by a tenant-in-chief.
Hundred, Wapentake	subdivision of a shire, with its own court.
Infangtheof	the right of a lord to hang a thief caught on his land.
Justices in eyre	justices commissioned to travel on a judicial circuit to try cases and to review administrative procedures.
Manor	jurisdictional and territorial holding.

Messuage	house with surrounding land.
Outfangtheof	the right of a lord to hang a thief wherever caught.
Oyer and terminer	commission issued to royal justices empowering them to hear and determine trespasses within a specified area.
Palatinate	semi-independent 'principality', the lord of which possessed some quasi-royal powers.
Polyptych	estate survey.
Quo warranto	royal writ inquiring by what warrant land or rights were held.
Right close, writ of	royal writ initiating land actions and transfers in ancient-demesne manorial courts.
Scriptorium	writing-office.
Scutage	shield-tax paid in lieu of military service.
Serf	lowest-ranking unfree peasant with very few legal rights.
Serjeanty	tenure by personal as opposed to military services.
Sheriff	king's representative and principal administrator in the shire.
Shire	county.
Socage	non-military tenure, usually by rent.
Soke	jurisdiction within a given area, and the area so described.
Sokeman	a free peasant liable to attend the court of his soke and to serve its lord.
Tallage	tax levied by a lord from his tenants.
Tenement	a holding of land.
Terra regis	land of the king.
Thegn	man of high rank (Anglo-Saxon), who fought or carried out administrative duties for the king.
Vill	sub-division of a hundred; usually a village.
Villein	highest-ranking dependent peasant owing his lord duties and services in return for his land.
Virgate	one quarter of a hide.
Wapentake	*see* Hundred. Term used in former Danish areas.

Index

The figures in *italics* refer to the captions to the plates and maps. Assistant Keeper of Public Records is abbreviated as AK, Deputy Chamberlain of the Exchequer as DC, and Deputy Keeper of the Records as DK.